The Search for Understanding

Revisioning Philosophy

David Appelbaum
General Editor

Vol. 24

PETER LANG
New York • Washington, D.C./Baltimore • San Francisco
Bern • Frankfurt am Main • Berlin • Vienna • Paris

R. L. Franklin

The Search for Understanding

PETER LANG
New York • Washington, D.C./Baltimore • San Francisco
Bern • Frankfurt am Main • Berlin • Vienna • Paris

Library of Congress Cataloging-in-Publication Data

Franklin, Richard L.
  The search for understanding / R.L. Franklin.
    p.   cm. — (Revisioning philosophy; vol. 24)
  Includes bibliographical references and index.
  1. Comprehension (Theory of knowledge). 2. Knowledge, theory of.
I. Title. II. Series.
BD151.5.F72   121—dc20   94-45072
ISBN 0-8204-2722-5
ISSN 0899-9937

Die Deutsche Bibliothek-CIP-Einheitsaufnahme

Franklin, Richard L.:
The search for understanding / R. L. Franklin. - New York; Washington,
D.C./Baltimore; San Francisco; Bern; Frankfurt am Main; Berlin; Vienna;
Paris : Lang.
  (Revisioning philosophy; Vol. 24)
  ISBN 0-8204-2722-5
NE: GT

Cover design by James F. Brisson.

© 1995 Peter Lang Publishing, Inc., New York

Printed in the United States of America.

For Margaret-Ann

who waited
and trusted

ACKNOWLEDGEMENTS

I emphasize in this book how our understanding is embedded in our history, and this surely applies to the intellectual debts incurred in writing it. Outside my own discipline of philosophy, Miriam Dixson pointed out wide ranging implications and also tirelessly criticized obscurities, while Alan Roughley lessened my ignorance of aspects of postmodernism. Innumerable philosophers have also contributed to the argument by critical discussion; I remember with particular gratitude the comments of Dorothy Emmet and Jocelyn Dunphy. A happy contact with John MacIntyre while he spent time at my University of New England led later to a stimulating visit to the University of Edinburgh during a sabbatical leave, and especially to vigorous discussion within its Science Studies Unit. The same sabbatical involved valuable contact with Rom Harre at Oxford. In my own Department my views have been forcefully criticized in seminars, and in informal discussions with such colleagues as Jeff Malpas and Bill McDonald. Postgraduate students like Andrew Brian and Gordon Stanley have also helped me as much as I would like to think I helped them. Many resulting benefits of all this are acknowledged in the endnotes. Further, Peter Forrest and Fred D'Agostino in Australia, and Bob Forman in America, found time to read the manuscript, and made many helpful comments. Above all, there was a memorable set of joint teaching seminars with Marion Knowles, now Marion Kading. She subjected my ideas to a ruthless pruning which, I hope, eventually enabled them to bear more fruit, and which demonstrated what co-operative dialogue can achieve. Finally, Liz Kitto's meticulous proofreading has saved the reader from innumerable irritations.

I am grateful to the copyright owners for permission to use material from my earlier work as follows: "Knowledge, Belief and Understanding" in *Philosophical Quarterly* vol. 31 (1981) pp. 193-208; "On Understanding" in *Philosophy and Phenomenological Research* XLII (1983) pp. 307-328; "Creativity and Depth of Understanding" in J. Brzezinski, S. Di Nuovo, T. Marek and T. Maruszewski *Creativity and Consciousness* (Editions Rodopi, 1995) pp. 41-57.

The index covers authors as well as topics, but those who are merely cited in the Endnotes without discussion appear only in the works cited.

October, 1994   University of New England

CONTENTS

CHAPTER I

THE IMPORTANCE OF UNDERSTANDING

1. How the Exploration Began

We suffer today from a fragmentation of understanding. The explosion of knowledge in every field makes it increasingly difficult to find an integrated picture of the whole. Moreover, as we live in increasingly multi-cultural societies, which themselves are brought into ever closer contact by the revolution in communications, old assumptions and values are repeatedly challenged by new viewpoints that seem to erode any stable base from which to understand our world. Though the resulting problems are particularly acute for us, they are not new, for they raise issues with which Western philosophy has grappled for over two millenia. But today academic philosophy is an arena where experts talk to experts; so it also is easily trapped in the net of specialization and fragmentation, and becomes part of the problem rather than of the solution. This book aims to approach these issues in a way that those outside academic philosophy can follow. For in the end, if we are to grapple with the fragmentation of our times, we must all become our own philosophers. As war is too important to be left to the generals, so philosophy is too important to be left entirely to the professionals.

The explorations that I offer here began with a much narrower focus. Over a decade ago, I noticed that English-speaking philosophy had little to say about the concept of understanding. Yet surely, I thought, it was an important concept? Not only do academic disciplines, including philosophy, search for understanding in their own fields, but we all continually do so in innumerable ways. Understanding can be theoretical or practical, purely intellectual or warmly empathetic, and can concern limited problems or our whole world-view. We may show it by appropriate words, by efficient activity, or by silence. Moreover, it must link with, and yet differ from, one of the most discussed concepts in philosophy, namely knowledge. For to know why an engine failed is to understand why it did, and vice versa; but merely to know *that* it failed is not, in itself, to understand anything. So, since the question "What is knowledge?" gives rise to the whole branch of philosophy known as epistemology or theory of knowledge, should we not also ask "What is understanding"? Yet, I found, though philosophers use the word "understanding" repeatedly in the titles of their books, they rarely examine it;[1] rather, they use it as a code-word to point to one of two areas. One is philosophy of language, with its discussions of how we understand written and spoken words. The other is philosophy of social science, where some claim that, in interpreting human actions, we must employ what they call *Verstehen*, or understanding.[2] Yet these contexts are too limited. Understanding language is only a special case, however important, of understanding something, while *Verstehen*, too, is a technical use of the word. What of the general notion, of which they are examples?

This was where my inquiry broadened in scope. Gradually I found connections, not only with theory of knowledge but with other branches and other traditions of philosophy. Increasingly, an understanding of understanding seemed to offer a new approach to virtually all the great themes of philosophy. Moreover it had further implications. For, since all disciplines search for understanding in their own ways, they might also find the argument relevant; and, in general, if we are to overcome the fragmentation of understanding today, an examination of the concept itself might be a good place to start. So what began as an inquiry into a concept that my philosophical tradition had neglected, ended by asking what any form of philosophy might contribute to our situation today.

Eventually I realized that this expansion of an initial question into a wider one is typical of intellectual growth, so my explorations were exemplifying one of their own themes. For such expansion reflects a continual interplay between specific and general considerations that is a fundamental feature of understanding. Our overall beliefs, which are the background of any investigation, shape all our specific inquiries, while at the same time the inquiries may modify elements of the original starting point and so lead to new questions. For an adequate understanding we need both aspects. Only detailed investigations can lead to reliable knowledge; but unless we also have some overall picture of where we are going, we feel we cannot see the wood for the trees. It is, at present, the overall picture that we lack with the concept of understanding; we need a sketch map of the wood, not as a substitute but as a preparation for detailed examination of the trees. Hence I decided I must write so non-philosophers could grasp the point of the discussion and contribute to it. I therefore bypass much professional argument. On some key issues I argue at length, but on others I only outline problems which arise, and solutions which look attractive. This invites others to explore these possibilities, and so to develop or to criticize my views. I also needed to avoid unexplained technical terms, but the necessity to do so again turned out to illustrate how aspects of understanding interact with each other. In stopping to explain matters that professional philosophers expect their readers to know, I found that some of their current assumptions were just what needed re-examination. So the explaining of "elementary" points to outsiders sometimes became a first step towards re-examining the philosophical discussions.

2. Problems, Plans and Procedures

So where should I begin? One point the inquiry brings out is how any reflection — including my explorations — is shaped by both our cultural situation and our personal history. Yet we can all use the word "understand" correctly, so I start from that common ground. In Part A I offer an analysis of understanding, developed with little reference to cultural setting or to current philosophical debates. I use "analysis", not with any technical philosophical meaning, but in the broad sense of a systematic examination of the concept. Yet the examination has a specific focus. Usually a claim to understand refers, not to some mental activity, but to a state that continues even while we are thinking of something else; if I understand mathematical calculus, I still do so while I am busily mowing my lawn. But my analysis focuses on the *search* for understanding, and that *is* an activity we undertake. I examine chiefly what I call intellectual understanding, which is what philosophy and other academic disciplines normally aim to achieve, but I also extend the analysis beyond this. For understanding is practical as well as theoretical, so I consider reasoning about what to do as well as about how things are. Finally, the analysis defends the claim that there are deeper than purely intellectual levels of understanding.

After the analysis in Part A, I turn in Part B to some of its implications. Here underlying assumptions become more relevant, so I sketch my own understanding of my philosophical background. Then I examine current debates about the concept of knowledge, and conclude that understanding *is* knowledge of a crucial sort, namely knowledge of structure and connections. After that I turn to doubts about our capacity to obtain knowledge. Here I begin with discussions in my own tradition, but then go beyond them to face more radical current challenges. Against such doubts I defend a cautious optimism about our capacity to expand understanding, even across widely different convictions or ways of life. Then these issues within theory of knowledge lead on to even broader ones about the nature of reality, in the area that philosophers call metaphysics. I end by asking what the implications of the whole discussion might be for overcoming the fragmentation of our understanding today.

In all inquiries we must start from where we are, which will be, in practice, the beliefs we share with those whom we respect. But my approach contains more specific applications of that general point. When I meet a disputed issue, I often adopt a "minimalist" approach of searching for areas of agreement which all fair-minded protagonists would accept. For this common ground often gives me all my argument requires, without needing to settle the dispute itself.[3] But this, we shall see, has limitations, and some would reject it as naive. For the choice of who is "fair-minded" will be debatable; and while there are independent tests for it, such as how accurately we state the views we reject, my own judgment inevitably shapes my approach. So I may ignore some point that others regard as vital, while no doubt at other times I am just ignorant of relevant material. This is where an informed debate can supplement the deficiencies of individuals who engage in it. Finally, I adopt the working assumption that, in an honest dispute between intelligent people, each side is likely to have some insight worth preserving. Hence by probing our differences, and particularly our underlying assumptions, we may hope that whatever withstands criticism in each of them may be preserved in a more adequate view. So we may work towards better understanding, not merely in spite of, but actually by use of, our diverse starting points. This will emerge as the basis for my cautious optimism about our capacity to expand understanding.

3. Objections

Many today, however, reject even the most cautious optimism. One objection is that the attempt to expand understanding, or even to gain any knowledge whatever, is in principle impossible. Such skeptical doubts have been urged for over two millenia, and I shall face them in Part B, but two other objections should be mentioned now. One emphasizes the difficulties of any overall understanding in the light of today's knowledge explosion. For to investigate fully how the mind works when we search for understanding requires input from many rapidly expanding fields, so no one could master all the relevant material. In reply, I acknowledge the difficulties. But still, however we try to handle the situation, we should not merely retreat into our specializations. For, first, if we all do so, it is no-one's responsibility to see the wood rather than the trees; and then the debate is abandoned to those for whom dogmatic belief replaces reasoned discussion. Second, we cannot really fence off our areas, for new developments may always erode the famil-iar starting points that we have taken for granted. To ignore this is to adopt the policy of the ostrich, which must eventually fail. Finally, specialized intellectual activities depend on wider assumptions, including the reasons why we think them worthwhile. To ignore these assumptions is not to avoid having an overall outlook, but merely to operate from within an implicit and unexamined one.

Besides these reasons for not avoiding the issue, I believe there is a more positive response to the knowledge explosion. Specialization is indispens-able, but we can look for approaches that promise integration rather than fragmentation. In the present instance, no one, including myself, knows enough to grasp all that is relevant to the concept of understanding, but I still hope to start a discussion that may improve our grasp of it. If the inquiry were to generate debate, it might even become an area of specialization in its own right; for—to distort the original metaphor—the shape of the wood can itself become one more tree to be examined. But that particular inquiry might be relevant to others in many fields, and so might contribute to the integration rather than the fragmentation of understanding.

A final type of current objection, found in much postmodernist thought, fastens on the assumptions made in a discourse. It might, for example, point out that my minimalist approach of searching for agreement between opposing views presupposes a whole background of Western philosophy. We need only imagine searching for agreement between, say, ourselves and a primitive tribe, to see how much I presuppose. Moreover, it may say, the project is not merely too difficult but undesirable. For it assumes there is such a thing as *the* way the human mind works; in technical language, it looks for the essence of understanding. But this is an outmoded notion which today must be discar-ded. There are no essences, and, further, a search for them is pernicious. For if we believe they exist, we will end by claiming to find them; and this will amount to claiming that everyone—or every "rational" one—should see things as we do. Such claims are only disguised attempts at intellectual domination.

These currents of thought are not simply opposed to my own approach, but resonate with it in complex ways. I have, for example, already emphasized how a search for understanding can erode its initial assumptions, so we can never be sure we have reached the essence of a phenomenon. Yet, I shall argue, we must also investigate the assumptions of views that set out to question all assumptions. Many of them assume that we must either claim some absolute, unshakeable truth, or else accept all viewpoints as ultimately of equal worth. I reject those alternatives; for even if we cannot reach truths beyond possible future challenge, we may still find answers to the issues we actually meet. Specifically, I offer an analysis of understanding. Insofar as it is adequate, it hardly matters whether or not we say it captures the essence of the notion. Insofar as it is oversimplified or distorted, its faults can be pointed out. We do not know in advance that we can get an overall picture which could be useful to those working in many areas, but neither do we know we cannot. The proof of the pudding is in the eating, and will emerge from debate between those with initially different views. No doubt, if we were to reach agreement, or at least to narrow our differences, future ages might uncover new assumptions that we had all taken for granted. But then the process of examining them could begin again, and the expansion of understanding could continue.

4. Recurring Themes

Others must judge for themselves what they find important in my argument, but I end by foreshadowing what seem to me some of its most striking conclusions. Above all there is the continual interaction between wider background and specific inquiry, between the wood and the trees or, in general, between the whole and the parts within it. The more I reflected, the more I was struck by how this produces an unpredictable unboundedness of understanding. As with a growing embryo, what is central at one stage of development is less important at another, while the final result often cannot be guessed from its present form. This whole-part interaction within the search for intellectual understanding leads, I found, to deeper questions. For, first, conscious thought is only part of our total mental activity, and in the relation between conscious and unconscious we find the same pattern: conscious thinking is influenced by factors we do not know, but we may set ourselves consciously to search out and reshape those factors. Beyond that lies a further question. Individuals, with all their mental complexity, are parts of a larger social whole. So how far does the interaction between individual and society parallel that between part and whole *within* an individual? Is change in society the product of individual action, or is that action only the manifestation of social forces; or, here as elsewhere, do whole and part reciprocally interact?

Another aspect of the inquiry that repeatedly struck me is the extent to which mental processes reflect conflicts between rival tensions. The human mind, it seems, works by a sort of polarization, whereby any claim to insight provokes a rival reaction. We have already met one example, for postmodernism is a reaction against earlier intellectual syntheses which were felt to be too sweeping. Both this polarization and the unpredictable unboundedness of understanding, seem different aspects of the perpetual whole-part interaction. It is because different parts of our belief system continually interact with each other and with the whole, that conflicts between them emerge as polarizing tensions where the results cannot be foreseen. But this in turn only raises further questions. May we hope to map the general tensions of the human mind, or do they so vary from age to age that any classification would reflect only the cultural situation of the classifier? And might we hope for a general method of resolving them, or are they an ineluctable aspect of the human condition? My cautious optimism about the power of reason does not itself answer these questions, though it claims we can always penetrate to a deeper understanding of them. But my further belief is that we can get valuable, but never final, answers; for we can endlessly illuminate, but never exhaust, our understanding of ourselves and of our world.

ENDNOTES

1 There is Wittgenstein's discussion of aspects of understanding in *Philosophical Investigations* (1953), but I can find in it no overall analysis of the notion. P. Achinstein *Law and Explanation* (1971), discusses understanding in relation to scientific explanation. There is not much more. But a list of books on philosophical topics which use the word in their titles would include: D. Z. Phillips (ed.) *Religion and Understanding* (1967); G. H. von Wright *Explanation and Understanding* (1971); Paul Ziff *Understanding Understanding* (1972); S. E. Toulmin *Human Understanding* Vol. I (1972); Richard Campbell *From Belief to Understanding* (1976); J. Manninen and Raimo Tuomela (eds) *Essays on Explanation and Understanding* (1976); F. R. Dallmayer & T. A. McCarthy (eds.) *Understanding and Social Theory* (1977); D. W. Hamlyn *Experience and the Growth of Understanding* (1978); G. P. Baker and P. M. S. Hacker *Wittgenstein: Understanding and Meaning* (1980); H. Hormann *To Mean—To Understand* (1981); H. Parrett and J. Bourveresse *Meaning and Understanding* (1981); F. Collin *Theory and Understanding* (1985). As for books which are not about philosophy, I have counted over 200 recent ones which use the term as the first word in their title, ranging alphabetically from *Understanding Abnormal Behaviour* to *Understanding Yourself*.

2 The books listed above either discuss one of these two areas, or else use the word generally but offer no significant analysis of it.

3 This minimalist approach should not be confused with various others. Thus logicians often seek the weakest axioms sufficient for their reasoning. But whether a theorem may still be derived after dispensing with an axiom depends purely on formal implications, while my approach concerns what is in fact believed, and looks, not for the logically weakest premisses, but for the actually accepted ones. It has more affinity with W. V. O. Quine's notion of semantic ascent, whereby we ascend "to a common part of two fundamentally disparate conceptual schemes, the better to discuss the disparate foundations" (*Word and Object* (1964) p.272); but I do not use the notion as he does. There is also an affinity to the notion of bracketing in phenomenology, whereby we put aside ontological truth claims while examining experience; but again my use is different.

PART A

ANALYSIS

CHAPTER II

INTELLECTUAL UNDERSTANDING

1. Understanding and Structure

When we set out to explore a concept such as understanding, we start simply from the fact that we know how to use the word. We must begin by marking out some more specific area for investigation, however vaguely and provisionally. Understanding, we may note, is used in such ordinary contexts as understanding why an engine failed; but in other cases it seems to make a larger claim, for we may speak of penetrating below the surface of our ordinary thinking to reach a deeper understanding. I focus first on the ordinary cases, which I call *intellectual* understanding. "Intellectual" at this stage is as inchoate as "understanding", but I identify it now just as the sense found in what we would ordinarily call intellectual investigations. I now try to clarify that vague notion.[1]

At the outset of the exploration I found, surprisingly, that we have no single word for that-which-we-are-trying-to-understand. However an analogous problem faced philosophers of science when they began to examine the notion of scientific explanation, and they solved it by calling that-which-is-to-be-explained an explanandum. So I too go back to the Latin, and call what we are trying to understand an *intelligendum*.[2] How, then, do we come to grips with intelligenda, and so achieve understanding? I start by noting that many words which do duty for "understand" have concrete as well as abstract senses. Two are specially important. The first is seeing: we talk of vision, insight, a new perspective, throwing light. The second is grasping: we take the point, we comprehend an argument as a monkey grasps a branch with its prehensile tail. Yet, at the concrete level, grasping and seeing are not at all interchangeable. What makes each of them suitable as a recurrent stand-in for understanding? The answer is, I suggest, that they both improve our control, or ability to cope: we have taken hold of something, so it cannot get away; we see it clearly, so its features are obvious. The initial clue is: what a good grip or sight is in concrete contexts, understanding is in abstract ones. It is an as-it-were grasping or seeing, because we gain an ability to cope with the data. Such a transfer of meaning may disclose either a useful clue, or merely a weird and tenuous association of ideas;[3] but here surely we can sense its *appropriateness*, and so grasp, however dimly, a feature of how our minds work.[4]

Another notion also found appropriate in both concrete and abstract contexts is that of fitting together. We fit together items of information to suggest an answer, or pieces of Leggo to build a crane. What these have in common we must non-visually see, but they point to something at the heart of understanding. To fit together we must see the *form* or *pattern* or *structure* of the intelligendum. These three words are often equivalent, though each has its own flavor. I primarily use "structure", with "pattern" as a variant, but my concern is with that to which they all point. Understanding is discerning structure. This in itself says little, for the notion of structure here is as wide as the sorts of understanding we can achieve. Still, the point is less vague than the mere ability to cope with data; we cope with data *by* discerning its structure, so that we can organize and deal with it effectively.[5]

Discerning structure in turn seems to depend on a basic capacity to discriminate likeness and unlikeness: "This and that are both X", or "This is X and that is not". This point applies not only with clear patterns, such as the symmetrical facade of a building, but even when there is no obvious repetition, as in discerning the structure of a play. "This scene takes up one thread in the previous one by ..."; in saying this, we note a similarity and imply differences. But items are like and unlike each other in indefinitely many ways. To understand, we must discern the *relevant* or *significant* ways, for only they enable us to cope with the data; and seeing something as significant involves relating it to the rest of our knowledge.   So here we meet again that interaction between part and whole which we already met in Ch. I. It is so basic to understanding that to describe its complexity is perhaps the central task of Part A. The process is already shaped by the concepts our language provides: we see the facade, not merely as a collection of shapes, but as the front of a *building*; without seeing words as a *play,* we would not know what structure to look for. But the capacity to use language is only the start.

2. Whole and Part

Coming to understand involves both connecting parts to form a whole, and distinguishing them within one.[6] If we have established a standard constant in physics, we would explain it if we could fit it into a theory which showed why it must have that value. Alternatively, we may have a whole that we will understand by analyzing it into its parts; a standard example would be a chemical analysis. But in these cases what is "part" and "whole" is fixed by the context, and other cases are more complex. If I say of a chess game, "I don't understand that move", I mean that I do not understand its particular strategy. But is this strategy a "whole" into which the move fits, or a "part" of an overall goal of checkmating the opponent?   Such questions lead on to greater complexity. For what we think of as part and whole often *interpenetrate*, so that we understand each better as we grasp more of the other. A central example is one which today is often taken as the paradigm of all understanding: reading a text. We understand a passage better as we see its role in the overall theme, and at the same time we grasp the theme better as we interpret the passage. This is just the situation we are involved in now, where our "whole" is the concept of understanding, and our "part" is what we tentatively distinguish as intellectual understanding. In such cases, connecting and distinguishing are not an either/or process but a both/and which proceed simultaneously, and part and whole are only provisionally distinct. Moreover, our whole intelligendum may be transformed by jumping, as it were, into a new dimension, if we call in question something we had taken for granted. If we come to suspect that the chess player has been bribed to lose, our former puzzle about strategy no longer applies.

Clearly our understanding is as varied as the types of structures we can find, and we integrate data in many ways. But for a unified account, I think we must start from the cases where connecting and distinguishing interpenetrate, as in reading a text. In the earlier examples from physics and chemistry, the strict assumptions controlling scientific investigation determined what was whole and what was part. But the less the framework of the inquiry is fixed, the more we must shuttle between the whole intelligendum and specific aspects of it, while improving our grasp of each at the same time. Analogues of this appear even within the confines of scientific theory. If, say, a physical constant had been established only within a range, a new theory might entail that it must lie at one end of the range; here theory would alter fact. Conversely, in a chemical analysis, prolonged failure to understand our results might lead us to postulate that some unknown reaction was involved; here fact would alter theory. So we may see these as special cases of the primary mode of understanding, where the interpenetration of whole and part is central. Yet we must realize that to call it primary is not to say it is the most important mode. If, say, we hold that science gives us the final truth about the world, then for achieving an overall understanding of our human situation the results of the scientific method take precedence, while the primary one yields only commonsense or proto-scientific understanding. I face that issue in Part B, but I leave it open now.

It is common to say that the primary mode of understanding is *holistic*, but that word can be both misleading and vague. Misleading, because it empha-sizes only the influence of the whole on the part, while I stress the reciprocal influence of each on the other. Vague, because it conflates two different cases. The first is the process of connecting parts and distinguishing within wholes. This applies to all understanding. The second is the typical but not universal interpenetration, in which our grasp of the whole and of the various parts continually modify each other. The first, general, connecting-and-distin-guishing process I call "articulation" (its root meaning is the joint of a limb, which both connects and separates the parts). To come to understand is to increase our discernment of structure by articulating our data. For the second, interpenetrating process I avoid the ambiguities of "holism" by speaking of the *mutualistic* interaction between part and whole. So understanding always articulates, and is primarily, but not universally, mutualistic.

3. Working Towards a General Formula

We are now on the way towards a general formula for the nature of intel-lectual understanding. We can reach it after noting four other points, which arise out of what I have so far said and are discussed more fully later. They are the role of (a) depth and (b) significance in understanding, followed by the contrasts between (c) theoretical and practical and (d) inner and outer aspects of understanding.

(a) Our grasp of structure is essentially a matter of degree. A scholar who is fluent in Greek and has mastered the details of the Platonic corpus claims to understand Plato. But what if he always reads him through his own precon-ceptions? In one sense, we might say, he understands, but in another sense he does not really do so. The natural metaphor here is that he lacks *depth* of understanding. This shows in the word "understand" itself.[7] If "under" means inside or beneath, as in "She inserted the knife-blade under the bark", the picture is that to understand is to penetrate to a deeper standpoint inside or beneath the surface.

(b) While depth is a matter of degree, some cases of discerning structure seem so unconnected to the rest of our knowledge as not to amount to understanding. If we merely notice a pattern in the wallpaper, without relating it to anything else, surely the notion of understanding does not get a grip at all.[8] We often put this by saying that the pattern has no significance outside itself; for, as we saw in Sec. 1, understanding involves grasp of relevant or significant connections. So from now on I shall speak of understanding as discerning *significant* structure.

(c) What is the relation between the intellectual ability to articulate data, and its practical consequences? The two need not go together. Passengers in a shipwreck may lapse into panic, or into a frozen inability to act at all. They understood that this was a shipwreck, as they interpreted the data of jolts, alarm bells, etc. But once they understood the situation, they could not understand what to do. So intellectual understanding need not induce, and may even destroy, practical understanding. Yet, we shall see, the two are linked. For if intellectual understanding did not *normally* improve our practical capacities, the value we give it would be radically changed.

(d) There is an analogous relation between our inner mental activity and its outer manifestation in behaviour.[9] When we test students' understanding by setting exams, the excuse that they knew it all but could not express it is not good enough. So in some way understanding is linked to appropriate behavior, such as the capacity to explain what we know. Yet we have tacit understanding we cannot fully explain, as when we recognize that something is troubling our friend; and, more generally, a paralyzed person might understand a conversation, but be incapable of any behavior at all. So understanding and behaving appropriately cannot be the same; yet, as in (c), the two are linked. In each case, I later argue, the relevant notions must normally go together, but the nature of the link is one that philosophers have not adequately grasped.

I can now offer a general formula for what I mean by intellectual understanding. I started with the vague notion of "the sense found in what we would ordinarily call intellectual investigations". I conclude that it is *the articulation of data so as to discern a structure with an adequate degree of significance*. Normally, but not always, such understanding will improve our capacity to act, and will issue in appropriate behavior. This formula is very broad, because it must cover the vast variety of cases in which we claim to understand; and we should see how these cases cut across many classifications that philosophers commonly employ. Often understanding is based on causal relationships; in understanding why a light failed, the significant fact is that the filament burnt out, and this is the end result of a causal chain. In other contexts it depends on logical relations, as in understanding an argument or a theorem. Other cases, such as a chess move, involve seeing an act as a means to achieve a goal. And besides causal, logical and means-end relations, we may claim to understand a symphony, which seems different again. Moreover, many relations may be involved in a single case. If someone were reckless enough to claim to understand Kant's *Critique of Pure Reason*, they must show that they grasp at least its overall structure, its fundamental aims and strategy, its historical context, and the logical structure of its arguments.

Further, in all the examples, the *criteria* for showing we have understood are different from the *relation* involved. In the case of the light, the criterion for understanding might be a capacity to explain, however sketchily, why filaments melt. In understanding an argument, the criteria include some capacity to put the point in our own words, and to apply it in new situations. With means-end relationships, they involve a capacity to state the actor's reasons correctly. In understanding a symphony, we must be able to show how its elements form a coherent structure. For *The Critique of Pure Reason* the multiple criteria include having a reasonable capacity to answer the question, "What would Kant have said to that?". But how do we find these criteria? I did so by reflecting on the sorts of significant structure we would need to discern, so I offer this as the common element. Those who reject it may be asked for their own suggestions, but I doubt if any formula less general than mine would cover all cases.

As a strict definition of intellectual understanding, the formula is hardly adequate. For one thing, it will turn out to apply to other cases of understanding also, and so would be too broad. But it points us, I believe, towards the core of intellectual understanding, which is in turn the central focus of Part A. For the rest of this chapter, I shall explore its different aspects in more detail.

4. Floating Contrasts

We now meet an unavoidable complication: namely, that many of the concepts needed in our analysis cannot be sharply distinguished from each other. Consider first the whole background against which we formulate our intelligenda. We would normally speak of this background as our "beliefs", though, as we shall see, philosophers often use that word in rather technical ways.[10] Yet, though we may isolate individual beliefs in a specific context, they are, we shall see, so closely interrelated that they are best seen as only quasi-independent elements of a *belief system* which is the background to our understanding. This system includes our factual beliefs and working assumptions, our expectations and sense of possibilities, our ideals, principles, evaluations, etc., whether now conscious, not currently attended to, or unable to be made conscious. It is called a system because of the strong interconnections between its elements, so that a change in any one may affect indefinitely many others. Yet our beliefs need not be systematic in the ordinary sense, and we may hold conflicting ones. As we shall see, to make our system more systematic requires arduous effort, and may not be completely attainable.

The background of any intelligendum, then, is an overall system where individual items can only provisionally be isolated, and we find that this pattern repeatedly recurs. Within an intelligendum, we normally attend to a series of things in succession, and disattend from the surrounding context. So the whole belief system is the background for the intelligendum, while the intelligendum is the background for our specific focus. But we will find we need to distinguish another level, intermediate between belief system and intelligendum. For our belief system covers both conscious and unconscious knowledge, and our intelligendum is our current problem, but between them lies the directly relevant, but currently unquestioned, background to our thought. This I shall call our *standpoint*. For example, in a chemical analysis the nature of the substance to be analyzed is the intelligendum, and within this the analyzer's attention will move between different aspects of the problem. The intelligendum's immediate background, which is the standpoint from which it can be formulated as a problem, is the analyzer's relevant scientific knowledge. But this presupposes a background of beliefs about the relation of chemistry to the rest of knowledge, and why the investigation is worthwhile. Similarly, if we are trying to understand a chess move, this is our intelligendum; within it, the immediate focus of our attention shifts, as we explore possible strategies; beyond that, the standpoint from which we approach it will be, say, that of a chess enthusiast; and the whole situation presupposes such elements of our total belief system as our knowledge of what a game is, and of the human propensity to play games. But this series of levels—belief system, standpoint, intelligendum and focus of attention—can be only provisionally distinguished from each other, for they not only mutualistically interact but continually shift. For example, paying attention to the background brings it into the foreground; so trying to draw a definite line between an intelligendum and its broader standpoint only gives us a new intelligendum, namely the question of just what our former one was.

All these terms have a feature also apparent in "whole" and "part". They mark a constant contrast, but their referent, or what they refer to in the world, depends wholly on context. A chemical sample, which is a whole for analysis, is a part of the whole from which it was taken. The chess move is part of a game, which may be part of a competition. Similarly with our attention, in one sense we attend to the whole intelligendum as our problem, while in another we focus on a part. Further, in an intelligendum we have projects within projects. I aim in this Part to analyze understanding; within that project, I have themes for this chapter; of them, I now focus on my present one; within

it, I must relate its various points; and each of these could be called my
intelligendum. The same applies to a standpoint. With all these terms (other
than "belief system", which does not vary with context because it is defined as
the sum total of all mental contents), I shall say that they *float* with the
context.[11] Floating notions are frustrating if, say, we are trying to classify
phenomena, but we cannot avoid them in analyzing understanding.

 For similar sorts of reasons, we cannot pinpoint the beginning of understanding, for our mental activity relates elements which are already structured by
the language we use in formulating the intelligendum.[12] Investigating the
implications of this fact will raise deep philosophical issues, but the point now
is that our structures build on each other hierarchically, as sub-systems
enclosed in super-systems. We can put this in more traditional language by
saying that the *form* of one structure is the *matter* of another; some aspect of
the structure or form of what we know becomes the subject matter of new
understanding. The form-matter distinction also floats, applying from the
minutest acts of thought to the largest re-examination of our whole belief
system.[13] Yet we must not suppose that the resulting hierarchy of structures is
a neatly ordered one. If it were, then in expounding what we understand we
could follow Lewis Carroll's immortal advice: "Begin at the beginning, and go
on till you reach the end; then stop". But the different aspects of our
understanding are related in ways far more complex than this, so it will be
better to say that structures within our belief system are *many-levelled* rather
than hierarchical.

5. Delimitation and Transcendence

 In trying to apply these floating contrasts, a basic distinction is whether the
standpoint from which we approach the intelligendum is fixed, or is itself
being put into question. All articulation within a standpoint I call *delimitation*;
it structures more clearly what previously was by comparison inchoate. However we may be led to focus on some previous assumption, as in wondering if
the chess player had been bribed. Standing back and reflecting on what we
have been taking for granted, and hence asking whether the intelligendum
could be better posed, I call *transcendence*. But these notions also float;
whether a specific mental act is seen as delimitation or transcendence depends
essentially on context. The most profound innovation is never independent of
its cultural milieu, and so employs beliefs it does not question; but the notion
of reposing the problem fits many a bright child's flash of intelligence. If
working on the development of children's intelligence, we might speak of transcendence in very simple cases, while with movements in the history of
thought we apply it only to large achievements. Yet however context-

dependent the contrast is, it marks an indispensable distinction.

In many of the contexts we will meet, the focus will be on transcendence. For though it does not necessarily yield improvement in understanding, still on a large scale this unpredictable creative shaking of the foundations is found in our greatest intellectual achievements. Yet they need delimitation as well. For delimitation provides the discipline and testing, without which transcendence is wild and unreliable. As a branch of knowledge develops, an act of transcendence that questions what is taken for granted may establish a new standpoint from which to approach its problems; but the later, systematic development of the standpoint is basically delimitation. Yet, since the distinction floats, the transcendence might be seen as delimitation within that whole branch of knowledge; while its development, which I called delimitation, will, on a smaller scale, transcend the ways that issues were previously posed.

Philosophers will realize that the distinction relates to many others. In philosophy of science, Kuhn has distinguished between normal science, in which a paradigm is taken for granted as a standpoint, and revolutionary science in which it is questioned; the former may be seen as delimitation, the latter as transcendence.[14] However I have extended this notion from scientific to all human thought. Again, Hegel inherited and transformed a distinction found in Kant between *Verstand* and *Vernunft*, that is translated as a distinction between "understanding" and "reason" respectively.[15] *Verstand* is a definite but limited standpoint where assumptions are not up for question, while *Vernunft* dissolves all such standpoints till it reaches an overall perspective. Thus the Hegelian English distinction between understanding and reason reflects the contrast in English English between two aspects of understanding, namely delimitation and transcendence. However no discussion, I believe, has adequately emphasized how the distinction floats with the context.

What we may glimpse so far is a rhythm. Usually we are trying to establish a clear and definite picture; this, at a suitably selected level, is delimitation. Yet from time to time our efforts become unsatisfactory, because the standpoint we have accepted has come to seem inadequate. So, like insects which depend upon and yet must outgrow their exoskeletons, we moult the older structures, and establish new ones which will later in turn be discarded. Then we meet a further question: is this cycle a mere change, whereby we exchange one view for another without ultimate improvement; or can it also be a spiral leading to progress in understanding? That, too, will later become a crucial issue.

6. More about Mutualism

I now return to a closer examination of the primary mode of understanding:

the mutualistic interpenetration of whole and part by which each modifies the other.   Since virtually anything may be seen either as part or as whole, mutualism applies everywhere.   Thus in understanding language, it is the delight of linguists and the despair of machine translation.   The influence of the whole appears in how we give a word meaning by fitting it into its context. When we meet the sentence, "Well well, he dug the well well", we see, even if we cannot formulate, that the first two "well"s are a joint exclamation, while the third is a noun and the fourth an adverb.   How we do so depends on unconscious rules too complex to be yet fully discovered, which is why programming them for machine translation is so difficult.   Or consider the newspaper sporting headline: SCRATCH PAIR STILL CYCLE TIP.   All the words can be two or more parts of speech, and some are multiply ambiguous. Yet most people can correctly construe it as elliptical advice to potential bettors that two bicycle riders who have been given a scratch handicap are still most likely to win.   Conversely, while we give sense to a word by referring to the whole passage, our understanding of a passage can be affected, in equally unformalizable ways, by changes in wording.   Consider how the sense of the headline alters, if we transfer the "s" in "still" to the end of "tip".

Language, however, is only one example of mutualism.   Another important one is our sensory experience of the world.   Here the part is the incoming information and the whole is our belief system.   Part affects whole, as our senses tell us about the world, but whole also affects part, as the system shapes what we experience.   Again, consider such cross-cultural conflicts as Evans-Pritchard's account of how the Azande invoked witchcraft to explain *inter alia* what we call disease.[16]   The occurrence of disease is interpreted in terms of their whole belief system; conversely, an acceptance of the value of Western medicine might force their whole worldview to change.   As three further random examples, consider designing a bridge, diagnosing a disease, and literary analysis of a text.   The first involves practical understanding of how to produce something not yet in existence, while the other two are theoretical investigations of what is already there.   The second infers a hidden cause from observable effects.   The third is a much debated enterprise, but one which most theories would see as very different from the other two.   Yet in each case the mind shuttles between whole and part; some element suggests a clue, which is tested by relating it to others, which in turn reject, confirm or modify it.   The part gains its significance by its role in the whole, while the whole is understood through an increasing grasp of the nature and relations of the parts.   Experience tests theory, while theory makes sense of experience.

Thus mutualism also floats.   Though ultimately the whole is our total belief system, interaction is typically between standpoints or other sub-systems within it.   However in the interaction between any sub-systems A and B, each is also potentially influenced by others throughout the whole system.   So we may also think of A as interacting with the whole, though that whole has B prominently in the foreground. Both conceptualizations, as part-part or as part-whole interaction, are acceptable, though in a given context one may be the more illuminating. Mutualism applies to all aspects of a strongly inter-acting system, where any change may lead to unforeseeable ones elsewhere. Yet, finally, the resistance of either the whole or the part to the impact of the other may vary greatly. Thus, though the meaning of a word depends on context, the range of *possible* meanings is given by the language, even if it is repeatedly modified by influences varying from scientific discovery to slang. I also later consider how formalization of language can reduce mutualism.

7. Related Aspects of Understanding

Other important aspects of the search for understanding are so closely related to each other and to mutualism in general, that it is difficult to tell whether *prima facie* separate ones are really distinct. However if some do reduce to others, then by considering them separately, and later realizing their identity, we would still gain insight.

(a) **Multiple Sub-Systems.** It is conceivable that we might structure data with only one concern in mind, and sometimes we may approximate that process. But typically, reaching a conclusion involves multiple considerations with imprecise relations between them. Thus a university librarian, in deciding policy, might consider the needs of undergraduates writing essays, of academics doing research, of budget constraints, etc. There is a multiplicity of competing sub-systems within the whole, which is what militates against achieving a completely systematic belief system. A sub-system typically contains sub-sub-systems while being part of other super-sub-systems, and "system" can float over them all. Each system presents an *aspect* of a given situation, with its own significance, which we fit into an overall structure in varying ways. This notion of an aspect also plays a crucial role in Part B.

(b) **Blurred Boundaries.** Each system typically fades away into an imprecise penumbra, rather than having a precise boundary. Not only do we have centers of expertise surrounded by vaguer beliefs shading off into complete ignorance, but even where we are competent expertise varies from total grasp to mere adequacy. This structure is also reflected in language. Words have many senses, and the senses themselves typically apply to a central core of cases, surrounded by increasingly off-center and then border-line ones.[17] The pattern is again one of multiple sub-systems, each with a core and penumbra. That is why achieving precision within a natural language can be so difficult.

(c) **Fluidity.** Our beliefs are continually being altered, both by new information and by re-articulation of old. Cases range from correcting false impressions by more careful observation, to overturning a whole worldview, and from unnoticed adjustments to intensely emotional conversions. This continual change I call the fluidity of our thought. It also appears in language, where words over a period can develop or decay. For new information may change old meanings, or new attitudes may bring emotional connotations of a word into favor or disfavor. So we extend the use of a word by giving it a new sense, or contract it to give a new precision. The extension may at first be metaphorical, though we shall see that the distinction between metaphor and literal use is difficult; but in time it can become a central paradigm, so the word changes its whole meaning.[18]

English-speaking philosophy commonly says, however, that a notable exception to fluidity arises with concepts. This involves issues where I can take a very minimalist position. All grasp of structure, we saw, depends on discriminating likeness and unlikeness by connecting and distinguishing; and concepts, I suggest, are our means for doing this. Thus in understanding a chess move we might apply the concept of "threatening the queen". In so doing, we connect it to other moves with the same purpose, and distinguish it from those with different ones. So for my purposes, I can treat A's concept of X simply as that by which A takes an X to be both distinguished from non-Xs and connected to other Xs; where "takes to be" is a technical term covering all cases of thinking about X, including wondering or doubting whether there are Xs.[19]

The problem in relation to fluidity is the philosophical claim that concepts cannot change. Certainly people speak as if they did, as in "Concepts of naval strategy had barely developed in Tudor England". But the problem arises: how can we individuate them, or distinguish one from another? With a physical thing, including the sound or mark of a word, we can say that it continues with changing properties; but concepts are not spatio-temporal things. They can be defined, it seems, only by their logical relations of compatibility and incompatibility with other concepts. Since any change alters some of these relations, it must produce a "successor concept" which replaces the old one. But if each change is a replacement rather than an alteration, concepts cannot have fluidity.[20]

Yet in contrast to this approach stand such views as Hegel's notion of dialectic, which see concepts as inherently fluid. Pressing a concept in the right way, they say, reveals the necessity for its opposite; as when a conception of justice as the subjecting of everyone without qualification to the law leads to a harshness which is seen as injustice, and so breeds a more flexible approach.[21] So there is a tension between the powerful arguments in philosophical logic that any alteration to a concept produces a new one, and the need in analyzing understanding to talk of concept-like things that persist while they develop

Errata

Regrettably, there are some textual omissions and repetitions in the latter part of **Chapter IV: Significance, Theoretical and Practical.** The following are the necessary corrections. The text enclosed in square brackets appears in the text.

Page 44, section 4: [We now meet a second major theme for this Chapter: that potentiality and significance, like understanding itself, have not only theoretical but practical] applications. We shall later see that the theoretical/ practical distinction may be drawn in different places, for what is unimportant for one standpoint may be central to another. But to understand understanding, the relevant distinc[tion is between thinking about *what is the case*, and thinking about *what to do*....]

Page 46, lines 1–4: Delete the words "they draw ... ask how the distinction".

Page 46, bottom line: [To ask how significance-judgments are rationally assessable, I begin by] asking whether they are objective. In a given context, often they surely are. For a detective, giving a clue too great or too little significance is as much a mistake as misdescribing the color of a suspect's hair. The significance of a fact may even be more obvious than the fact itself; it may be more difficult to determine the blood group of a bloodspot, than to see the significance of [determining it....]

Page 48, lines 1–6: Delete the words "point contains ... amount to finding".

Page 48, bottom line: [The actual words] are often interdefinable, and so may be individually dispensable; thus I could in principle, though not so conveniently, have focused on the philosophically familiar term "knowledge" rather than "understanding". But my terms, or others in the same circle, seem to me rock bottom in understanding understanding. By repeatedly going round the circle, we learn more about them all, and so come to recognize underlying features of the human mind.

[Yet, we might wonder, what if people should just fail to understand the terms,....]

Necessary corrections will be made in subsequent editions.

over time.[22] Here my minimalist position is simply to speak *as if* concepts could change. So talk of, say, improving a concept may be construed either as changing it, or as producing a more appropriate successor.

(d) Unboundedness. Despite constraints on *current* understanding which we shall later meet, the strong interactions within a belief system give rise to unforeseeable *future* developments.   Not only can we learn more, but transcendence may always lead to new understanding. In reconciling different aspects of our thought, we may take the form of the situation—that there are conflicting structures—as the subject matter of new reflection, and look for a new structure which resolves the conflict. The vagueness and multiplicity of our sub-systems of understanding means that there are always things we do not quite know, evaluate from potentially inconsistent aspects, etc. We may focus on any feature of any situation, make that element of its form the subject matter of a new structure, and so see another aspect of things. The tracing of new structures can start anywhere, can lead in any direction, and stops only at the accidental boundaries of the present moment.

These points present an interlocking picture. Within the belief system, the whole and the sub-systems continually interact with each other. Sub-systems have vague boundaries, and present different aspects of situations. As understanding grows, systems confront each other, and new ones develop to reconcile them. Their impact on each other may produce instability in any area of our thought, and so lead to fluidity and unboundedness. So our understanding has an amorphousness, reflected in our language, which is both a blessing and a curse. A blessing, because it gives us the flexibility to transcend current assumptions; a curse, because it resists the delimitation needed for precise reasoning. It is no accident that computers, which are constructed without amorphousness, can calculate with supreme efficiency, but cannot think creatively.

8. Conscious and Unconscious Tensions

A crucial modern insight is that mental activity extends far beyond conscious reasoning. Here mutualism applies in yet another context, in the interaction between conscious and unconscious elements in the whole belief system. How different sub-systems develop at different stages, how they interact in the progression from birth to maturity, and how they may misdevelop to produce distortions of personality, raises hotly debated questions. But we already know that some basic sub-systems precede a sense of individual identity, while some forms of insanity involve conflicts between sub-systems not under the control of any unified personality. For all of us, growing up involves the repression of fears, angers and guilts which are too threatening to be acknowledged, but which linger as powerful unconscious attitudes. In fact, the major difficulty in unifying our overall belief system may stem from the influence of repressed sub-systems which pull us in conflicting directions. These have a quasi-independent inertia, which maintains them against others. So it is sometimes convenient to speak of them as striving to maintain themselves, just as we sometimes talk as if biological species had a goal of survival, or as if genes had the purpose of propagating themselves.

The conscious-unconscious interaction intrudes even on what seems purely intellectual reasoning. Large and well-established systems, such as academic disciplines or branches of science, absorb new information in ways that make it difficult to tell whether their underlying assumptions need radical change.[23] That itself is a logical point, but new information that challenges cherished beliefs may also be threatening. So arise not only anger and hostility, which do not help our reasoning, but rationalization and wishful thinking by which we ignore the implications of awkward facts. We meet here a point foreshadowed at the end of Ch. I, that such conflicts generate *polarization*; the fear of change leads to a reassertion of the values under threat. So each value fosters its opposite, as when a half-conscious recognition of the unboundedness of future thought stimulates a yearning for beliefs that will stand firm amidst the flux. Such motives drive much intellectual inquiry, but, we shall see, to face them we may have to go beyond intellectual understanding.

Polarization again reflects the Hegelian notion of dialectic, of each concept stimulating its opposite. Yet Hegel also held that this is an inherently rational process, which should take a single proper course; and we shall later see that many today dismiss this as gross over-optimism, or as intellectual imperialism. At present, we need only note the ambivalence of the phenomenon. One person's threatened values are another's intellectual excitement, depending on the nature of their involvement. To a greater extent than logic usually acknowledges, we can *choose* whether to treat rival viewpoints as conflicting or as potentially complementary. Even if they see themselves as opposed, we may still either accept the conflict, or seek to transcend it by finding a new view that preserves what seems central in each. This further question of whether to attempt or to reject reconciliation, will open up its own issues.

9. The Individual and the Tradition

There is a further extension of mutualism; we may consider the individual person as a part, and the group to which they belong as the whole. Here "group" again floats with the context, covering everything from the emerging global village, through nations, down to any sub-culture or academic discipline, and including as a most powerful group the family. For many purposes we must distinguish between the nurturing value of small friendly groups and the alienation produced by large impersonal ones, but my present points apply to groups as such. As a correlative, and equally floating, term, I speak of a "tradition", which is, in effect, the belief system of a group. It includes the language we learn, the beliefs we absorb, and whatever our group takes to be knowledge. From our tradition, modified by our individual history, we inherit our personal belief system. We absorb and take for granted more of it than we can know, even if we are consciously challenging it. This is an ambivalent process. Without a tradition we would not become human at all, but it presents reality to us in ways we can question only with difficulty. So it both makes understanding possible, and yet restricts it. We may transcend the assumptions we inherit and so produce partly new ways of thinking, which will, in turn, both empower and restrict our successors; but always we are historical beings, funmdamentally conditioned by our past. Any new view, however radical, originates as a modification of accepted ones, and continuity with the past constrains the possibilities of the future. What limits our thinking is, in part, facts we do not know and capacities we do not have; but, more importantly, it is *the possibilities we do not think of, or do not take seriously.*

There are both parallels and contrasts in how we speak about groups and individuals. Among the parallels, we say a group has a viewpoint, makes up its mind, etc. As individual belief systems contain sub-systems, so do traditions; though, since these notions float, each sub-tradition can also be seen as the more homogeneous tradition of a sub-group. Fluidity also applies; even apparently static societies alter, while in modern ones the erosion of accepted beliefs is a major challenge. As sub-systems in a belief system conflict, so pressure groups, vested interests and classes struggle with each other. So we find polarization too, by which attitudes provoke their opposites; a sub-group's pressure for a goal commonly produces a backlash, while, conversely, dominant intellectual viewpoints rarely totally suppress others.

Let us turn to the contrasts. Because a group's viewpoint seems to stand solidly over against the individual, people may turn to it in the face of change to seek what will stand firm. This contrast is partly a delusion, since the viewpoints of groups are also fluid, but it can still be a powerful influence. Further, as our whole society has vastly greater information than we do, we may be tempted to assume that it maps the geography of knowledge in essentially *the* correct way. Yet again the contrast is misleading; for a culture, like an individual, can grasp only aspects of reality, having some areas of competence while others are neglected and downgraded. Again, much effort has gone into showing how the official viewpoint of a group may be shaped by a dominant sub-group such as a ruling class, and how this influences other groups by giving them a false consciousness that leads them to accept the authority of their rulers. Here there are parallels with how unconscious attitudes influence individual thought, but also a contrast. For though a ruling class may believe its own ideology, its views normally serve its interests, while unconscious influences often subvert, rather than serve, all rational goals.

As examples of the vast literature on the relation of individual and group, sociology focuses on the impact of group on individual; Marxism takes the relevant group to be the social class, as determined ultimately by its relation to the means of production; and depth psychology emphasizes the importance of the family. My analysis of understanding in itself provides only a minimalist way of posing these issues, but it also suggests a further point which I explicitly endorse: that, here as elsewhere, the relation is genuinely mutualistic. So we should pose questions in terms of the *degree* of influence of group on individual or *vice versa*, and *how* they continually interact. This allows that in a particular case the influence of either on the other might be negligible, but it challenges all views which suggest that either the creative powers of the individual, or the social pressures of the group, exclusively determine the human condition.

When we assess the value of our tradition, we can emphasize either its disabling or its enabling qualities. The former occurs when some sociologists talk of "social conditioning", with an overtone of being on our guard against accepted views. The latter is found in Gadamer's insistence on the value of "Bildung"—an untranslatable notion involving the acquisition of culture, character formation and true education.[24] Such conflicts are difficult to settle, because each side seems to acknowledge how we are influenced by society, but gives it opposite significance. Another issue here is whether the social sciences should aim to guide the momentous choice of whether to accept, transform or reject our tradition, and whether they could do so while retaining the value neutrality they usually seek. The nature of human freedom is also involved in various complex ways.[25] Further, we meet the question of whether any rational assessment of such issues can be made at all; for since we are so embedded in our own tradition, how could we objectively appraise any other? Yet perhaps the deepest question arises from the fact that a person's search for understanding can also be seen as a process whereby the group develops its tradition. So is a tradition ultimately only a way of talking about the beliefs of past and present members of the group, or are our own beliefs only the manifestation of our tradition's self-understanding? English-speaking philosophy usually assumes the first view; to talk of a group's understanding, it holds, is at best a metaphor, and at worst a sinister exaltation of society over the individual. But some English-speaking social science and Continental philosophy takes the second view. It sees us as midwives rather than originators of our ideas, so that our activity is, in effect, the tradition's acting through us. Is this a conflict where one view must prevail—and if so, which? Or is it a tension to be transcended in a more inclusive standpoint? These are among the questions we must face in Part B.

ENDNOTES

1 Linguistic analysis of "understand" would show it has many senses, which have only what Wittgenstein (*op.cit.*, Secs.65-67, pp.31e-32e) called family resemblances; neither a common core of meaning, nor clear-cut ambiguities, but overlapping similarities which appear and disappear like features in the faces of a family.

2 For how this notion relates to the debate between realism and idealism, see Ch. XII.1.

3 An example of the latter is the word "pattern", which I shortly use. Its origin is "pater", i.e. "father". From this came the notion of a patron as a father-surrogate; hence, later, a patron saint. Such a saint came to be thought of, not merely as a protector but as an example to be followed. Hence quite late (c. 16th century) "pattern" (with a second "t") took on the meaning which it has today in, e.g., a dress pattern. From this developed the sense in which I use it.

4 Moving to this conclusion from a remark about two English verbs raises other large questions. It suggests the picture that language starts with concrete words, and extends them to abscract senses. It also suggests, what I think is true, that equivalent words are likely to function similarly in other languages, as natural pictures of understanding. However I avoid these investigations here.

5 This point applies even to such protests as poststructuralism, for challenges to structure still establish structures.

6 Again the relevant words slide between concrete and abstract uses. We connect gas pipes or ideas, we separate arguments or fighting dogs. Concrete roots from Latin and Greek such as binding or putting together appear in such words as "connect" and "synthesize", and loosing, splitting or arranging apart in such words as "distinguish", "separate" and "analyze".

7 Besides this, and seeing and grasping, there are other notions worth investigation. Sometimes we speak of understanding as really listening; cf. the repeated biblical injunction, "Those who have ears to hear, let them hear" (Mat. 11.15 and *passim)*. This seems basically an appeal to something beyond purely intellectual understanding. Again, the Latin root of "intelligendum" represents gathering or picking up. This is close to grasping, and is appropriate to picking out or discerning structure.

8 There are many borderline cases. Suppose I discern the pattern that a spot on my pet piranha grows brighter when she is hungry. Do I simply know this as a brute fact, or do I understand *when* to feed her, though not *why?*

9 Philosophers will realize that I by-pass intricate controversies here, including those about behaviorism, or Wittgenstein's notion of a criterion.

10 In particular, beliefs are often contrasted to value judgments about how things ought to be. Yet in ordinary speech we say as readily that someone believes abortion is wrong, as that they believe there is cheese in the refrigerator.

11 Strictly, but less conveniently, it is the referents rather than the terms that float.

12 So arises a paradox: if we cannot try to understand unless we already have some understanding, how can it ever arise? A full reply would turn on the point that there is a broad spectrum of cases, whether in babies or in animals, where information is processed in increasingly complex ways; and at some more or less arbitrary point we could stipulate that this begins to amount to understanding.

13 Today some philosophers reject the whole form-matter distinction. But the objection seems to apply only when the distinction is used in a non-floating way (as often in the Aristotelean tradition) to treat specific aspects of things as being either their form or their matter. If we use it as a floating contrast, I do not think the objections can hold. For any argument against the distinction focuses on the form of the thought of those who, like myself, use it, and makes that form the subject matter of a claim that it should not be used;

so it uses the distinction in my sense in the very process of rejecting it.

14 T. S. Kuhn *The Structure of Scientific Revolutions* (1970).

15 *Verstand* is a different concept from the *Verstehen* mentioned in Ch. I.1, which is also translated as "understanding".

16 E. E. Evans-Pritchard *Witchcraft Oracles and Magic among the Azande* (1937).

17 Words have both open texture and vagueness, which are not the same. For many purposes the starting point on these matters is still F. Waismann's classic papers "Verifiability" and "Language Strata" (A. G. N. Flew, ed., *Logic and Language* Series I (1951), p. 117, Series II (1953), p. 11). But there are intricate later discussions on various matters; e.g. those concerning the implications which vagueness has for natural languages as means of communication. As one example, cf. the articles in G. Evans and J. McDowell (eds.), *Truth and Meaning* (1975). I do not think their points need conflict with what I say.

18 Some fine examples can be found in the essay "Living Language" in L. Thomas *The Lives of a Cell* (1976). Cf. also "pattern" in fn. 3.

19 This is compatible with most philosophical positions. My approach owes much to excellent, but as yet unpublished, work on concepts by my former colleague, Dr. Marion Knowles, now Marion Kading. She is not responsible for my use of it.

20 Another problem with individuation is that some say the criterion for it must be a precise one; for otherwise in borderline cases we cannot say whether we have one entity or more.

21 See the discussion of Hegelian dialectic in H. G. Gadamer *Truth and Method* (1979) pp. 423-5.

22 We might suggest that even if *the* concept of X cannot change, *my* concept of X can; but that threatens to drive a wedge between the concept and my concept, which would be as unsatisfactory as any other solution. This problem arises not only for concepts but for beliefs, intelligenda, word meanings, etc.

23 Kuhn's discussion of scientific paradigms (*op. cit.*) makes this point forcefully.

24 Gadamer (1979) esp. Part One, I, 1, (b)(i).

25 In analytic philosophy, the problem of freewill arises if we ask whether our choice to reject or accepting a tradition is itself free or determined. For this, see my *Freewill and Determinism* (1968). Then there are questions of political freedom; for, however much we are embedded in our traditions, groups certainly vary greatly in their suppression or stimulation of questioning and diversity. Finally, there is the relation between freedom and awareness: insofar as we come to see how we have accepted a tradition, in what sense may this give us a new freedom to choose, rather than merely to follow it?

CHAPTER III

COHERENCE AND DEPTH

1. Coherence

I now examine more closely the processes involved in the articulation of data into understanding. I do so primarily by exploring what we mean by *coherence* and *depth* of understanding, though other matters also arise. Let us begin by noting how mutualism applies not only to sub-systems within our belief system, but between that system and incoming information. Consider first the pressure of the system on information. Our belief system shapes what we do or do not notice, and hence heavily influences even our direct perception. Dramatic cases occur when we "see" what we expect to see, as when we mistake a piece of rope for a snake because we have been warned to beware of one. These can be corrected by more careful perception, but even then we see only what we have learnt to see, for all our beliefs use concepts that ultimately involve the whole system. Illiterate people see only marks on paper where the literate find information; an aboriginal tracker reads a story in the sand where other eyes see nothing. Conversely, new information puts pressure on the belief system, as it continually modifies and updates our beliefs—not only consciously, as when we learn new facts by reading a newspaper, but unconsciously as when we alter our stride to avoid a puddle.

As a result, we develop a complex attitude towards our perception of the world. We have a fundamental belief that our senses are normally reliable, so that what we see and grasp under good conditions is a basis for the internal seeing and grasping which is understanding. But we also know our senses can mislead us, through illusions, hallucinations or sheer error in unfavorable conditions. So while sometimes we allow perception to overthrow a currently held belief, at other times we may reject purported new information as unreliable. The general point which emerges is that from infancy onwards we develop a picture of the world, which is continually updated, consciously and unconsciously, in both small- and large-scale contexts, by new information; while at the same time the information is assessed in terms of the current picture. The traditional word to express this mutualistic process is that we seek *coherence* in our belief system, and we assume we have understood when we achieve it.

Yet, as we shall see, these apparently straightforward remarks raise immense philosophical issues.[1] The element of unconscious interpretation, which appears when we see what we expect to see, goes far deeper than we easily realize; and today we know that even our most direct perception is the end product of extremely complicated processes in the central nervous system. So to ask how "what we see" is related to "what is really there" raises fundamental problems. Moreover, we can only adjust our beliefs to what we *believe* to be new information, yet we assume that the information represents how the world is independently of us. One way of answering this problem has been to develop coherence theories of *truth*, which relate beliefs to an external world by saying that to call a statement true simply means that it coheres with our other beliefs. Those who reject that view may be suspicious of the concept of coherence. But I too shall reject coherence theories of truth; what I have outlined above is a coherence view of *reasons for believing* something to be true. Yet this distinction raises its own problems. For if we say that we justify beliefs by making them coherent with others (including new information), but that their truth depends on their relation to an outside world, do we not drive a wedge between justification and truth? Could not even a completely coherent set of beliefs be false? In such ways, the simple point that we seek coherence in our belief system opens up profound issues for Part B. But now I am still examining the process itself.

2. Depth

An increase in understanding is not just an addition to knowledge but a restructuring of it, as we reshape our sub-systems in the light of new information. This leads us to the crucial notion of *deeper* levels of coherence. Depth involves an asymmetry, where the deeper explains the more superficial and not *vice versa*, but it takes many forms. With people it may mean that we see their real motives and attitudes; with nature, that we find laws explaining already known ones; with a symphony, that we grasp the structure, both of individual passages and of their relation to the whole. There are depths below depths, for a new structure is not seen as giving deeper insight if it conflicts with an even more basic one. Leibniz rejected Newton's theory of gravitation, though it explained so much, because of a conviction that action at a distance was incomprehensible.[2] Such convictions may themselves be challenged; as science accepted Newton it rejected the rejection, but in turn some may say that relativity theory today is a belated victory for Leibniz. Moreover the notion of depth extends beyond the intellectual understanding we are now discussing, when we speak of a deeper empathetic insight into someone's situation, or of deeply experiencing the impact of a work of art.

I have found it extremely difficult to see common elements here, but in our culture I think we should begin the exploration with the centers of advanced knowledge we call disciplines. They represent our customary structuring of our vast store of knowledge—indispensable for careful inquiry, though needing, like all delimitation, to be transcended when their boundaries become artificial. We cannot distinguish disciplines simply by their subject matter, for they may study different aspects of the same things; but they are shaped by the inquiries they undertake, using the methods they find appropriate. Often we group them into families, such as the twofold Continental division into *Natur-* and *Geisteswissenschaften*, or the common threefold English-speaking one of natural sciences, social sciences and humanities. I believe an adequate theory of understanding transcends these contrasts, and presents a continuum of inquiries, within which disciplines define their own approaches; but still some such division seems a useful starting point. As we shall see, much philosophical conflict today turns on whether the natural sciences or the humanities provide a better clue for integrating our understanding, so a conflict between what I shall call science-based and humanities-based views is a prominent feature.[3] I shall work with this broad contrast. For I believe that the social sciences, in working out their distinctive methods, will draw analogies from both these sources, and what they may need for that task is a clearer grasp of the features of each.

I begin by suggesting a common element. All articulation—in science, in the humanities and outside specific disciplines—seems to involve what we may call *selective description* of the data. We describe the intelligendum, to ourselves or to others, by selecting the significant features which bring out its structure. Philosophers often contrast mere "description" with an "explanation" which gives deeper understanding; but though that contrast has its uses, selective description remains at any level. The skill in the process lies in selecting what is significant and omitting what is irrelevant for a coherent picture. But this common element applies in very different ways, and here we may draw a broad distinction between science and the humanities. The scientific family of disciplines centers on selecting variables that can be experimentally observed and measured in such a way as to permit mathematical treatment; its central method is a mathematico-experimental one. In typical cases, the selectivity in its selective description lies in formulating the hypothesis that is to be tested, while the description involves the language of mathematics. The family of the humanities, by contrast, seems unified more by subject matter; it studies human products, varying from the documents of historians to works of art. Here, by selectively describing the intelligendum we may, for example, integrate facts into a new perspective in history;[4] draw attention to what we had not noticed in criticizing a work of art; or make explicit aspects of our grasp of language in philosophical analysis.[5]

I have not found any method in the humanities which dominates as the mathematico-experimental one does in the sciences. Certainly, most of its disciplines are involved in one way or another with the interpretation of texts, and today this point is often generalized so that any structure is called a "text" to be interpreted. But if this means that all the humanities should study texts in a way developed in such a discipline as literary studies, then it tries to impose a unity of method before it has been shown to be desirable. If, on the other hand, it merely stipulates that whatever the humanities study may be called a text, then it disguises the variety of their methods. In any case, in drawing our distinctions we must avoid a common confusion. We contrast the mathematico-experimental and other methods, and we also contrast science and the humanities; but we then easily assume that, apart perhaps from the social sciences, the two contrasts coincide. Yet they do not. As one example, classical evolution theory, on which biology depends, is a basic part of science. But methodologically its form of selective description has affinities to history, though using its own sort of evidence, and only now is it being mathematicized through the application of molecular biology, etc. Again, logic is a sub-branch of philosophy in the humanities, but is a formal discipline like mathematics. Yet the contrast is a useful place to start. For the notion of depth is found in both the sciences and the humanities, but with significant differences which are related to their typically different methods.

3. Depth in Science

With science, we can draw on current discussions in English-speaking philosophy of science about why scientists prefer one theory to another. Various factors are acknowledged to be relevant; a typical list speaks of "accuracy, consistency, scope, simplicity, and fruitfulness".[6] Just what these mean has kept philosophers busy, but my concern is their relation to depth. As for the first two, to show that theories deal accurately with the phenomena and are consistent both internally and with other theories, rarely in itself gives greater depth of understanding; but scope, simplicity and fruitfulness typically do. Scope means that the theory explains other matters beyond its original field. Simplicity is a difficult notion to explicate,[7] but it is easily grasped intuitively, and is widely acknowledged to contribute to deeper insight. So does fruitfulness, which refers to opening up new lines of research. I use "elegance", stipulatively, to cover these criteria, together with any analogous ones. Elegance is seen in such achievements as the theory of electro-magnetic radiation, which unified earlier knowledge of electricity, magnetism, heat and light. In many-levelled scientific understanding, the most striking advances come as higher-level laws are found from which lower-level ones can be deduced, so that we are not so much explaining sheer new facts as deepening our understanding of previous explanations.

Elegance, however, is not the only criterion, for we meet depths below depths. As we saw with Leibniz and gravity, an elegant theory may not cohere with other parts of our total belief system. Despite the unquestioned elegance of quantum mechanics, such physicists as Einstein denied that it gave real insight into how nature works; for it seemed to challenge strict causality, and so to conflict with the overall structure of science. Science can hope that, as in Einstein's case, such issues will eventually become experimentally testable, so that attractive speculation can be disciplined by experiment.[8] But this is only part of the answer, for we inevitably meet questions *about* science that the scientific method itself cannot answer. A sociological inquiry might show what proportion of scientists agreed with Einstein's view of causality, but that would not show who was right. Still less could we devise an experiment to show what the proper place of experimental science should be in our overall worldview. Such issues lead, in the first place, to philosophy of science, and beyond that to still broader ones in general philosophy. I later argue that today our overall understanding of science has itself become a problem. But my present point is only that, powerful though the appeal to elegance in science may be, it is not the only thing to consider in an analysis of depth.

4. Depth in The Humanities

Increasing depth in science depends on the types of laws discovered, but the humanities have no such laws. A deeper understanding of how elements in *Hamlet* cohere to produce its power, does not give a formula by which to write equally powerful plays.[9] New insights do show analogies to scope, simplicity and fruitfulness as they extend to other fields and open up new questions, so we may extend the broad notion of elegance to the humanities too. Yet here the issues are less precise, reasoning is less conclusive, and, above all, evaluation of what counts as improvement is more debatable. Today, we shall see, the very goal of seeking deeper understanding may be rejected. However I see two dimensions of what we normally take to be deeper insight here. Each involves a family of cases, with complex intra- and inter-family relationships.

(a) One dimension is to expand our personal awareness of ourselves and of the human situation: of our potentialities and limits, of the factors that influence us, and of the values and attitudes we may adopt. This is often a motive in the study of novels, of drama and of history, not to mention the social sciences. Such understanding covers two aspects: individual character, and relationships within society. Yet the two closely interact. We can, I think, neither understand individuals without seeing how they are influenced by the family or by larger social structures, nor understand the forces operating in society without seeing how people respond to them.

(b) The other dimension is esthetic understanding, which concerns art, including literature, rather than the human situation. Traditional approaches here involve two claims. One is that a work of art has the capacity to challenge us if we open ourselves to it, and that unless we do so our understanding of it will be superficial. That involves an element of going beyond purely intellectual understanding. The second traditional claim is that a work of art is an autonomous whole to be appreciated for its own sake. While no doubt our knowledge of the relevant art contributes to our insight, yet still understanding a work is grasping its own structure. For only in this way, it is said, can we distinguish good art from bad, and on that all proper judgment depends. By contrast, some contemporary views treat a work of art as something to be understood by the same criteria as other artifacts.[10] My general analysis of understanding is compatible with either, but has a special application to views which see a work of art as autonomous. Always there is interaction between foreground and background, but for autonomy views it takes on a specific form. The foreground is the work itself; the background is everything we bring to it. Their interplay means that a great work may speak to us over generations in indefinitely many ways if we open ourselves to it; but though we see new aspects, it is the work itself which makes the impact.

I suggest that, insofar as the humanities aim at deeper understanding, the search moves in the two dimensions mentioned, which cut across disciplines and complement each other in varying ways and degrees. The point of studying novels and drama involves esthetic appreciation as much as expanded awareness. A great history may be appraised as a work of art, while a work of art may be treated as a historical document throwing light on the past. However I have not found a significant connection between the two dimensions themselves, which might provide a relatively unified concept of depth in the humanities.[11] Moreover, apart from these complexities, we lack decisive criteria for depth within each of them. We easily assume our latest insights are superior to old ones. But, in the esthetic dimension, may not taste decline, so that what one age sees in a work of art is more superficial than in the past? As for expanding awareness, a selective description, whether using real events as in history or fictional ones as in a novel, may explicitly or implicitly present a vision of the human situation. But, in typical mutualistic fashion, while the vision expands our awareness, we must judge whether it is ultimately a true or a distorted one in the light of what we already believe. The criteria by which we do so are too subtle to be made fully explicit, and in the end the search for them leads, I believe, beyond intellectual understanding.

As a result, though in the humanities the apostles of new visions may proclaim the inadequacy of previous views, we often find ourselves speaking of complementary, if not equally profound, insights into different aspects of phenomena. In science, by contrast, claims to understand are usually rivals, and use the idiom of distinguishing truth from error.[12] There are exceptions; philosophers usually speak of seeking *the* truth rather than complementary insights, however unsuccessful they may be at finding it. Conversely, science has sometimes had to live with complementary insights, as when wave and particle theories of light could not be reconciled. Yet the distinction is pervasive enough to have suggested an invidious comparison. When, as in science, we have adequate criteria for depth, we talk of truth and error; when, as in the humanities, we have not, we talk perforce of competing insights. But that comparison is incomplete. For we have seen that elegance may not be enough even in scientific contexts, and at the final level of combining all insights into a worldview, we shall meet new complexities.

5. Depth, Coherence and Transcendence

The previous discussion, which is itself a typical piece of selective description, on the whole brought out the merits of science rather than the humanities. Science has relatively clear criteria for depth of understanding, until its deepest assumptions are questioned. But in the humanities, I found two dimensions of depth—awareness of the human situation and of works of art—which I have not effectively unified. Criteria for depth may seem to lie in the eye of the beholder, and complementarity largely replaces rival truth-claims. The differences seem to turn on the *degree* and the *sort* of constraint on transcendence. When a delimited context is not up for question, the direction of depth may be set also; but the more we transcend our assumptions, the less this holds. The strong constraints in scientific contexts mean that elegance signals success. Yet in reflecting *about* science, we cannot use the mathematico-experimental method; and then, however much scientific knowledge the inquiry may require, and whether it is undertaken by reflective scientists or by philosophers, we must fall back on less specialized forms of selective description which impose fewer constraints.

Not that constraints are lacking in the humanities. Most work is done within some school of thought which provides criteria for acceptability. But debates about criteria frequently challenge the schools, so that disciplines more often re-examine their assumptions; and in any case, "issues are less precise, reasoning is less conclusive, and ... evaluation of what counts as improvement is more debatable" (Sec. 4). Overall, what we meet is a trade-off: the greater the depth, the more difficult the resolution of an issue. Though some methods —particularly scientific ones—have more powerful decision procedures than others, we can only use a method appropriate to our context. As a species may flourish because of an adaptation which may still become disastrous if the environment changes, so a method may succeed because of its specialization, but be inappropriate in different circumstances. So in, say, the search for an overall worldview, we must retreat from the specialized success of the scientific method towards more general ways of seeking coherence.

In general, then, coherence, transcendence and depth are interrelated concepts. As we make our understanding more coherent by re-organizing our picture of the world, we need both delimitation and transcendence. Not all transcendence gives depth, for reflection on what we had taken for granted may lead in any direction. But depth is one form of transcendence, which arises from the many-levelled nature of understanding. The mere adding of new information may obscure understanding; but as we struggle for more coherence, one aspect of doing so is to question previous assumptions. It is here that metaphors of digging below the surface saturate our thought. The assumptions *underlie* our thought, so unearthing them gives *deeper* insight. In this way the search for greater depth is at the heart of the process of creating greater coherence between our levels of understanding.

6. Ultimate Depth—Constructive or Critical

The previous points apply in many ways to my own discipline of philosophy. Later I shall use the trade-off between depth of penetration and resolution of issues to explain why philosophy seeks final truth but never seems to reach it. But now let us consider our capacity to transcend a standpoint, and ask where it might end. We may then conceive a possibility which philosophers have often seen as their ultimate ideal: to transcend all limited standpoints, and to see the ultimate structures that relate everything within the whole. This is the most ambitious of philosophical goals. It arises naturally from reflection on transcendence, and may even seem self-evident: why should we *not* aim at a coherent overview? Yet here we meet a great conflict. For an opposite reaction is found repeatedly in the history of thought, particularly when some overarching system has grown tired and stale. This reaction rejects grand intellectual constructions as a pretentious goal beyond our reach. Its attitude towards them may vary from the contemptuous to the wistful. But always it says that, even if the search for them is inevitably suggested by our capacity for transcendence, it is a temptation we must learn to resist.

The two approaches have been given various names, such as speculative and critical metaphysics respectively, but I shall speak of constructivist and criticalist approaches. We may approach the difference as follows. When we set out to articulate some intelligendum, we cannot always find a coherent or interesting or significant unity. We may end with a collection of sub-systems that represents only the disconnected ways we have managed to make sense of our information. The result may have the merely "formal" unity of being *our* knowledge, rather than having the "material" unity of being a coherent whole. Constructivism asserts that ultimately our thought must have a material, coherent unity, while criticalist opponents say it has at most the formal one of being *our* beliefs. The choice between the two is as live an issue today as ever it was, and so far my argument shows only that each side has deep roots in how we think. As we shall see, current English-speaking philosophy arose in a strongly criticalist *milieu*, but today a particular form of constructivism is widespread within it. Elsewhere, however, the cluster of views broadly called postmodernism reflects a strongly criticalist position. This will be a central issue in Part B, where I eventually defend a cautiously optimistic attitude towards constructivism.

7. Creativity

I now turn to consider the inherent creativity of the human mind.[13] When we work within a delimited standpoint, we can not only assess proposed new knowledge by asking how it fits what we already know, but can sometimes foresee the form of new understanding by asking what gaps in our knowledge remain to be filled. Yet the more the framework is challenged, the more our foresight withers, so that our recognition of deeper insight is often only retrospective. This applies both to the sciences, where relativity and quantum mechanics were unforeseeable, and to forecasting the future of the arts and humanities. So how does our understanding, in its unboundedness, reach the achievements which we can perhaps assess when they confront us, but which we could not foresee?

The unpredictable creativity that forms new structures and challenges old ones seems to have two elements, each a matter of degree. The first, which will later lead us beyond intellectual understanding, is an *opening* of ourselves. Essentially creativity happens to us; it draws strength from sources beyond our knowledge, and is not ours to command. But, second, what distinguishes it from fantasy is control or discipline. In intellectual contexts insights must be tested against possible objections, while in art also the original glimpse is only the starting point. Without the vision that comes from self-opening, work has no flair or inspiration; without discipline, its potential will not be realized. These two elements are specially important cases of transcendence and delimitation respectively. They are in a tension with each other which varies in different individuals from the stimulating to the agonizing: to open ourselves is one attitude, to impose order is another, and combining them is never easy.

I believe that our response to proposed insights has analogies to the two elements that are involved in creating them. The reasons we offer for acceptance or rejection will depend on how we articulate it with our other beliefs. In rigorous contexts such as academic disciplines, our reasoning will respond to the rigor that was originally applied to the creativity. But the process goes deeper. Even scientists find that, in their trained judgment, a radical new proposal "feels" right or wrong; and though such feelings are highly fallible, they powerfully influence the direction of scientific effort. The point holds even more strongly for the humanities. Here, in our attraction or hostility to the proposal, our own creativity reacts to that of the creator. So our response, like the original, eventually goes beyond intellectual understanding.

8. Coherence and Truth

We now meet a final point. Though we acknowledge depth and creativity most easily with views we accept, we may also do so with those we reject. So why do we reject them? Because, creative though they may be, we take them to be *false*. In searching for a more coherent picture of the world, we seek *true* beliefs, in a different and stronger sense than when we may speak of the truth of a work of art. I discuss the concept of truth in Part B, but we meet now its inescapable role in better understanding. Though the many-levelled structure of understanding forces on us a notion of levels of truth—though, therefore, a deep understanding contrasts with one that is superficial but not necessarily false—yet my discussion of coherence, depth and creativity is still a complexity in, and not a substitute for, the claim that better understanding gives us more truth about the world. And the mere exhilaration of finding coherence, or even of creative intellectual breakthrough, is no guarantee we have reached it.

Here as elsewhere, the more we question our assumptions the more our difficulties increase. To raise the problem sharply, I focus on science; for whatever view we might hold of its ultimate significance, few deny the power of its method in its own sphere. For this discussion I can borrow sterotyped examples from current science-based philosophy, without asking whether they are fair or accurate; so I take the natural sciences as the paradigm of true knowledge, and witchcraft and astrology as false. The problem is to find criteria that distinguish the two. The attraction of pseudo-knowledge lies largely in claims to disclose hidden structure—how magic affects the world, or stars our destiny. To those who accept them, these give a sense of depth through explaining manifest phenomena by hidden causes. But that is just what gives depth to scientific understanding. So the difference is said to lie in method and in result: the superiority of scientific method is its openness to empirical test, and the superiority of result is that its theories work. By contrast, it is said, pseudo-sciences either resist empirical testing, by offering built-in explanations that can account in advance for any possible failure; or else they allege results which depend only on the will to believe of adherents.

Yet current English-speaking philosophy of science is acutely conscious of the difficulty of these claims.[14] Science, like all thought, has its standpoint, and the more this is challenged, the less applicable the scientific method becomes. In fact, if we focus on the large-scale issue of the rise of the scientific outlook itself, we find the same reliance on glimpsed and unverified structure as in pseudo-knowledge. In the case of witchcraft, historians debate why the great 17th century concern with it died down, but certainly it was not because of scientific proof that no-one had the power to put a murrain on their neighbors' cattle. Nor could it have been so, since all who might have claimed such powers knew that a successful demonstration of them would lead to a painful death. The change occurred before a germ theory of disease, and was based simply on the general conviction that all causal mechanisms in nature were like those in the physical sciences. Belief in witchcraft withered away because there was no *room* for it in the explanatory scheme of the new natural sciences. Similarly, astrology was not so much disproved as *squeezed out* by the new astronomy. A few new discoveries were projected to create a new sense of possibilities and impossibilities in nature, and so whole branches of learning were rejected. Not only superstition and carelessness have jumped to conclusions, but our greatest intellectual triumphs also.

So we find a dilemma. Knowledge surely has advanced since Galileo rejected Aristotle, and the science which lands a man on the moon is superior to primitive speculation. Yet an embarrassingly plausible case can be made that whether we accept witchcraft and astrology on the one hand, or science on the other, depends on the culture into which we are born.[15] This is the challenge of relativism, that no view can ultimately be shown to be better than any other. In reply, I shall later argue that we can properly trust our broad tradition of knowledge, though there may be more things in heaven and earth than are dreamt of in our science. But now we must note how the challenge arises not only from the extent to which our culture shapes our thought, but from the unboundedness of understanding itself. If knowledge and understanding require truth; and if nothing can be established as unquestionably true, because our present beliefs might be transcended in some unforeseeable way; then, however bravely we call such transcendence "creative", do we really know whether even our best justified current beliefs amount to real knowledge? So our capacity for creative transcendence not only gives rise to the sense of deeper understanding, which we so often seem to achieve, but also inevitably questions the reliability of all claims to knowledge.

ENDNOTES

[1] For the most general ones, see Ch. XII. More technical ones include the following. (1) Since coherence can apply only to our beliefs, I might seem to be saying that perception is *nothing but* the acquiring of beliefs. But though some philosophers do hold this view (e.g., D. M. Armstrong *A Materialist Theory of Mind* (1968)), I take a minimalist position. I do not need to offer any "theory of perception", or even to deny that unconscious sensory interaction might occur in ways too simple to amount to acquiring beliefs. (2) My view has a complex relation to J. L. Pollock's *Contemporary Theories of Knowledge* (1986). The role I accord to perception is not, I think, in his technical sense a coherence view at all. (3) Coherence and conservatism have been contrasted as opposites (G. Harman "Positive versus Negative Undermining in Belief Revision" (1984) p. 154). But as I use the words, conservatism is simply one of the values we use to bring about coherence.

[2] For this and other examples, cf J. S. Mill *A System of Logic* (1947) pp. 157-8.

[3] Our language has no neutral vocabulary here. Science-based views often call themselves "scientific"; but that borrows the prestige of science for views which are *about*, rather than *part of*, science, and which cannot themselves be established by the methods that give science its reliability. Opponents call such views "scientistic", but that word is always used pejoratively. There is also a problem for humanities-based views, for "humanist" not only is rarely used neutrally but also has widely different meanings. It goes back to a pre-scientific Renaissance tradition which contrasted humane learning, or the humanities, not with science but with a medieval, narrowly *religious* concern. Since the religious outlook was also challenged by the success of science, those who call themselves humanists today are often friends of science, though foes of religion. On the other hand, postmodernist views in the humanities today reject "humanism", but they mean by it the notion of a human subject found in the Enlightenment.

[4] British children, learning their Empire's history, used to read of "The Indian Mutiny" (1857-59). Today, Indian children read of "The First Indian War of Independence". This simple descriptive change carries a wealth of significance.

[5] For how much of our ordinary knowledge is implicit, cf. M. Polyani *The Tacit Dimension* (1967). See also Ch. VI.1.

[6] T. S. Kuhn *The Essential Tension* (1977) p. 322.

[7] Cf. e.g., E. Sober *Simplicity* (1975). The variety of theories he notes (p. vii) shows the philosophical difficulty of the notion.

[8] I have in mind here the Einstein-Podolsky-Rosen paradox, which later, after Bell's theorem, was found to be experimentally testable, and shown to be false.

[9] In practice, however, what the humanistic and the scientific expert both acquire is not a set of laws which can be straightforwardly applied, but a repertoire of considerations which are likely to be relevant.

[10] Such views vary from Marxist or Freudian ones to deconstructionism. There are also other conflicts. Views appealing to esthetic experience leave little room for understanding, while hermeneutic theories may insist that understanding in art illuminates all other; cf. H.-G. Gadamer (1977) (1979), R. E. Palmer *Hermeneutics* (1969). I am neutral here, and also in the conflict over whether or how the creator's intention is relevant. I believe that there is a valid point in the autonomy view, but that in general complementary insights are too often treated as rivals.

[11] Since esthetic understanding asks why art moves us as deeply as it does, we might say, very generally, that the humanities seek understanding of ourselves and of what moves us. However "understanding ... what moves us" is ambiguous here as between understanding the thing which moves us (the work of art), and understanding what it is about human nature, in virtue of which we are moved. So the phrase does not represent a concept which usefully unifies the two dimensions.

[12] Technical debates about degrees of verisimilitude concern approximations to, not aspects of, the truth.

[13] I have taken some aspects of this question further in my "Creativity and Depth in Understanding" in J. Brzezinski, S. Di Nuovo, T. Marek and T. Maruszewski *Creativity and Consciousness: Philosophical and Psychological Dimensions* (1993).

[14] The vast literature stems particularly from K. R. Popper *The Logic of Scientific Discovery* (1959), and T. S. Kuhn *The Structure of Scientific Revolutions.* For one sample of the debate, cf. I. Lakatos and A. Musgrave (eds)., *Criticism and the Growth of Knowledge* (1970). A valuable introduction, going beyond mere exposition, is A. F. Chalmers *What is This Thing Called Science?* (1982).

[15] Some add that *within* science choices are ultimately arbitrary. See P. K. Feyerabend *Against Method: Outline of an Anarchistic Theory of Knowledge* (1975).

CHAPTER IV

SIGNIFICANCE, THEORETICAL AND PRACTICAL

1. Significance and Importance

The next stage in the analysis returns to the point in Ch. II.3 that understanding involves *significant* structure.[1] Philosophers and linguists are often concerned with significance. But they use the word in the specialized sense in which it indicates that a term has meaning, as in the Oxford English Dictionary example:

(1) -kin is a significant termination.

However the relevant sense for our analysis is the more general one in which the two most authoritative dictionaries of English interdefine significance and importance.[2] If we consider such cases as

(2) A more (significant/important) development in the growth of agriculture was...

we see the difference. "-kin" may be a significant termination, but it is not an important one.[3]

As seeing and grasping gave a clue to understanding, so I turn to the concrete senses underlying significance and importance. "Sign" comes originally from a battle standard, which showed the presence of a leader; and the significant is what will, in a variety of contexts and senses, signal, represent or indicate the presence of something else. The root of "important", on the other hand, is carrying into, as when we speak of a country's imports. What do these two notions have in common? In articulation, that which is taken as a clue to a structure is a sign that indicates its presence. The significant is *that which is to be taken into account* if our grasp is to be satisfactory. The forensic expert takes a barely noticeable stain on a coat, and shows it to be blood of the same type as the murder victim's; it thereby acquires immense significance. Another similar looking stain turns out to be mud, and has no significance. What then of importance? To see what is significant carries us, imports us, into the position from which we can understand. This seems the common element of meaning. "They do not see the (significance/importance) of ..." indicates they do not see that something they already know is also a sign which should carry them to a deeper standpoint.

Sometimes, however, "important" is a stronger, rather than equivalent, term.

(3) Smoking is an important factor in lung cancer

surely says more than

(3') Smoking is a significant factor in lung cancer.

For (3), but not (3'), suggests it has *more* influence than many others. Another example, the content of which also makes the point, is:

(4) The fact that "significant" and "important" are sometimes equivalent and some-times not, is enough to show there must be a significant difference in meaning, but is not itself enough to show the difference is important.

Both the dictionaries earlier mentioned give a further word as a synonym for importance but not for significance: "weight". This is another natural meta-phor for aspects of our thinking, and the root of "to deliberate" is to weigh in a balance. To say a factor has weight does not mean it must override all else, but it means more than merely that it should be taken into account in our deliberation. "Important" has come to carry the sense of being weighty, of something which should not merely count but count for a great deal. Yet if "significant" means "is to be taken into account", while "important" means "is to count heavily", how can they ever function interchangeably? Well, in contexts of comparison the difference vanishes. To say X is *more* significant (more to be taken into account) than Y, or *as* significant, is to say it is more important (is to count more heavily), or as important. Similarly, if we have eliminated all but one of the relevant factors, "This is *the* (significant-/important) factor", leaves no room for a distinction between counting and counting heavily.[4]

I have used "significant" and "important" only as crossbearings to locate the crucial notion of that-which-is-to-be-taken-into-account. Other words also cluster here, such as "relevance" and "interpretation"; often seeing the signifi-cance of a relevant fact represents an interpretation of the data. But as I earlier picked out "structure" from a collection of near-synonyms, so I use "significant" as the general term. In any form of selective description, we need what I shall call significance-judgments if we are to articulate our data.

2. Significance of Part and of Whole

Since there is continual mutualistic interplay between foreground and background, in which each must be taken into account, significance applies as much to a larger structure that makes sense of a fact, as to a fact that suggests a structure. In the bloodspot example a fact was significant because it suggested an overall picture, but police faced with multiple murders might see significance in a pattern, such as that the murderer stabbed with the left hand. What is to be taken into account may be either a fact which points to a structure, or a structure which highlights a fact.   The notion of significance floats, for the relevant background of a significance-judgment is our particular standpoint.   It is from the standpoint of wanting to catch criminals that the examples above have significance.   The intelligendum of the police might be, in typical floating fashion, the solving either of a crime or of a series of them, and the standpoint from which they approach it includes their professional skills, their concern to catch criminals or to achieve promotion, etc.   Here there are fairly clear-cut criteria for what is relevant, but not always.   Unless we have a relevant standpoint, we cannot grasp what is significant—as when an expert immediately diagnoses the fault we could not discern.   Or, as a very different case, some pattern may register unconsciously in our belief system, so that we do not know why something seems significant to us.   Yet always phenomena are significant only from some standpoint.

Significance, fact, structure, relevance, standpoint and intelligendum are a package deal of concepts, all involving each other and essential to our understanding.   Because they float, they reappear at many levels.   To illustrate with "fact" and "structure", if we explain observed facts about chemical reactions by the law of their combination, then relative to the observations the law is a structure.   At another level, it may be a fact to be explained by laws of molecular structure, while those laws might in turn be facts derived from quantum mechanics.   The intermediate members of the series can be called either facts or structures, leaving at one end the facts of observed reactions, and at the other the laws of quantum mechanics which cannot be fitted into wider ones. The constant factor is that, in each context, a fact is the part, while a structure is the whole.   We also easily shift, not merely between levels but to radically new contexts: chemical reactions take on quite different significance if we focus on their beauty, or on the skill of the experimenter.   But always we articulate by seeing the significance both of facts and of structures.

3. Potentiality and Possibility

The previous examples of facts represent how the world is, so they may tempt us to think of all true beliefs as representing actual states of affairs.   But this masks the crucial point that significance also inherently involves the notion of *potentiality* or *possibility*.   We pick out items in the world, from boots to butterflies, largely in terms of potentiality: boots are things that could fit an appropriate foot, and that will not turn into butterflies; butterflies exemplify the potentialities of caterpillars, and cannot turn into boots; things of which this was not true would not be boots or butterflies, even if they looked the same.   Similarly, the discussion in Ch. III.8 noted how "a new sense of possibilities and impossibilities in nature" led to the rejection of whole bran-

ches of learning. Again, laws of nature, and the causal relations by which we
make sense of the world, state not merely what does or does not happen, but
also what *can* or *cannot* happen.[5] They involve what are called counterfactual
statements, that, say, *if* this piece of cold metal *were* to reach X degrees centi-
grade, *then* it would melt. In general, grasping the significance of things
depends on knowing what is or is not possible, and why.

English-speaking philosophy has dealt with possibility primarily as the
notion of *logical* possibility, which is what can be asserted without self-
contradiction: it is logically possible that butterflies might turn into boots, but
not that 2 + 2 might equal 5. This notion has elegant uses in modern formal
logic.[6] It also plays an important role in clarifying concepts; for to ask if a
state of affairs is logically possible is, in effect, to ask whether the description
of it is conceptually coherent, so that incoherent uses of concepts emerge as
logical impossibilities. It is logically possible that I might burgle Fort Knox,
but not that I might burgle my own home—not because my home is safer than
Fort Knox, but because burglary is breaking into *someone else's* property.
Besides this, philosophers recognize a notion of nomic possibility. It is
usually defined as what can occur in accordance with the laws of nature, and
is used in the analysis of causal and scientific laws. But, just as we had to
move beyond technical uses of "significant", so again we need now a concept
that is not precisely covered by logical and empirical possibility. To avoid
confusion, I call it "potentiality".

A search for understanding can take into account only what we *believe to be*
potentialities, though we will normally take them to hold whether we had
believed them or not. The believed ones are a subset of the real ones, for the
world presumably contains more potentialities than we know. But our beliefs
may also be false, so believed potentialities include some that do not really
obtain. Believed and real potentialities are separate but overlapping classes.
Believed potentiality is an untidy notion, compared to the relatively clear-cut
ones of logical and empirical possibility, but its role in significance-judgments
is indispensable. It applies not only to the world, but, crucially, to ourselves.
Our hopes and fears, our plans, predictions and precautions, concern what is
possible rather than actual, both for ourselves and in the world. Without these
we would not be what we are. To be human is essentially, and not merely
accidentally or occasionally, to live with mental horizons bounded by what we
believe to be potentialities.

4. Theoretical and Practical

We now meet a second major theme for this Chapter: that potentiality and
significance, like understanding itself, have not only theoretical but practical

tion is between thinking about *what is the case*, and thinking about *what to do*. The significant is what is to be taken into account, but, as the earlier examples showed, this may be either for theoretical or for practical purposes. Similarly, while theoretical potentialities represent how the world operates, practical ones present possible alternatives for our actions.

In exploring the search for understanding, we must ask not only how but why we think, and then we find that theoretical and practical concerns are intimately connected. Our standpoints are sub-systems which, like our belief system as a whole, contain both factual and evaluative elements—even if what we value is simply knowledge for its own sake. My distinction between theoretical and practical is itself a practical one, defined in terms of whether our *goal* is to discover how things are, or to decide what to do. We may ask the theoretical question why people pursue their goals, without judging if the goals are appropriate. But even this asking is something we *do*, and so we may raise the practical question of whether and why we should do it. So the theoretical and the practical each provide standpoints from which the other can be assessed. Further, the distinction floats, and where we draw it may depend on our standpoint. A pilot notices the aircraft is losing altitude, and immediately takes corrective action. We could distinguish a "theoretical" recognition of the facts from a "practical" response, but the theoretical process occurs within a practical one; instruments are scanned, not just to gather information but to fly the aircraft. Conversely, in a theoretical scientific investigation, a printout of data might show a fault in the programming and immediately set off practical reflection on how to remedy it. In each case observation shows something to be the case, and by a movement of the skilled mind so spontaneous as to be unnoticed, the fact is seen as significant for action.

Indeed my basic formulation of intellectual understanding in Ch. II.3—"the articulation of data so as to discern a structure with an adequate degree of significance"—applies to practical no less than to theoretical understanding. We articulate by adjusting conflicts within and between sub-systems, in deciding either what is the case or what to do. Our reasoning involves whatever potentialities we see, and even the words we use are largely the same: we speak of laws of nature and laws of the land, rules for prediction and rules of conduct. The parallels between theoretical and practical reasoning are far closer than philosophers often realize. Yet there remains a difference between what we may conveniently call theoretical *statements* and practical *evaluations*. In theoretical cases, articulation concerns how the world works; in practical ones, it makes coherent such things as our wishes, goals and obligations. Many have held that this difference makes all the difference. For they draw a sharp distinction between theoretical "facts" and practical "values", and often claim that, while factual beliefs may be rationally confirmed or rejected, we have no way of similarly assessing values. I discuss this in Ch. XIII, but now we must ask how the distinction they draw a sharp distinction between theoretical "facts" and practical "values", and often claim that, while factual beliefs may be rationally confirmed or rejected, we have no way of similarly assessing values. I discuss this in Ch. XIII, but now we must ask how the distinction between statements and evaluations operates in the search for understanding. Here my approach reformulates the problem, by asking whether and how we can rationally assess the significance-judgments that play so indispensable a role.

5. The Problem of Objectivity

I now introduce a distinction between *objective* and *subjective* claims. These two words always mark a contrast, but are used in many ways.[7] To grasp my own use, consider the difference between saying "Joe likes yoghurt" and "I like yoghurt". The two facts are similar, but the utterances are not. For I could be wrong about Joe, but not about myself; though I can lie about my tastes, if I believe I like yoghurt I like it.[8] I apply "objective" and "subjective" to beliefs or utterances, rather than to what they are about; and the central notion is that they are objective if our sincere belief may still be *mistaken*.[9] So the remark about Joe is objective, and the one about me subjective (though if *you* said I liked yoghurt, that would be objective). I shall clarify this point by relating it to some others, and then use it to discuss the assessment of significance-judgments.

The objective/subjective contrast is not the same as the earlier statement/ evaluation one. As the yoghurt examples show, statements can be either objective or subjective, and we can leave open whether this is also true of evaluations. So when I discuss the fact/value distinction in Part B, I need not beg questions about whether evaluations can be objective. Next, objectivity —the notion that we might be sincerely mistaken—is linked to truth, for to call an utterance true seems to say that it represents how things are independently of our beliefs. But there are two problems here. First, as we shall see, some philosophers deny this notion of truth. Second, "true" is more at home in theoretical than in practical contexts. Many philosophers, and not only those attached to a gulf between facts and values, say that only statements, and not evaluations, can be true or false. However, even if we agree with them, we can still ask if evaluations may be (not true but) objective. Finally, objectivity links with the notion of rational assessment, for normally we have some idea of how objective utterances could in principle, even if not in practice, be confirmed or rejected. But we must not confuse the two. For, as we shall see, it at least seems conceivable that a belief might be right or wrong, even though we had no way of finding out which it was.[10]

To ask how significance-judgments are rationally assessable, I begin by determining it. We cannot *directly* observe significance as we can hair color, but this applies to many facts, including scientific ones; complexity of confirmation is different from objectivity. Certainly, not *all* significance is objective. If I enter a gift shop to look for something that takes my fancy, the significance of what I see is that it does or does not do so; and that it takes my fancy is subjective, true if I take it to be so. But this subjectivity exists because my standpoint is a subjective one. In general, significance must be judged from a standpoint, and it is subjective only if the standpoint makes it so.

Now the question shifts to the nature of standpoints: can we treat them as objective starting points that might be mistaken? Well, first, as we have seen, some of them make no claim to objectivity. Among those that claim to represent the world correctly, some surely are objective, *given* that others are. Since the notion floats, this applies particularly to sub-standpoints within larger ones: if we accept the general standpoint of scientific investigation, we can rationally defend, say, the results of chemistry. But the larger standpoint has its own assumptions, which we presuppose in defending the sub-standpoint. If we hold, as a paranoic might, that all scientists distort information because they are trying to take over the world, why should we trust chemistry? So, finally, the question now shifts to such problems as we met in Ch. III.8 in contrasting science with witchcraft and astrology. Can we find some criterion by which to show that our broadest, most overarching standpoints are objective? And if not, are they ultimately subjective and a matter of opinion?

Now we approach, from a new direction, an old set of philosophical issues. The most general one is the skeptical claim that we can never show that we have any knowledge at all. This has a long history that I sketch in Ch. VII.1, but, putting that aside now, my whole approach acutely raises the problem of deciding between rival large-scale standpoints. For if, as we saw in Ch. II, our nature as historical beings embedded in our culture influences even what we observe, then even more it shapes what we can only indirectly confirm. So we meet the challenge of relativism, that ultimately no view can be shown to be better than any other. For relativism amounts to the claim that, because there is no super-standpoint from which to judge all others, purportedly objective utterances are in the end subjective. Relativism is an issue for Part B, but the point now is to distinguish two forms of it. The first, which is, I believe, the deeper of the two, is what we have just met: that all standpoints are ultimately subjective. This must apply to statements as well as evaluations, for a standpoint contains both elements; the paranoic's suspicion was as much about facts as about values. The second form turns on the contrast, not between objective and subjective as such, but between statement and evaluation. When statements conflict, it says, we can hope to explore the issue and arrive at the truth. Yet if evaluations clash, we may debate differences, and perhaps negotiate agreement; but this cannot amount to finding point contains both elements; the paranoic's suspicion was as much about facts as about values. The second form turns on the contrast, not between objective and subjective as such, but between statement and evaluation. When statements conflict, it says, we can hope to explore the issue and arrive at the truth. Yet if evaluations clash, we may debate differences, and perhaps negotiate agreement; but this cannot amount to finding out how things actually are, independently of us. So, despite parallels between theoretical and practical reasoning, the conclusion is that evaluations, but not statements, must be ultimately subjective. My analysis highlights these questions, but cannot itself answer them. It emerges in Part B, however, that the answer must focus on the role of significance-judgments in the search for understanding.

6. Metaphors and Starting Points

A final point applies to my whole analysis so far. I have examined various terms that are unfamiliar in English-speaking philosophy, such as transcendence, depth and significance. Some philosophers might feel that these should be taken as mere pre-philosophical *metaphors*, which can at best be a starting point for analysis. I reject that view. The contrast between metaphor and literal language is notoriously difficult, and I take a minimalist position. But my analysis suggests that metaphor arises from the same unboundedness of our thought as gives us our creative capacities. A metaphor connects one conceptual sub-system to another in an unfamiliar way, and the shock of bringing them together produces its power. With familiarity the shock may disappear, so we have a dead metaphor. Thus "transcend" does not seem metaphorical, but its Latin origin of "climbing beyond" the standpoint may once have seemed so. If a word is still found in two contexts, we tend to take the more concrete sense as the literal one. Thus "see" and "grasp" may seem metaphorical in relation to understanding, but not so in sensory contexts.

Yet, however we define the metaphorical-literal contrast, I suggest the real issue here is a different one: that to call something a "mere" metaphor makes an implicit contrast with the *real* truth. "Real", as I later discuss, marks many contrasts in different contexts, but with metaphors *sometimes* it contrasts only with what we are used to. I think this is the case with any feeling that the terms I have used are "merely metaphorical". Many of them, such as depth, are totally dead metaphors. They are familiar terms, providing no shock of connecting new conceptual systems, that are used continually, unselfconsciously and effortlessly. The problem is that we are not *used* to them in philosophical contexts. The remedy is not to replace them, but to become used to them, and then to clarify them as much as we need. The actual words

Yet, we might wonder, what if people should just fail to understand the terms, so we had no shared vocabulary to point to these features of the mind? This, however is a problem for any approach, and not just mine. The activity of philosophizing presupposes our ordinary grasp of reality, and if we really lacked an initial, pre-philosophical understanding of the terms, discussion could not proceed till it was acquired. We could only offer examples and explications till people caught on; but, in the end, only the mentally defective cannot catch on. What we reach as philosophical rock bottom is that people just can grasp talk about features of the mind.[11] Yet for our unbounded understanding, what is rock bottom from one standpoint may not be from another. We might, perhaps, explain biologically how our central nervous system evolved so as to produce our sort of consciousness. This would have its own presuppositions, but could still explain those from which our ordinary understanding starts. But explanations of why we have our sort of understanding must produce either what we already accept as understanding, or at least what we have learnt, starting from our present notion, to accept as a satisfactory successor to it.

In saying this, I have assumed that our minds work in recognizable ways, so that I and a reader can judge the correctness of the analysis and correct its inadequacies. Yet in emphasizing similarities we must not forget differences. My selective description of intellectual understanding must reflect in subtle ways not only the influence of the philosophical tradition that has shaped my thought, but also my white, middle-class, male assumptions. No doubt it needs to be supplemented or challenged by those who differ from me in these or other respects. But this, I hope, is part of that process by which we may use the diversity of our standpoints to achieve better understanding.

ENDNOTES

[1] For some more technical assumptions that underlie my argument here, see Ch. VIII.
[2] *Concise Oxford English Dictionary:*
Significance: Being significant, expressiveness.., covert or real import.., importance, note-worthiness.
Importance: Being important; weight, significance.
Webster's Third New International Dictionary:
Significance: Something signified: import, meaning, bearing... The quality of being important: consequence, moment.
Importance: The quality or state of being important: weight, significance ...*Syn*: consequence, significance, import, moment, weight.
[3] Two interesting earlier discussions of this notion are A. N. Whitehead *Modes of Thought* (Camb. U. P., first edn. 1938), and D. M. Emmet *The Nature of Metaphysical Thinking* (MacMillan, 1945). There has not been much since.
[4] A possible counter-example comes from Webster, where certain factors were said to have "not the major significance but some importance". Though on my analysis this is permissable, because the element of comparison makes the words equivalent, if "important" is the stronger notion we might have expected "not the major importance but some significance". But I believe the latter phrase would be slightly more appropriate.
[5] See A. Sloman *The Computer Revolution in Philosophy* (Harvester, 1978). I am also

deeply indebted here to discussion with Brian Ellis.

[6] It marks off "contingent" statements about the world, which might be true or false ("Today is Tuesday"), from those with which formal logic deals. The latter are logically necessary truths ("If p and q are true, then q is true"), and logically impossible falsehoods ("p and q are true, but q is false"). Here possibility and necessity are interdefinable: "possibly" = "not necessarily not", and "necessarily" = "not possibly not". Their formal treatment in modal logic is presented as a logic of relations between possible worlds, which in turn leads to further intricate debates. We can mark the relevant distinction in standard terminology by saying that logical possibilities are expressed by analytic propositions, and potentialities in my sense by a certain type of empirical ones.

[7] English-speaking philosophy may use "objective" either to indicate a rationally supported belief as opposed to a biassed or unsupported one, or to mark off statements from all evaluations, whether rationally supported or not. Nearly always "objective" is a term of approval, opposed to the "merely" subjective. But in Continental philosophy, subjectivity may be the approved notion. Here objectivity is roughly equivalent to intellectual understanding, while subjectivity goes beyond it. My use is closer to the English-speaking ones. For an example of a very different one, cf. M. Deutscher *Subjecting and Objecting: An Essay in Objectivity* (Queensland Uni. Pr., 1983).

[8] Many philosophical issues arise about what is called the "incorrigibility of first person utterances", but I do not think they are relevant here.

[9] Philosophers might object that necessary propositions, which cannot be wrong, are certainly objective. But I am talking about beliefs, not propositions. I might believe and say that $1723 + 876 = 2589$, even though that proposition is necessarily false.

[10] For me, objectivity involves the possibility of being mistaken, but not necessarily of knowing that we are.

[11] So Wittgenstein could end an investigation simply with, "This language game is played", or say: "What has to be accepted, the given, is—so one could say—forms of life". *Op.cit.*, Sec.654 (p.167e), p.226e.

CHAPTER V

FORMALIZATION

1. The Path to Formalization

In the course of the analysis, we have noted the power of formal language, which is found in mathematics used by science. So what gives formalization its power, and how far does my analysis apply to it also? We must answer these questions before we can later assess the strength of science-based views in philosophy. I skirt here some very technical issues, and try only to capture some key features of formal language that practitioners often take for granted.

We may approach the drive to formalization as follows. Exploiting the resonances and overtones of ordinary language has its own rigor; poetry may be as tough a mental discipline as science, and perhaps can penetrate to deeper levels of understanding. But developing precise structures of argument in context-dependent language can seem like building a house with bricks of blancmange. Analysis of ordinary meanings may increase our grasp of how we use words, but it only brings out the very features that make reasoning so difficult. To reduce them, as opposed to understanding them better, we must regiment our terms more formally. This begins when we stipulate a term's meaning for a given purpose. That reduces ambiguity, but still the power of context remains. Consider the philosophical terminology of necessary and sufficient conditions: that if A is a sufficient condition for B, then always if A is the case B is the case, while if A is a necessary condition for B, then unless A is the case B is not the case. In these stipulated meanings, contextual connections between A and B are ignored.[1] Hence sufficient and necessary conditions are reciprocal; if the presence of oxygen is necessary for the occurrence of fire, then fire is a sufficient condition for oxygen. Yet beginners in philosophy resist the point. They import from the context the notion of a causal connection, and so hear the remark as saying that the occurrence of fire is sufficient to *bring about* the presence of oxygen. They must control the mutualism of their understanding before they can understand. Even for experts using technical terms, there is a danger of ambiguity—of establishing a conclusion in a technical sense, and then taking it as true also in an ordinary sense which set the original problem. So with philosophers such as Spinoza, who have complex technical vocabularies, it may be relatively easy to see they have proved something in their technical sense, but difficult to know if any implications follow for ordinary thought. Again, if we define "intelligence" operationally, we may not know whether intelligence tests adequately measure what we want to know about intelligence.[2] In such cases experts, like others, can be misled by mutualism.

So we may move beyond stipulation to the full-blown formalization of mathematics and formal logic. Well before our current achievements, Descartes reported:

> I especially delighted in mathematics, because of the certainty and self-evidence of its reasonings.

Later, using "geometer" in 17th century fashion as virtually equivalent to "mathematician", he speaks of

> those long chains of perfectly simple and easy reasonings by means of which geometers are accustomed to carry out their most difficult demonstrations ...[3]

It is formalization that makes possible these "long chains of...reasonings"; and, when joined to precise terms that apply directly or indirectly to what we can observe, it leads to the success of modern science. We must investigate what its practitioners can take for granted, namely what gives such reasoning its power; and here the key notion is that of a *formal system*.

2. Formal Systems

While stipulation produces a new concept within a natural language, a formal system is a new artificial language, or fragment of one, which is to be free from just those features of ordinary language that make long chains of reasoning so difficult.[4] The modern notion of a formal system depends on a basic distinction between variables, on the one hand, and constants or operators on the other. A variable is a sign that marks a gap; it may be filled by any term appropriate to the system, provided the same sign is filled by the same term. Constants are signs with a fixed meaning, which state that some relation holds between variables, or that some operation is to be performed on them. Thus in "$10 + 10 = 20$", "10" and "20" are variables that apply to any collection which can be taken to consist of ten or twenty items, while "+" represents the operation of addition, and "=" the relation of equality.

At this stage we must note an important distinction between two senses of "form". Since Aristotle, who began the study of logic, it has been a truism that the validity of sound reasoning depends on its form: that is, it depends, not on the particular subject matter of the argument, but on general or formal relations between the terms used. However in the context of formalization and formal systems, the contrast is not with matter, but with what is informal or non-formal, where the formal is more regimented and less sensitive to context.

In logic, Aristotle's doctrine of the syllogism combined terms in a small number of relationships to produce valid patterns of inference: as in the classic pattern, all M are P, all S are M, so all S are P. Here M, P and S are variables, and "All ... are" is a constant. So his logic is, in retrospect, a formal system; not because it deals with logical form (for there the contrast is with matter), but because it deals with it in a formal as opposed to a non-formal way. However mathematics was also developing, and for over two millenia the paradigm of what we now call a formal system was Euclid's geometry.

From the 17th century, though logic at first remained static, mathematics and science developed rapidly together. But while in a broad sense such developments as the invention of the calculus by Newton and Leibniz were achievements in formal thought, they often used inadequately defined notions and procedures.[5] The great development in formalization came in the 19th century. Euclid had based his theorems on a small number of apparently self-evident truths, which were by then called axioms.[6] One, the axiom of parallels, had long seemed less obvious;[7] so new attempts were made to prove it by a *reductio ad absurdum*, assuming its falsity so as to derive a self-contradiction. However the attempts only produced consistent non-Euclidian geometries. This focused attention on the general characteristics of formal systems, at a level so abstract that the boundary between mathematics and logic eventually blurred. It produced a total revision of logic, which ceased to be Aristotelean and was redeveloped into modern "symbolic" or "mathematical" logic. Above all, there occurred the most fundamental change in two millenia in the conception of a formal system. Instead of seeing axioms as self-evident truths, which therefore guaranteed the applicability of the system to the world, mathematicians and logicians began to conceive them as merely the chosen starting points for their formal elaborations. While axioms were often chosen in the expectation of their applying to the world, this question could be put on one side in the elaboration of the system.[8]

The concept of a formal system continues to expand at breathtaking speed, and its theory becomes ever more abstract as existing notions are seen to be special cases of more general ones. Any adequate account would be too difficult for non-experts to understand, and also soon out of date. But we need consider only the most general features of a formal system. These seem to be precision and explicitness.[9] By precision I mean that the concepts used avoid the ambiguity, vagueness, etc., of ordinary language. By explicitness I mean that context-dependence is replaced by explicit rules determining meaning. These two features are what permit the long chains of reasoning, though both of them are matters of degree; 17th and 18th century mathematics was rigorous enough for its purposes, but standards have steadily risen. The relation to our non-formal thought seems to be this. Ordinarily, the obstacle to precise reasoning is what I called in Ch. II.7 the amorphousness of understanding, which has at least three aspects: blurred boundaries of terms; untidy, many-levelled relations between sub-systems, which lead to floating terms; and mutualism, which makes meaning context-dependent. To remove these, the central principle of formalization, I believe, is that *the meaning of the elements (constants and variables) is unchanged by the relations into which they enter, and the meaning of sub-wholes and wholes is determined by context-independent rules relating the elements.*[10]

3. Formalized and Ordinary Thought

The ultimate relation between formalized and ordinary thought is a topic for Part B, but now I pave the way by examining some specific aspects of it. We may start by noting again that with formal systems "formal" contrasts with "non-formal", while with logical form "form" contrasts with "matter". We cannot assimilate the two, because there are valid inferences—valid, as always, in virtue of their form—which we cannot formalize. Thus linguists accept the following as valid:[11]

> Fred knows who won the prize.
> Annabelle won the prize.
> Therefore: Fred knows that Annabelle won the prize.

But at present they have no formal theory of what they call wh-clauses ("who won the prize") to show how validity depends on features of "who" and "know". They only know that any adequate theory must preserve validity. This brings out that there is mutualistic interaction between formalization and the inherent sense of rational connection which logicians call our intuitions. Intuitions are fallible, and may be abandoned because they conflict with others or with a proven formalism, but unless we could simply see elementary inferences, we could not judge the soundness of a formalism. So there are simple cases, as above, where we can see the validity but cannot state the form, while in complex cases we often cannot decide validity without adequate formalization. To a formalist, preformal inference seems only an elementary criterion to which systems must conform, or else a challenge to further formalization; yet neither it nor formalization can dispense with each other.

Hence we may gradually pass from using our intuitions to judge the reliability of a system, to trusting it beyond where intuition can reach. To illustrate both the development and the limits of this process, we may consider the practical reason discussed in Ch. IV. Logic has concentrated on propositions that assert how the world is, but has also examined thinking about how to act; Aristotle himself investigated the practical syllogism. Today there is growing discussion of the theoretical bases of practical inference,[12] while decision theory and games theory formalize some factors involved in making choices. Where we can formulate specific goals, decision theory can be more reliable than our intuitions; and though its scope is still limited, we may expect improvement to continue.[13] Yet some cases are of quite another sort. A man may set his heart on being managing director, no matter what the cost; then suddenly, when his wife leaves him, he feels it was not worth the effort. The problem is not that he lacked technica! expertise to model the considerations mathematically, but that he did not know his own motives; he lacked the wisdom of self-understanding. This goes beyond all intellectual under-standing, even of a non-formal kind, and is something to which decision theory, as currently conceived, would not even aspire to contribute.

What this brings out is that formal thinking occurs within the wider matrix of our overall understanding. As a result, some points mentioned in Ch. II, which might seem typical of non-formal understanding, actually apply throughout the connecting-and-distinguishing that is found in all articulation, and so appear in formal contexts also. In particular, while the mutualistic interpretation of words and sentences presents a clear contrast with context-independent formalized meanings, the unboundedness of understanding applies everywhere; for we can set no more limits to the development of formal than of non-formal thought. I see the resulting situation as follows. Some formal reasoning is algorithmic. Algorithms are specifiable procedures, however complicated, for reaching a result in a finite number of steps. They exclude amorphousness, so are readily programmed for computers. But, since formal reasoning is embedded in general understanding, even seeing that we have a situation to which an algorithm applies, is a matter of skill for which we normally have no algorithm. Far beyond this lie such complex achievements as finding proofs within non-algorithmic systems, and developing new formal systems or theories about them. These tasks, like non-formal ones, depend on seeing the significance of relevant elements in unpredictable ways.[14] So we can no more program our present computers to be creative, than we can easily do the things for which we construct them. In general, while formal systems vastly reduce amorphousness, the seeing of new significance remains. The search for coherence here proceeds under new conditions; for the precision and explicitness of formal symbols and structures allow effective methods of testing new claims, and so facilitate long chains of reasoning.[15] But creative advances still depend on transcending given structures to glimpse new signifi-cance, and they reflect in this new context the complexities we met in the previous analysis of understanding.

4. Reasons and Entailments

Another aspect of the interaction of formalized and ordinary thought is the relation between formal logic and the actual processes of human reasoning. Logic began with the question "What makes an argument a good one?", and "logical" is still often a synonym for "rational". Hence it has a close but complex relation with good reasoning; yet, surprisingly, this is a delicate philosophical issue. Much 19th century philosophy saw logic as "the morphology of thought", seeking the norms of correct thought by examining our best reasoning.[16]   But early modern logicians saw this as confusing logic and psychology, and the older view replied by denigrating the new logic as lacking philosophical insight.   So, as modern views triumphed, "psychologizing" became the deadliest insult in the logician's vocabulary.   Yet the debate was confused as well as heated.   I take the value of formal logic to be unquestionable, but our reasoning processes are less tidy than its elegant structures. So we have two issues.   One concerns the structures which give arguments validity, and here modern logic has made enormous strides.   The other is how we articulate data, and this modern English-speaking philosophy has largely neglected.   My question is how the two are related.

Logic divides reasoning into the branches of deduction and induction. Deductive arguments are those such that if the premisses are true, the conclusion could not be false, while the premisses of inductive ones only make the conclusion more probable.[17]   Applied to the process of articulation, this means that the connections we forge may be either so deductively tight that we cannot break them, or else may leave room for other possibilities and so be only inductive.   In either case, the logical notion that the *premisses* of the argument *entail* its conclusion, is closely related to having a *reason* for *accepting* it, and this is how logic can apply to our thinking.   But the parallel does not always hold.   An entailment will not be a reason if it is either too trivial or too difficult.   Trivially, any proposition entails itself, for it is a premiss from which we can deduce it; but it is not a reason for itself.   On the other hand, a reason cannot be too difficult to be grasped.   Mathematicians know many entailments where I cannot even understand what is meant, let alone see the connections.   These entailments are reasons for them, but not for me, to accept the theorems.[18]   Beyond that, there are surely entailments which are too difficult for any human mind to grasp.[19]   "Reason", in short, operates to bridge the gap between pure logic and the search for coherence.   Only insofar as we can appropriate entailments in our articulation of data, can they be reasons for us either to believe or to act.

The question, therefore, is how entailments become significant for us. Logical relations not only exceed the limits of our minds, but are timeless: 2 + 2 eternally = 4, and premisses always entail or fail to entail their conclusion. Yet their application occurs in limited, time-bound, context-dependent reasoning, where the sub-systems in our thought mutualistically interact.   A formal system prevents other questions from intruding; within it, we can only ask whether something can be proved, and not what the significance of a proof might be. But this only exports outside the system the question of whether the results within the system are significant for us as reasons. This applies not only to what we can grasp, but also to how we finally assess what we grasp. Though formalization is invaluable in many contexts, we cannot escape responsibility for a final judgment of how far it can actually help our search for coherence. And just as we saw that the ultimate value of science cannot be assessed by the scientific method, so we shall see that the final judgment about the value of formalization must be a non-formal one.

5. Other Senses of "Formal"

"Formal" is not itself a formalized term, but has all the blurred edges, context dependence, etc., from which the process of formalization aims to deliver us. Beyond the central senses of "formal system" and "logical form" lie an array of others. Philosophy, for example, is not a formalized discipline as, say, physics is; outside logic, its basic medium is ordinary language, supplemented by some standard logical symbols and a fairly extensive technical vocabulary. Yet it often distinguishes between formal and informal analysis. Informal, or ordinary language, analysis aims to improve our grasp of our actual language, with all its amorphousness, while formal or ideal language analysis aims to work with new and more rigorous concepts. In this context, formal analyses use formalization as an ideal rather than a method. Thus in philosophy of language, they may take the basic structure of symbolic logic as revealing the skeleton of ordinary language; then, since some aspects of language do not conform neatly to the principles, debates turn on whether we need more complex formalisms, or whether any are adequate.[20] As always, we may expect unpredictable future advances; for example, while formalization aims to eliminate vagueness, fuzzy set theory may increasingly permit formal treatment of it. So formalization may later impinge in new ways on the analysis of understanding.[21] We meet here a general point, which applies not only in philosophy but throughout science: that we often formalize by successive approximations, first selecting aspects of a situation that we can handle, and hoping later to take into account the complexities we had earlier bypassed. So in many contexts what is "formal" is a matter of degree, indicating only that it has some larger element of formalization than what it replaces.

Are formal and non-formal approaches, then, to be seen as complementary or as rivals? In many contexts, though there may be hostility between the two camps, they surely are complementary.[22] Specifically, an analysis of understanding might well benefit from relating it to more formalized concepts, yet the development of those concepts may need a grasp of their ordinary language predecessors which my informal analysis may provide. But there are deeper conflicts. Thus for formal philosophy of language, the problems arise when natural language does not conform to its models. But for hermeneutic views that take interpreting a text as the model, the problems stem from our being embedded in inherited language and thought-forms, which we cannot control like our constructed formal systems. Thus far there is complementarity, and each side can acknowledge the problems of the other. Yet formal views not only note that ordinary language lacks the precision of formal ones, but take formal ones as *ideal*. Hermeneutic ones, in acknowledging the difference, *exalt* ordinary language as the vehicle of true understanding. Since formalization is an essential part of science, but not of the humanities, these conflicts in method both reflect and feed the deep tension between science-based and humanities-based views. Here we meet again what will be a central issue for Part B. For behind differences in many fields about what formalization can achieve, ultimately lies the deeper question of the proper place of science in our worldview.

6. Formal and Non-formal Generalization

A particularly important aspect of the contrasts between formal and non-formal reasoning appears in that sort of transcendence which generalizes concepts by treating them as special cases of a wider notion. This is typical of advances in formalization; as a random example, consider how elementary algebra generalizes arithmetic by using variables (x, y, etc.) that stand for any number whatever, so that its truths hold generally no matter what numbers we substitute for x and y. But how does generalization work in non-formal contexts? The examples we meet here are such cases as the theological notion of "demythologizing". A story such as the Resurrection of Christ is reconceived as making a more abstract point—say, that God's love will rise triumphant over all evil. In both formal and informal cases we rise above a level of discourse by seeing it as a special case of a more general one; but despite this parallel, the process is strikingly different.

In formal contexts we can hope for a clear cut decision on whether generalization succeeds. If it does, we gain deeper understanding of underlying formal structures; if not, we learn from our mistakes. That is why mathematics and logic grow today at so breathtaking a pace. But in non-formal contexts we find another pattern. When relevant background beliefs are shared, the decision may be clear; but if they differ, the debate may be agonizing, divisive and inconclusive. What to one person is illuminating demythologization, is to another total betrayal of Christian orthodoxy. On each side, multiple subsystems present different aspects of an issue, with intricate connections between them, and the rival significance-judgments inevitably downgrade some connections as they forge others. To some, the merit of demythologizing the Resurrection is that it eliminates the need for a miracle, while to others, God's miraculous act is crucial. For while formal structures dictate what sorts of transcendence can be relevant, non-formal ones ramify into our whole belief system, and so vary between individuals.

An important implication concerns the search for counter-considerations. Though formalized arguments may always have unnoticed shortcomings that critics will delight to point out, their merits can be tested by tracing out entailments. But in non-formal cases, we should look for the costs as well as the benefits. It is no accident that the law takes as its most elementary maxim of natural justice that we must hear all sides to a dispute, and this applies no less when we are both advocate and judge in our own reflection. A useful precaution is to ensure that we state any position we oppose in a way our opponents would accept, but this is easily overlooked. For, as we noticed in Ch. II.8, when new generalizations challenge underlying assumptions, they produce powerful emotional reactions. This may occur even in the purest formal contexts, as the venom of mathematical debates sometimes shows; but it is more common and intractable in non-formal contexts, where decision procedures become less conclusive at the same time as our convictions may be more deeply challenged. That questioning of assumptions, for example, which consists of asking whether our country's cause in wartime is really justified, may seem sheer treason. Such reactions lead us to ask whether reasoning can penetrate beyond the purely intellectual understanding with which we have been concerned.

ENDNOTES

[1] We may have a causally sufficient, a logically sufficient, or even an accidentally sufficient condition. (i) To say that striking a match in the proper conditions is sufficient for its lighting is a causal condition. (ii) If one logical formula entails another, it is a logically sufficient condition for its truth. (iii) Suppose the largest number of planets circling any star is 45. Then being a star is a sufficient condition for having less than 46 planets, even if this is a quite accidental fact.

[2] The point applies, even if we discover that intelligence is more multi-dimensional than we had realized, and so discover we had been confused about what we thought we meant.

[3] *Discourse.* Parts I, II, in G.E.M. Anscombe and P.T. Geach *Descartes: Philosophical Writings* (1966), pp.11, 21.

[4] In this Section I have been greatly helped by discussion with David Londey. I have also relied heavily on W. and M. Kneale *The Development of Logic* (1962).

[5] At that time mathematicians distinguished between the new developments, which they called "analysis", and the "synthetic" method of Euclid's formal system. They took the latter as the ideal in exposition, while analysis was the method of discovery. Thus in *Principia Mathematica*, Newton presented his results as synthetically, or geometrically proven, and ignored the analytic calculus by which he had reached them. See W. and M. Kneale, *op.cit.*, p.309.

[6] Euclid himself had divided them into two groups; "common notions" taken to be

fundamental in all sciences, and "postulates" which were specific to geometry.

[7] This has more than one mathematically equivalent statement. In Euclid it is that if a straight line falling on two straight lines makes the interior angles on the same side less than two right angles, the two straight lines, when produced indefinitely, meet on that side on which the angles are less than two right angles.

[8] The discovery that Euclid's "obvious" truth could be denied, together with the austere fascination of the new rigor, led to a demand to remove the role of intuition not only from axioms but also from proofs. This "syntactic" approach conceives of a formal system simply as a set of symbols, with rules for manipulating them to obtain more sets, which are theorems. The question of interpretation, or what the system was about, was distinguished from its syntax as being its "semantics". At first many logicians ignored semantics. Today, however, logicians not only work in and construct formal systems, but also theorize metalogically about them, with formal semantics being important branch of metalogic.

[9] This point has been made to me by Cliff Hooker.

[10] More specifically, formal systems avoid disorderly, many-levelled structures by regimenting their sub-systems into hierarchies governed by the sort of rules called recursive. These generate a continuing sequence of instances; a basic example is the rule which starts with the numeral "one" and generates an infinite sequence of numbers. Further, the meaning of formal constants is unaffected by context. Finally, since the values of variables must fit the slots available, they are conceived, however artificially, as being: (a) discrete, i.e. not modified in meaning by entering into combination with others; and (b) distinct, without borderline cases, so we have clear-cut answers to the questions, "Is this an item or not?", and "How many items are there?". All this raises many problems in philosophical logic, but I can avoid them here.

[11] I have borrowed this with modification from J. Groenendijk and M. Stokhof "Semantic Analysis of wh-complements" (1982), p.173. As Fred D'Agostino has pointed out to me, the example may be more questionable than they assume.

[12] Most theories try to base it on imperatives or on intention. They link with deontic logic, which began as the examination of moral inferences. A useful place to start investigation of the issues is B. Aune *Reason and Action* (1977).

[13] Effective formalization is often unavailable for multi-dimensional choice, where we could opt for many possible objectives; and it is not even currently available for some cases of agreed objectives. With the latter, we may be unable to go beyond an ordinal ranking of alternatives in order of preference to a mathematically more useful interval scale, let alone to a fully tractable ratio scale. For a useful discussion of these concepts, see D. W. Miller and M. K. Starr *The Structure of Human Decisions* (1967), pp.87-95.

[14] Lakatos brings this out strikingly in showing how proofs in complicated cases are negotiated, and how mathematicians may adjust formal structures rather than accept unwanted conclusions. I. Lakatos *Proofs and Refutations* (ed. J. Worrall and E. Zahar) (1976).

[15] By contrast non-formal debates *about* formal structures, such as those between classical and intuitionist accounts of concepts like negation and implication, are as difficult to settle as any others in philosophy.

[16] This is the Absolute Idealism mentioned in Ch. VII.2.

[17] The distinction is different from, but related to, Aristotle's orginal one. For convenience I join some, though not all, logicians in applying to each branch the notion of premisses' entailing conclusions, though inductive arguments entail only a probability.

[18] They would function as reasons for me only if I could first grasp the meaning (it would be an inadequate grasp compared to a mathematician's), and then accepted them on authority. That would be a non-formal judgment of probability ("These experts say so, so they are probably right") which is quite different from the entailments themselves.

[19] If we try to avoid this point by stipulating that something is a reason for a conclusion independently of our capacity to grasp it, we must still ask how we appropriate these reasons-as-such when we actually reason. We then open up a gap between reasons-as-such and actual reasons, which is just the gap between what I call premisses-and-entailments and reasons-for-acceptance.

[20] Here philosophy merges into linguistics, which may have a different approach, for

linguists may not share philosophers' reverence for symbolic logic. I am also avoiding other debates, such as those concerning the notion of reference.

[21] Thus "pattern", which I use as a synonym for "structure", has a formal definition within Information Theory. "A pattern may be defined in general as an ordering among elements of a set such that when the arrangement of a subset is given the remainder is indicated at a probability greater than chance occurrence in proportion to the size of the given subset." K. Sayre *Cybernetics and the Philosophy of Mind* (1976) p.152, quoting his *Recognition: A Study in the Philosophy of Artificial Intelligence* (1965), p.153.

[22] In philosophy there has been rivalry between formal and informal analysis, but in principle they seem complementary. Before improving a concept we need to grasp its actual use, but successor concepts are often valuable.

CHAPTER VI

BEYOND INTELLECTUAL UNDERSTANDING

1. Passing Beyond The Detached Intellect

In my analysis, I began with the vague notion of intellectual understanding, and concluded that it was "the articulation of data so as to discern a structure with an adequate degree of significance" (Ch. II.3). Part A developed this notion; but it also foreshadowed that depth of understanding not only operates within intellectual understanding, but may also point beyond it. To many philosophers this will seem highly dubious. For it suggests to them an appeal to intuition or mere feeling, that allows no rational decision procedures by which to adjudicate rival claims.[1] But the sort of passing beyond intellectual understanding I shall defend does not involve that. For though there are many problems in relating various senses of "understand", this one is only another case of transcending a standpoint to move to a more inclusive one.

I begin by focusing on a particular case of intellectual understanding, which I call the standpoint of the *detached intellect*. By this I refer to situations where we attend solely to the information content of what is before us. A central example is where we consider the content of written or spoken material. Here we disattend from the authors, not asking why they trouble to speak or write, etc.; and so, by attending solely to their information content, we treat them and ourselves as detached intellects. I extend this standpoint to cases where scientists analogously focus solely on instrument readings, etc. This standpoint of the detached intellect is probably our central paradigm of intellectual understanding. But it may be transcended in favor of others, by taking into account more than just the information content of what is heard or seen. We then find a whole set of new standpoints, which fit the general formula for intellectual understanding, but differ among themselves in many ways. For they have in common only the negative feature that, by bringing something more into account, they are *not* confined to the detached intellect. Thus, rather than attending solely to an argument, we might search for its implicit premises; or, quite differently, we might treat the book in which it appears as an example of 20th century printing. These are cases of intellectual understanding, but they transcend the detached intellect as I defined it. For just as formalization abstracts from the mutualism of ordinary understanding, the detached intellect abstracts from intellectual understanding. *Within* intellectual understanding we can move beyond the *detached* intellect, in ways no more (and no less) mysterious than any other act of transcendence.

Intellectual understanding, then, is a cluster of cases, and some are far removed from its central paradigm of the detached intellect. We will be helped to grasp its multiplicity, if we remember that all knowledge and understanding depends on an unformulated background of tacit knowledge.[2] A standard example is when we recognize a face, but cannot say how we do so. We may make tacit knowledge more explicit, in such ways as the Identikit methods employed by police; but we still know more than we can tell, even when we can tell more of it. We cannot hope to escape our reliance on tacit knowledge, since even the detached intellect presupposes it; we cannot fully explicate how we recognize letters or words, or give sense to sentences. To be aware in this way of how all understanding is embedded in what we take for granted, encourages us to ask what assumptions we make in intellectual understanding, and how we might transcend them.[3] Then, since transcendence may lead to greater depth, we might find a deeper than merely intellectual understanding. I now explore that claim.

2. Involvement

All standpoints that drive the search for understanding include evaluative beliefs, so we may ask what values motivate intellectual understanding. Philosophers might think first of valuing knowledge for its own sake, but many others are involved. A desire for profit may drive a businessman's intellectual understanding, and even philosophy books may be written for personal advancement. As we shall see, motivation is so complex that some deny the existence of a pure desire for knowledge at all. But our question now is whether some motives may lead us to pass beyond intellectual understanding altogether. This involves adopting, not so much different intelligenda as a different, less distanced, *mode of involvement* with them. I note cases where that claim is made, point to common features, and suggest where the contrast with intellectual understanding lies. My illustrations are best seen as what sociologists would call ideal types, which may enter as an element into many situations without appearing in their pure form.

(a) In personal relationships, involvement comes from an attitude of concern for others, which is the best sense of the much abused word "love". Psychology emphasizes how love is needed for childhood development, and in common experience life without it loses much of its savor. The point now is that it also raises claims to deeper understanding. For, it is said, in our ordinary dealings with others, we hide ourselves in ways we rarely notice. We take on the roles of business executive, guest, parent, according to the situation, and these act as masks to conceal what we really are. Ordinary contact reinforces the masks, but in an atmosphere of love we can increasingly remove them, become aware of each other as we really are, and so achieve a deeper understanding. Love and friendship have many varieties, but involvement may enter all of them.

(b) Analogous claims are made about our understanding of ourselves. An example in Ch. V.3 was the managing director who lacked self-understanding. We could examine such cases as part of theoretical psychology. But we may also conclude that we who investigate are mysteries to ourselves—directed by motives we do not acknowledge, influenced by forces we do no know, ignorant of aspects of our own being. So we may struggle to penetrate the masks which hide us not only from others but from ourselves, and then we are involved beyond intellectual understanding.

(c) Another context is esthetic appreciation. As noted in Ch. III.4, it is said that we must go beyond intellectual understanding by opening ourselves to the work of art and responding to its impact. Criticism that does not do this will at best be clever rather than profound, and only involvement with the work makes the appreciation of art more than the elaborate game of social or academic prestige which it may often be.

(d) Much theology insists that involvement should be the basic human attitude towards God.[4] Drawing on the biblical notion of approaching God through the heart, it may reject a "theology of the head" as mere intellectual speculation. Religious understanding, it says, must be the head making sense of the heart, rather than the work of the head alone; that is, it must spring from involvement. For the believers' true response must be to open their lives to the divine challenge, and intellectual assent to propositions expressing the faith is insufficient.

(e) Finally, people may speak of experiencing such a relation of involvement with the whole of creation. This is Wordsworth's "sense ... of something far more deeply interfused", which came from the contemplation of nature.[5] Often it is related to religious mysticism, and some say it is the heart of all true religion. However others who experience it may be hostile to religion, which they see as attempting to conceptualize and control an experience that is beyond understanding.

These claims have been developed without reference to each other in very different contexts, but they present more than the negative point that intellectual understanding is not enough, for they have common features that manifest an underlying thrust.[6] They accept the "other" with which we are involved as it presents itself, trying to give it its full value rather than fitting it into categories we already have. So they have a passive element, a letting oneself be with the other. Involvement is essentially a response; we may prepare or long for it, fear or encourage it, repudiate or accept it; but we must wait for whatever may arise between us and the other. This applies even in (b), where the other is ourself, seen as having unknown aspects which we must accept.

Though this waiting on the other appears strikingly in these cases, it occurs as an element in many other contexts. Even scientists must occasionally just wait on the situation to see what it has to say to them. For waiting is at the heart of creativity, where, as I noted in Ch. III.7, we must also open ourselves to what will come. Yet, though the balance differs greatly between cases, opening ourselves should involve, not rejection of the critical intellect, but mutualistic interaction with it. While in science the waiting may be a rare moment that inspires rigorous investigation, even in the central cases the other comes to us already seen as a work of art, a revelation of God, etc., and we must struggle to grasp its import no less than we must open ourselves to it. What is different is that we must treat it as something we respond to, rather than *merely* analyze. In doing so, we transcend ordinary attitudes by coming to see intellectual understanding as an attitude of *mentally dominating the phenomena*, which we must pass beyond.

3. Involvement and Symbols

I now consider some applications of the need for involvement. A psycho-therapist listens to a patient by monitoring the conversation at many levels, hearing the words but also listening for what the patient is not aware of. The intelligendum is the total performance—the choice of these utterances, in this context, to convey that information, with those hints of anxiety or anger, while body language suggests tension, remoteness or trust. All this is evaluated to offer clues to quasi-autonomous, unconscious sub-systems within the patient's belief system that have been suppressed because they are threatening, so that by discovering and facing them we may better integrate our personality. My own view is that, while depth psychology affords great insight into how sub-systems interact in our growth from infancy to adulthood, no general theory, such as Freud's or Jung's, is fully established, and there is much about our-selves that we do not understand.[7] But my point now concerns involvement. Perhaps the mere notion of evaluating a patient's total performance need not go beyond intellectual understanding, though certainly beyond the detached intellect. But good therapy needs a state of trust between patient and therapist which is an involvement beyond purely intellectual understanding.

Moreover, in considering how depth psychology deals with its data, we meet the problem of interpreting symbols.[8] "Symbol" has many senses, including one in which any word is a symbol, but here it is something which both appears at the conscious level, and also bears a load of significance from the unconscious. The mark of a symbol is its emotional impact, such as the numinous force that ordinary objects may have in dreams, which indicates its connection to unconscious sub-systems. Primarily it is a symbol *for an individual*, because of its connection to their unconscious. But certain things commonly serve as symbols, with a typical significance; so in a secondary sense there are theories of how certain items tend to symbolize unconscious contents. Symbolism has levels. An item in a dream may represent a recent, easily recalled, event, but the event may be a symbol of a another, and that, if uncovered, may in turn be a symbol for a still more deeply buried fear. Further, in the deeper levels of the psyche we meet acute polarization, as unconscious systems pull us in different directions; so symbols manifesting them may be ambivalent, pointing to one sub-system and also hinting at its opposite. The therapeutic aim is to uncover and face the polarities, so as to integrate as complementary what had previously been warring aspects of the psyche. Then the symbol may lose its numinous power and become a mere metaphor, making a link with a previously unconscious system. It might even become a dead metaphor, used in a theory of symbols to name a commonly occurring state. But, while theories of symbols offer intellectual understanding, and books on them can be assessed by the detached intellect, *working* with symbols needs involvement. Patients who refuse to get involved may play fascinating games with their therapists, but no improvement results.

Symbols extend far beyond therapy, and we may study how their power is exerted in, say, myths or fairy stories.[9] Further, I said in Ch. V.1 that the "resonances and overtones" of poetry "perhaps can penetrate to deeper levels of understanding", and a similar point applies to other art. If we open ourselves to such things, we may gain deeper insight. We can then struggle to express them intellectually; but a crucial part of our intelligendum is that the symbols involved have a deeper than intellectual impact. Yet now a further question arises. Because of ambivalence and levels of significance, interpretations are tentative and consensus fragile. So can we adequately test our alleged insights; have we any decision procedures to lead to understanding? Before I examine that issue in Sec. 5, I must first consider another point.

4. Involvement and Emotion

What is the relation of involvement to emotion, and of emotion, in turn, to reason? An ancient tradition, starting in Greece, typical of the Enlightenment, and underpinning the fact-value distinction today, contrasts reason with what it may call passion, feeling or emotion. The task of reason, it holds, is to control the emotions; knowledge *is* intellectual, and alleged "deeper than intellectual" understanding is at best only ordinary knowledge, more or less distorted by emotion. My analysis, like many views today, challenges this tradition.[10] For if the standpoints that drive understanding have evaluative as well as factual elements, they also have characteristic emotions. Even the purest search for knowledge may produce the emotional "Eureka" experience of discovery.

I can adopt a minimalist attitude towards many of the debates here, but my own position is as follows.[11] Certainly, emotion can interfere with reason. Anger may make us unreasonable, jealously may distort our perspective, even the exhilaration of discovery may blind us to the need for mental discipline. Yet involvement requires emotions, from the calm but powerful stirring of great art, through the therapist's detached compassion, to the warmth of friendship. In such cases emotion is an aid to, rather than an enemy of, deeper understanding, for without the appropriate emotion we could not gain the insights. So there is no *overall* conflict between reason and emotion. This is true in a different way when we set out to penetrate the masks in self-understanding. The process produces intense emotions as suppressed fear and hostility come to light, and these are indeed great hindrances to good reasoning. Yet they are both necessary and valuable. Necessary, for unless we accept involvement and experience the emotions, the masks will not drop, and we will not get the insights. Valuable, because we can *use* emotions to obtain insight. If we are prepared to face them, their very painfulness points to the areas where deeper understanding can emerge.

So, against the traditional opposition of reason and emotion, I hold that, though emotion sometimes hinders reasoning, and though emotion-filled situations need careful assessment (which has its own emotional drive), in cases requiring involvement emotion plays an essential part in gaining insight. Beyond that, the tradition that equates involvement with emotion faces a deeper criticism, which questions not merely its disparagement of emotion but how far the emotion-reason contrast is even relevant. For involvement, with its openness towards the other, is not *in itself* an emotion, but is related as much to the will as to feeling. If it comes upon us spontaneously, we may still choose to adopt or reject it, and when it does not come we may set out to encourage it. Though emotion is sometimes inevitable, the true contrast is between non-involved and involved *attitudes*, while the reasoning process is basically the same in each.   For the central point is that intellectual understanding is an abstraction, however valuable, from our total mental activity. To go beyond it is a *transcending of limitations* rather than a mere adding of emotion. If we so fear the distortion of the intellect by emotion that we stand back and avoid all involvement, we will miss the point of the relevant situations, and so miss deeper understanding.

5. Involvement and Knowledge

In endorsing the value of passing beyond intellectual understanding, I must face the widespread philosophical objection that involvement cannot lead to objective knowledge of how things are, because it has no adequate decision procedures for assessing claims. My own account of the use of symbols in Sec. 3 may seem to make the point. If a symbol may ambivalently point to opposite values, while its interpretation depends ultimately on subjective acceptance, surely its assessment is immune to effective rational control? Such views see involvement as a threat to the precious value of rationality. To run through the cases in Sec. 2, talk of dropping masks through love, they may say, is metaphorical and dubious; love is proverbially blind, and only too often leads to *mis*understanding. The search for self-understanding can be a narcissistic cultivation of inner states that is frequently a subtle exploitation of others. Claims of art and theology to yield deeper knowledge are unverifiable, and a mystical attitude towards nature is worst of all. For science has grown by rejecting anthropomorphic categories which treated non-human things as if they were human; and does not nature mysticism threaten to reanthropomorphize the world?

Defenders of involvement appeal to their own values. Some accept this strict view of reasoning, and retort that there are deeper than merely rational insights; but others challenge that whole picture of rationality. Whatever the abuses of love or the search for self-understanding, they claim, involvement is an essential source of insight. For deeper contact with others is a mirror in which we see ourselves more clearly, while conversely, if we misunderstand ourselves we will misunderstand others. So these defenders may counter-attack. A refusal to go beyond intellectual understanding, they allege, is a typical unwillingness to take off a mask, and in the end is a shrinking from the painful process of deeper insight.

Unlike this counter-attack, I shall not claim to know the motivation for refusing to go beyond intellectual understanding. But I have endorsed the value of involvement, and my answer to the objection that it lacks decision procedures has already been foreshadowed. Our most powerful procedure is the scientific method; but it does not cover all cases, since we cannot even use it to defend science itself. Beyond it, we have weaker but still valuable procedures, involving more general forms of selective description. With involvement we meet such further complications as the ambiguity of symbols, and may find we can only offer insights for others to accept, modify or reject. But we can still rationally test those insights, by searching for coherence in the ways we have met. Then we find that not all cases are equally difficult. A straightforward therapeutic diagnosis may be easier than a complex issue *within* intellectual understanding. One such complex intellectual issue is this very dispute about decision procedures itself. For it is another example of that most difficult type of case, namely a clash of large-scale significance-judgments. Whether and how such cases might be resolved will become a central issue.

6. Stilling the Mind

There is a still deeper issue: can understanding extend even beyond these cases of involvement? This arises in debates about mysticism in philosophy of religion, and particularly in the practice of stilling the mind through meditation.[12]   The claim here starts from the point that our minds are continually active, with an unceasing stream of thought. Meditation aims at stilling this activity. It may be practised simply to remove stress and enhance the quality of life,[13] but my concern is with the claim that it gives us a radically new insight into reality. In stilling the mind, it is said, we find that our mental activity, including our search for understanding, essentially *conceals* reality, much as chatter at a cocktail party may conceal people's real concerns. When we stop the mental chatter we reach, first fleetingly, then more readily, a deeply peaceful state, which is totally conscious and alert, yet in which conceptual thought dies away.   So it transcends the ordinary distinction between the knower and what is known. Then we find that the boundaries we draw with our concepts are in some sense illusory or unimportant, and that the unbounded oneness represents the true reality.[14]

This provokes intense disputes, and in places here I must move beyond a minimalist position. Tough-minded views reject the mystical claim as absurd: what is beyond concepts is beyond words, and to pretend to speak of such an indescribable state is self-defeating. But this is surely too cavalier a rejection, for the claim retains many threads of resemblance to other cases of understanding. It claims objectivity, that this is how things are whether we know it or not. It involves an openness and a waiting on what comes, like that needed for involvement and creative thought. And it claims that, here as elsewhere, we reach a deeper state by transcending limitations—in this case, the limitations of conceptual thought itself. As for its indescribability, this applies in a sense to all experiences, for our tacit knowledge of their flavor goes beyond what we can fully convey; yet we can provide useful and recognizable descriptions of them. In the present case, since I myself experience the loss of boundaries in the stillness of meditation, I cannot doubt that it occurs, or believe that my brief description of it is self-defeating.

A quite different controversy connects with my repeated emphasis on how our thought and experience is embedded in our culture. We must later ask whether this prevents us from reaching any objective truth at all, but now it raises a different issue. Defenders of mysticism have often claimed that the experience of unbounded oneness is the same across all traditions. Yet how, it is asked today, could any experience be common to such diverse belief systems? Must not mystics' cultural expectations shape not merely their interpretation, but the experience itself? Elsewhere I have argued that the impact of the cultural tradition is greater than many scholars have realized, but is not as dominating as some today insist.[15] But now I take a minimalist position by merely drawing attention to some similarities and differences. I see two common elements in all mysticism. The first is that by stilling the mind we reach an experience which is in some sense one of unbounded oneness. Whether or not this is identical across cultures, as is currently debated, it has this recognizable common feature. The second element is the mystics' agreement that, because the experience goes beyond ordinary conceptual thought, attempted descriptions push language to the edge of intelligibility. Their writing points beyond itself—often in ways closer to poetry than to prose—towards what it sees as an ultimately inexpressible reality.

Given these similarities, mystical traditions certainly explicate the unbounded oneness in different ways. As an example, two basic models are used to point towards the ultimately inexpressible relation between the one reality and the world we know: communion and merging. Communion is a dualist notion that appeals to the experience of involvement through love. For such mysticism, though the *ordinary* distinction between knower and known is transcended, there remains a relation between two centers of consciousness. Thus theistic mysticism speaks of the soul and creation as bound in communion with God. Merging, by contrast, is monistic, with two things becoming one; its classic image is a raindrop falling into the ocean. So Hindu advaita vedanta says that the true self, and all creation, merge totally with Brahman. These models are not exhaustive, and Buddhism avoids them both by speaking only negatively of the ultimate unreality of all distinctions. How far such differences affect not only the interpretations but even the experiences of mystics, is an important question. But we must not miss the more general point, that all their language struggles to point beyond itself.

How far then, must their experience of unbounded oneness be inexpressible? Here, too, they vary, though all agree that language is stretched to the uttermost. Some emphasize the contrast with ordinary understanding, risking accusations of absurdity so as to jolt listeners into new attitudes.[16] Others insist on a continuity. And with them we can see how, in this limiting case, involvement and intellect still mutualistically interact. However different the experience may be, their efforts to express it show the same search for coherence. So the allegation of unintelligibility, like the refusal of involvement, is not so much refuted as shown to be protecting one view of rationality. In the end we can largely *choose* whether to see mystics as strain-ing against the limits of intelligibility, or as passing beyond them.

Finally, even granting that we can understand the claim that stilling the mind contacts the deepest level of reality, we must still ask whether it is true. Here we meet further objections, which attack the link between having the experi-ence and concluding that it represents a deeper reality.[17] They accept that it *seems* to do so; but they insist that no experience can interpret or justify itself, and then reject the mystics' interpretations on other grounds, such as what they see as its incompatibility with scientific inquiry. This is another large-scale clash of significance-judgments. It is often treated as a relatively peripheral issue in the sub-discipline of philosophy of religion, but surely it is more central than that. If the claim that the unifying oneness presents the true nature of reality is false, it is dangerous illusion; if it is true it should ultimately be the central point of our worldview. My own conviction is that the mystics' vision of a unifying oneness is correct. But just as I hold that no current theory of depth psychology gives a full understanding of ourselves, so here I believe that we cannot yet articulate the insights of various traditions into a least inadequate overall picture. However, to explore that issue would take us not only beyond my analysis of understanding, which I have completed, but beyond the current philosophical debates to which I now turn.

ENDNOTES

[1] This is the main charge levelled, rightly or wrongly, against the notion of *Verstehen* in the social sciences.
[2] M. Polanyi *op. cit.*
[3] This links with many aspects of human communication. Face to face communication involves elements of body language, etc., which may be much more important than intellectual understanding usually realizes. That is why children must learn to use a telephone as a separate skill from ordinary conversation. The situation changes again if tone of voice is eliminated, as when people communicate by typing onto computer screens. Written language also differs significantly from spoken. All this makes expansion beyond intellectual understanding less surprising.
[4] A central modern source has been M. Buber *I and Thou*, trans. R.G. Smith (1937).
[5] *Tintern Abbey* ll. 95-6.
[6] I owe this point largely to the valuable comments of Miriam Dixson.
[7] I place considerable trust in the position of K. Wilber, as in *The Atman Project* (1980).
[8] As a particularly relevant reference in this vast literature, cf. C. G. Jung and others, *Man and His Symbols* (Pan Books, 1978).
[9] See, e.g., the many works of Joseph Campbell, such as *Hero with a Thousand Faces* (1956).
[10] See here W. Lyons *Emotion* (1980), R. M. Gordon *The Structure of Emotions* (1987). The complexities of the subject perhaps come out best in A. O. Rorty *Explaining Emotions* (1980).
[11] There is a complex relation between emotion and motive, and both words derive from the notion of what moves us. I am now concerned with emotions when they act as

motives.

[12] There are immense complications even in defining the field of discourse here. Some have the relevant experience as an unsought flash of awareness, as in the classic cases in William James *The Varieties of Religious Experience* (1960). More often the experience occurs within the practice of a religious tradition, but some religion is hostile to mysticism. Psychological approaches may group mysticism with other "altered states of consciousness". These may include either the results of psychedelic drugs, etc.—though many religions regard these as dangerous aberrations—or else exaltation sought by dancing or chanting. What I call meditation is often also called contemplation, while "meditation" is applied to disciplined devotional use of the imagination as well as to stilling the mind.

[13] See, e.g., the research collected in D. W. Orme-Johnson and J. T. Farrow *Scientific Research on the Transcendental Meditation Program* (vol. I) (1976). Further volumes are in preparation.

[14] Cf. my "A New Science of Consciousness?" (1983).

[15] For the objection, cf. S. Katz (ed.) *Mysticism and Philosophical Analysis* (1978), *Mysticism and Religious Traditions* (1983); especially the former, at p. 26. For a reply, see my "Experience and Interpretation in Mysticism", and other contributions to R. K. C. Forman (ed.) *The Problem of Pure Consciousness* (1990).

[16] An example is Zen Buddhism. Yet even it typically claims that the inexpressible insight of enlightenment may interact with later reflection to produce what is the least misleading account of reality.

[17] An example is N. Melchert "Mystical Experience and Ontological Claims" (1977).

PART B

IMPLICATIONS

CHAPTER VII

STARTING POINTS AND ISSUES

1. The Historical Background: Foundationalism

In my analysis of understanding in Part A, my claim was not that it was uncontentious or without presuppositions, but that discussion of it could start from appeal to the word's meaning by asking: "Do we use it as I have said, or do we not"? I now turn to apply the analysis to current philosophical problems. Here my background assumptions become centrally relevant, so I begin by sketching how I see my position within European philosophy. My perspective is fairly orthodox within my tradition, but is certainly not uncontroversial, for today orthodox views are under attack.

The great flowering of Western philosophy that began in the 17th century approached its problems largely through the lens of one question: what can we know and how do we know it? In understanding why that approach was adopted, I emphasize two points. First, we may see it as a response to a skeptical challenge to all knowledge in Greek philosophy.[1] If our beliefs are questioned, the challenge went, we need a criterion to which we can appeal in settling the issue. Whatever we offer, we can be asked for a criterion for this criterion, and a further one for that one. So we can never find an agreed criterion to prove the truth of our starting point. That we need some criterion of certainty to counter this argument, became part of the intellectual tradition inherited by Christianity. Till the Reformation, the accepted criterion was the teaching of the Church. The Reformers replaced it by the authority of the Bible. A central tactic in the resulting polemics was to attack rival criteria by arguing they did not yield real certainty. But some found the criticisms of each side more impressive than their defences, and so felt the need for more general reflection. Then the theological search for a criterion of certainty returned as a dominant theme of philosophy.

The second point is this. Not only was Europe being racked by Reformation and Counter-reformation, but the long-established Aristotelean worldview was feeling the first impact of what was to become modern science. Throughout the period, these new developments had a double-sided impact on the search for certainty. On the one hand, certainty seemed particularly urgent yet particularly remote when the accepted fabric of belief was being questioned. On the other hand, within its own field science seemed to present an unprecedented growth of that knowledge which skepticism said we could not attain. Faced with this situation, thinkers reacted in many ways. Some lapsed into skepticism, many others reaffirmed old certainties amid the flux. But the future lay with those who could bear to challenge old assumptions and search for a new approach, precisely because they retained an optimistic faith in the possibility of new knowledge.

Such thinkers needed to distinguish between old beliefs that must be cast aside, and new, trustworthy knowledge. So, influenced by the need for a criterion, the search took the form of what is today called foundationalism. This is the conviction that any radical attempt to justify our beliefs must build on some starting point that *could* not be wrong. As a building can be no firmer than its foundations, so genuine knowledge must rest on an unshakeable base. Descartes began foundationalism, by setting out to doubt whatever could be doubted so as to find a sure foundation for knowledge. In his argument two notions appear, that appealed to many even when they rejected his own application of them. One was that of innate ideas of human reason, which need only be understood to be accepted: an example was the belief that every event must have a cause, which seemed to underlie all rational investigation. The other notion was that, though I might be mistaken in what I thought I saw, at least I knew I *seemed* to see things, or had sensory experience. From this two streams diverged. The Continental Rationalists took up the first strand, and aimed to develop metaphysical systems based on innate ideas of reason. The British Empiricists emphasized the other strand, starting from what they called "simple ideas", or sheer uninterpreted experience.[2]

While the need for a criterion spurred the search for an unshakeable base, the form the search took was influenced by the increasing prestige of science. For science had two aspects. One was the use of mathematics, where the exemplar was still Euclid's geometry with its "self-evident" axioms. The other aspect was the testing of theories by careful observation, which made sensory experience the final court of appeal. So we can see both the Rationalist appeal to self-evident truths, and the Empiricist appeal to experience, as inspired by one aspect of the most conspicuous intellectual achievement of their day. Certainly, Rationalists extended the notion of self-evident truths far beyond mathematics, while Empiricists sometimes focused their critique of knowledge on science itself; but all thinkers had to come to terms with the impact of science. "Come to terms with" does not mean "accept"; rather, it means that in whatever ways they assumed, supported or resisted it, we can see it as shaping their agenda. This was to become a longer-lasting issue than the search for certainty itself, for we find here a recurring phenomenon: that one type of knowledge—in this case, science—becomes the standard by which others are judged.

2. Later Developments

Behind the specific arguments of Rationalist and Empiricist philosophers lay a general optimism, fuelled by advances not only in science but in many fields. This led to the great 18th century confidence in the power of reason to solve our problems, that proudly called itself the Enlightenment. The notion of innate ideas of reason, evident to all who understood them, extended far beyond technical Rationalism to such moral and political principles as the proclamation of inalienable human rights. Similarly, the criticizing of traditional beliefs by asking how they actually worked echoed, but went beyond, Empiricist claims to ground knowledge in experience. But by the 19th century, new doubts were emerging. Some were concluding that science, by ignoring what cannot be measured, had a dehumanizing effect, and that the humanities gave deeper insight. Thus, while Hegel's vast synthesis still reflected the optimism of the Enlightenment, natural science played a thoroughly subordinate role in it.

On the whole, the English-speaking Empiricist tradition retained an admiration for science, while Continental philosophy tended to emphasize the humanities. Yet the two traditions have been neither isolated nor monolithic. In particular, British philosophy in the later 19th century developed a neo-Hegelianism known as Absolute Idealism.[3] This placed an extreme emphasis on the importance of understanding the part in the light of the whole. Whatever is less than the whole, it claimed, is to that extent inadequately conceived, or "unreal".[4] So it deprecated both scientific thought and ordinary commonsense;[5] for they both examined specific problems in isolation, without relating them to the whole, and so needed correction by metaphysics. It was for the philosopher to produce the true account of reality. But by the beginning of the 20th century, Absolute Idealism was tired and complacent. Its presentation was so obscure, and so scornfully unwilling to explain its basic assumptions, that it came to seem a model of how not to do philosophy. Hence there was a revolution, which returned to some aspects of the Empiricist tradition. It came to be known as linguistic analysis, philosophical analysis, or, as I shall call it, analytic philosophy. After the 1930s, it merged with a continental challenge to Hegelianism called Logical Positivism, or simply Positivism, and it remains the dominant English-speaking philosophical tradition.[6] As it is my own background, which I partly accept and partly react against, I must sketch it in rather more detail.

In the terms used in Ch. III.6, the analytic revolution was overwhelmingly a criticalist rejection of metaphysical synthesis. What began as an attempt to clarify the baffling concepts of Absolute Idealism, concluded that there was nothing worth clarifying. This led to a rejection of all constructivist metaphysics, which left only the question of why people might have thought it was a worthwhile activity. Analytic philosophy's first answer appealed to how we can be misled by grammatically similar but logically different expressions. "I see nobody on the road" has the same grammatical structure as "I see someone on the road"; but we cannot conclude that nobody is a mysteriously invisible someone. Similarly metaphysicians, it was said, had been led into confusion by assuming that their abstract language must function as in simpler contexts. This not only gave a reason for ignoring what they said, but opened up important new inquiries about how language actually worked. Later, the impact of Positivism produced a new argument, known as the Verification Principle. There were, it said, only two types of meaningful statement: those verifiable by observation, like "This is red"; and those that simply drew out the implications of the words or symbols involved, as in "All bachelors (that is, unmarried males) are male". This was an even more iconoclastic view. Though its central target was still traditional metaphysics, whole areas of discourse such as esthetics and religion were rejected as being beyond verification in either of the two possible ways.

While nothing unites like a common enemy, these strands in analytic philosophy contained tensions. All agreed that they should analyze problems into their constituent elements and find piecemeal solutions to specific problems. Thus in the connecting-and-distinguishing that is articulation, the Absolute Idealist emphasis on the holistic, connecting element was replaced by an analytic, distinguishing one. But the earlier rejection of metaphysics by distinguishing grammatical from logical form, appealed to the ordinary language which reflects our commonsense view of the world. Arising in a humanities-based literary and classical culture in Oxford and Cambridge, it took commonsense as the touchstone of reality; so it rejected any claim, whether based on Absolute Idealist metaphysics or on scientific discovery, that the world is radically other than as we take it to be. Positivism, however, though it was embraced by some with a background in the humanities, was a science-based view. For a scientific claim could be verified by observation, while, as we saw in Ch. V.2, its mathematics merely drew out the implications of the axioms. So though Positivism officially rejected all overviews, it inevitably tended to see science and formalized language as reflecting the true structure of reality. Thus the conflict between humanities- and science-based views reappeared within analytic philosophy itself.

So forceful was the analytic rejection of metaphysical synthesis, that this is still how many outside philosophy departments think of analytic philosophy. However, not only were some earlier analysts constructivists who used their analyses to improve rather than to eliminate metaphysics,[7] but today the critic-alist thrust has largely spent its force. A new sort of science-based constructivism has arisen which I discuss in Ch. XIV. Moreover, another change has come from work both on how scientists develop their theories, and on philosophy of language.[8] These, as we have seen, reveal the mutualistic interaction of whole and part; and so the analytic conviction that insight came only from reducing wholes into their components, is being replaced by a more holistic approach. Though these philosophers see themselves as being in the analytic tradition, and make no reference to the holism of Absolute Idealism, the wheel in some respects has come full circle.

In English-speaking philosophy today, while analytic philosophy is still dominant and has some impressive research programs, it faces a renewed contact with long neglected Continental traditions. Besides deep differences there are also convergences which often go unrecognized; thus aspects of analytic philosophy of science link with such Continental developments as hermeneutics, which has spread from its original meaning of the interpretation of texts to become an analysis of all knowledge.[9] In principle the parallels offer hope for new insight into the major themes of philosophy. But in practice the resulting turmoil sometimes seems too great to bridge, so that even at the same conferences some philosophers attend papers on analytic philosophy, others on hermeneutics or poststructuralism, and others on more practical issues such as environmental ethics, all without serious interaction. To set the scene for applying my analysis of understanding to these issues, I trace out two threads in contemporary thought: a widespread agreement that the foundationalist program has collapsed, and a more controversial attack on the whole optimism of the Enlightenment.

3. The Rejection of Foundationalism

The assumption of foundationalism, that secure knowledge needs an unshakeable base, is an entirely natural one; the problem today is that no such base can be found. The Rationalist appeal to innate ideas of reason had as its central mathematical model the "indubitable" Euclidean axioms. When these were downgraded to being only one starting point for formal systems, the whole approach was discredited. The Empiricist appeal to sensory experience had a complex history, and I offer a quasi-historical sketch of its logic as follows. Our experience, we say, gives us information about the world, but how? The natural view, known as direct realism, is that we perceive things just as they are. But in the search for certainty we soon realize that we make mistakes in perceiving, so to get knowledge of the world we must *interpret* our sensory information. Further, science suggested from the beginning what is now undeniable, that our central nervous system presents a highly selective picture. To avoid the possibility of error, it seemed, we must acknowledge that strictly speaking we are not *directly* aware of the external world, but only of the contents of our minds. Empiricism called those contents "ideas"; and though they took complex forms, basic "simple ideas" represented the uninterpreted raw material of our experience.[10] This suggested a "representative" theory of perception: that we know there *is* an external world, but can only know about it *via* the ideas it produces in us. Yet if we take seriously the belief that we always experience ideas and never the world itself, how could they ever show the world is really there? So we may seem cut off from the world by our ideas.[11] In the face of that difficulty, we might conclude that the external world is a "noumenal" somewhat, of which we know nothing; for all we can know are its "phenomenal" effects on us, rather than its own nature.[12] But then how could we even know it *causes* our sensations; and how would a something-about-which-nothing-can-be-known differ from nothing at all? So we may be driven to the view that, far from the world's being the *source* of "ideas", talk about that world is really only a *way of talking about* "ideas" —our actual and possible experiences—which are all we can know.

This last alternative was inherited from Empiricism by early analytic philosophy. Empiricist "simple ideas" became 20th century "sense data", and the goal of presenting our knowledge of the external world as a logical construction out of sense data was pursued with new vigor and logical expertise. But the result was to show, as conclusively as anything in philosophy, that the whole enterprise must fail. No set of sense-datum statements can imply a statement about the physical world, and, further, we must *presuppose* that world in formulating sense datum statements. Even if we can intelligibly talk of private experience at all (a point that is still debated), we can do so only by communicating in a public language. The world common to us all is the world from which theory of knowledge must start, despite the possibility of error and the inevitable interpretation involved.

If we generalize this point about philosophy of perception by applying it to all knowledge, we may say that we can never get back to any starting point which is inherently beyond challenge. We must abandon the search, not only for uninterpreted, indubitable experience, but for any unshakeable base. Moreover, insofar as science, with its appeal both to mathematics and to observation, had been the underlying inspiration of both Rationalist and Empiricist foundationalism, it too came to point in another direction. Till the 20th century, the Newtonian synthesis seemed the ultimate truth about the physical world. When it began to be undermined by relativity theory at one end of the scale and quantum mechanics at the other, science did not cease to advance. But it now presented a picture of successful knowledge *without* unshakeable foundations, and no other plausible foundation appeared. So whether and how we can have knowledge without foundations is the central issue in current theory of knowledge.

In the long process in which the need for a criterion of knowledge was theologized in Christianity, shaken at the Reformation, and resecularized in philosophy as foundationalism, skepticism and the search for certainty have fed on each other. The search aimed to ward off skeptical objections that we cannot justify our knowledge claims, while, conversely, it seemed that without a criterion for certainty we had no true knowledge. So the rejection of foundationalism would surely have stimulated a reappraisal of Enlightenment faith in the power of reason to achieve knowledge. But there were also other factors in a very complex process.

4. The Challenge to Enlightenment Optimism

For the Enlightenment, reason was essentially universal, and those who found difficulty in grasping its truths only showed they were lacking in it. As its impact would continue to spread, humanity could expect to progress. One challenge to this view came from a growth of historical consciousness, that showed how notions of what is reasonable differ from age to age. In Hegel, the inevitability of progress remained, and the new historical sense was used primarily to show how the past had culminated in the achievements of the present. Even Marx remained confident that, after an inevitable class struggle, progress would prevail. Yet powerful new concepts were being forged: a sense of how far we were shaped by our place in our culture; an awareness of how a dominant group could shape the ideology of a whole society; and a corresponding notion of false consciousness, whereby even those who stood to benefit from change would still accept their lot. These raised questions of how far Enlightenment ideals of progress and reason were themselves part of the ideology of a ruling class, which had the effect of keeping others in subjection. Later came such critiques as a feminist inisistence that appeals to innate human reason concealed assumptions of innate male superiority, and current deconstructionist emphases in many areas.

The spread of science into new fields reinforced these disturbances. The concept of evolution extended a historical perspective back into vast pre-human stretches of time. Anthropology and sociology re-emphasized, not only the possibility of diversity, but also how society shapes individual belief. Freud indicated how, even within the individual, surface reasoning is affected by rationalization. In principle, many of these discoveries could be used to modify, rather than destroy, the earlier vision; for example, evolution could be seen as extending progress far beyond the human time scale. But the intellectual challenges to Enlightenment optimism were strongly reinforced by others. Such experiences as the devastating emotional impact of two world wars, and the realization that "advanced" societies could perpetrate such unthinkable obscenities as the holocaust, made all optimism seem shallow. So today powerful attitudes replace the earlier optimism by an equally deep pessimism about progress and the power of reason.

Such attitudes not only accept the widespread rejection of foundationalism, but often see it as only one of at least three Enlightenment errors. A second one is intellectualism. This treats the process of gaining knowledge as a detached investigation, in which involvement is only a hindrance. It both reflects and reinforces a belief that the task of philosophy is to uncover universal and eternal truths. Yet, its critics say, it is through praxis, or applying knowledge in action, that we acquire insight, particularly in understanding society; and what we learn depends on what interests guide our praxis. Further, intellectualism considers only the isolated individual, but in fact what we will be allowed to find out, and its acceptance as knowledge, depends on the negotiation of interests within and between *groups*. So we must replace intellectualism by a view centered on praxis and on conflicts between group interests.[13] The conclusion often is that both we and our knowledge are essentially constituted by our roles or discourses within groups. Besides foundationalism and intellectualism, a third error is held to be an imperialism, by which philosophers aspire to become the ultimate intellectual umpires who adjudicate all claims to knowledge made by others. Such imperialism depends on the intellectualist assumption that there are eternal criteria for knowledge that philosophers can discover, and it too must be discarded. Some see the rejection of this foundationalist-intellectualist-imperialist syndrome as demanding so totally new an approach that it marks the end of philosophy as we have known it.[14]

Analytic philosophy has grappled with these issues less than I would have liked. It often criticizes "relativism", or the view that all truth is relative to a standpoint, and would probably regard those who reject the syndrome as relativists, but it has failed to engage in detail with their critiques. It thus invites remarks about offering a safe haven for intellectuals who pretend to investigate the deepest questions while avoiding real involvement. But, conversely, those who reject the syndrome sometimes see analytic philosophy as still mired in it,[15] and this is unfair. In justifying our knowledge claims, the analytic tradition rejects the first element, foundationalism. As for imperialism, the English-speaking exponents of this view *par excellence* were the Absolute Idealists. Analytic philosophy, by contrast, has been diffident about its role, and has regarded commonsense or science as the benchmark of truth. The charge of intellectualism has, I think, more substance, and there has also been undue retreat into technicalities. Yet, I shall later suggest, analytic theory of knowledge has real insights to bring to the debate. All views on these issues, however, depend ultimately on our conception of the nature of philosophy itself, so my own view of that should now be made explicit.

5. The Nature of Philosophy

It is difficult here to separate minimalist points from my own, more specific views. But first, virtually all philosophers agree that they approach their problems by using reasoning, rather than by, say, relying on the authority of myth or revelation. This does not mean, however, that they must reject such authority; but only that if they accept it, as many have done, they must offer a rational defence of doing so. Virtually all philosophers would also agree, with varying enthusiasm, on two more points. First, they should be familiar with their tradition, which, as in any discipline, formulates the problems they face. Second, they acquire a specific skill of rigorous argument, which distinguishes professional debate from casual discussion of the same broad themes. If, as suggested in Ch. III.2, disciplines develop their own specialized versions of the general process of selective description, these common factors may point towards what marks philosophy off as a discipline, but they leave open a range of views about its nature. Much depends on the balance we hold between delimitation and transcendence, particularly the tension discussed in Ch. III.7 between vision and the need to discipline it. As philosophy has become a professional discipline, the rigor of its thought is central. But the figures who shaped the tradition are great because of their vision, even though some show a striking lack of rigor. Philosophers immersed in their debates easily forget that vision provides the ultimate point of their discipline; but if they do so the impact of their discussion withers, no matter what its technical brilliance. Analytic philosophy has often sacrificed vision for rigor, but I shall argue that it is capable of applying itself to the central themes of the human condition.

Now, however, I focus on a paradox: that even skilled philosophical debate does not permanently settle its central issues. Philosophers cannot even agree whether they have perennial problems which are reformulated in different ages, or whether they repeatedly formulate new ones with some resemblance to the old.   For convenience I speak as if the issues are permanent, but whichever way we speak philosophy cannot solve them.   No doubt in any discipline a radical new insight may always shake accepted assumptions.   But the great transformations which occur in, say, physics leave an increasing legacy of agreed knowledge, which philosophy does not seem to achieve.   No matter how rigorous the argument, other philosophers eventually question something that is explicitly or implicitly taken for granted.   The argument would establish its conclusion apart from the objection, while the objection will refute the argument unless it can be answered.   So arguments repeatedly switch the onus of proof from one view to another, as objections are raised and met.   In itself this shifting of the onus is not unique; it is, for example, the standard legal view of the effect of lawyers' arguments.   But philosophy has nothing analogous to the decision of a court, by which issues might be settled.

Faced with this paradox of inconclusiveness, a repeated response of philosophers has been to search for a new method or starting point that might settle their problems.   Examples in this chapter include the foundationalist search for an unshakeable base, and the appeal to ordinary language or the Verification Principle in early analytic philosophy.   But we have already seen that this also fails.   The new approach may yield fresh insight, but it fails to deliver all it hoped; and, in the end, either it is discarded, or else its defence becomes yet another issue about which philosophers disagree.   A similar situation arises in the constructivist-criticalist conflict mentioned in Ch. III.6. Constructivism hopes to escape the paradox of inconclusiveness by finding the true metaphysical viewpoint where others have failed, while criticalism aims to end sterile strife between constructivist claims.   But these rivals have failed to vanquish each other permanently, so again the very attempt to overcome the problem becomes another illustration of it.

This situation arises, I suggest, from the restless human capacity for transcendence, and the resulting unboundedness of understanding.   It is because we may always question what we had taken for granted, that philosophy repeatedly transcends its premises, methods and solutions.   There is, as suggested in Ch. III.5, a trade-off between depth of questioning and capacity to settle issues, and the paradox of inconclusiveness reflects what happens when we question our assumptions far enough.   Yet we cannot simply abandon philosophy, for the capacity for transcendence means that we will always continue to ask the ultimate questions.   Hence a striking feature of philosophy is that, while we cannot permanently settle its problems, we also cannot permanently avoid them.   This might suggest a criticalist conclusion that human reason is impotent on these matters, but that would be as contentious as any other view.   For it may still be that we can penetrate more deeply into problems that will always resist a definitive solution.

We can see how this situation both gives rise to, and also refutes, philosophical imperialism. If we reflect on the rationale of other disciplines—if, say, we ask what science or history can hope to achieve—we reach a stage where we no longer call these scientific or historical questions. Rather, we enter, first the philosophical sub-disciplines of philosophy of science or philosophy of history, and then even more general questions of theory of knowledge or metaphysics. So it is inevitably tempting to see philosophy as marking out the boundaries of other disciplines. Yet it does not follow. For philosophy could authoritatively tell other disciplines what their boundaries are, only if it could first find the answer. The fault of the imperialists is not to say, what is quite true, that the questioning of assumptions raises issues where they have special expertise; but rather to pretend, despite all philosophical experience, that any experts can finally answer these questions.

Transcendence, and the resulting unboundedness, also explain other problems met in Ch. III. One was the suggestion that philosophy, like science but unlike many of the humanities, insists on searching for *the* truth rather than complementary aspects, yet, unlike science, cannot achieve it. We can now see that, as philosophy's questions cannot be answered by scientific methods, it remains one of the humanities even when it most admires science. But since its questioning of assumptions may transcend any intelligenda, it must face the question of how they all fit together, and so cannot just take refuge in complementarity. For even if it argues, as some criticalists do, that we cannot overcome complementarity, it must present this as *the* truth about the human condition. Yet since it may question all assumptions, its candidates for ultimate truth meet challenges to their own presuppositions, and so end as one more debated insight into how things are. Its starting points are forever eroded by the unboundedness of understanding, as we rethink what had seemed so attractive or absurd to some other generation or culture.

How this might apply in the future is inherently unforeseeable, but I offer one consideration that arises out of the notion of passing beyond intellectual understanding. If we reflect on our philosophical practice, we may notice that underlying the cut and thrust of argument is the fact that we *want* to defend or attack different views. So if our criticism is parried we thrust again, while if our view is wounded we revive it in a new form. Then we may raise the question: *why* are some attracted to positions by which others are repelled? If argument has deeper than conscious roots, to explore these roots might give deeper insight, but it requires involvement beyond purely intellectual understanding. So should philosophers focus in a new way on what lies behind their skilled debate? Or should they leave this to others, even if this means that for their deepest understanding of their own activity they must rely on others? Should my initial truism, that philosophy approaches its problems by reasoning, be understood to mean that it is restricted to the merely intellectual, or only that it must bring reason to bear on all considerations?

Here as elsewhere, we may expect philosophers to continue to differ, but whatever answer they give, they still have the paradox of inconclusiveness. I later give specific answers to such questions as the constructivist-criticalist issue, but in all my answers I try to hold a delicate balance. On the one hand, since we cannot restrict the unboundedness of the human mind we must give up hope of once-for-all solutions, and accept that our voyage of philosophical discovery will never end. But it does not follow that we must be pessimistic about possible philosophical achievement. For that very questioning of assumptions which precludes a final end, is also the process that may lead to greater depth of understanding. So the possibility remains that philosophy will achieve deeper, though not final, insights into the human condition, and I shall argue that this is a reasonable hope.

6. Implications of My Analysis

Finally, I foreshadow some specific implications of my analysis. We shall meet various views that are more pessimistic than mine. Insofar as they aim at understanding the human condition, Part A should be neutral, in the sense of showing how they represent *claims*, whether correct or not, to insight. But they will also challenge my assumptions, and may see my allegedly minimalist starting points as begging questions against them. Here I believe my analysis is relevant in a deeper way, as providing a strategic starting point from which philosophical problems can be better approached.

Among the issues raised earlier, I endorse the widespread rejection of foundationalism. For to take anything, whether Empiricist experience or Rationalist intuition, as an undeniable starting point, conflicts with mutualism. Any starting point is one element in our whole belief system, and might be affected by interaction with others. Even the most apparently indubitable belief or experience occurs in a context, and we cannot know in advance that a new context will not challenge it. But then I must face a crucial contemporary problem. If we receive from our tradition what we initially take to be knowledge; if that putative knowledge must rest on unexamined assumptions; and if apparently sure assumptions may always meet new objections: then are we too embedded in our tradition to be able to stand back and assess it independently? These questions resonate so deeply with my approach that I cannot just accept analytic philosophy's dismissal of them as "relativist" doubts, but when I examine them at length I reach a twofold conclusion. Certainly I find the extreme Enlightenment confidence in reason to be shallow and indefensible. But I also find grounds for a cautious optimism about our capacity, in appropriate circumstances, to extend our understanding by rational investigation. That cautious optimism conflicts with those who reject the foundationalist-intellectualist-imperialist syndrome, and I argue that the syndrome is not as tightly connected as they suppose. I reject foundationalism, and agree we must pass beyond intellectualism, but I deny the anti-rational conclusions that are often drawn. I argue that, however much our thought is governed by social interests, a specific interest which we can acquire is just to find out the truth for its own sake; though it is a further question how influential this motive actually is. Finally, I foreswear philosophical imperialism; but though many disciplines contribute to understanding our human condition in their own ways, I believe philosophy has its own unique role.

The structure of Part B is as follows. Since understanding is closely connected to knowledge, I begin by relating Part A to analytic philosophy's theory of knowledge. In Ch. VIII I argue that understanding *is* knowledge of a particularly important type—namely, knowledge of structure and of connections—so whatever is true of all knowledge must apply to understanding also. In Ch. IX I examine analytic philosophy's view of knowledge, and offer my own version of it that emerges from my analysis of understanding. These discussions represent an internal debate within my own tradition, but I hope its nature and relevance can be seen by others. In Ch. X I present a broader, and crucial, argument, for here I defend my cautious optimism in the power of reason. In Ch. XI I face objections to it. Here I begin with debates within analytic philosophy, but go beyond them to discuss others. Those discussions lie broadly within the field of theory of knowledge or epistemology, but they raise crucial issues which belong to those most general questions of philosophy that are broadly called metaphysics. So Ch. XII centers on the question of the relation of thought to reality, which is traditionally called the conflict between realism and idealism. It also raises such issues as the nature of truth. Ch. XIII turns to the relation of theoretical to practical understanding, and also considers the relation of the individual to the group. Finally, Ch. XIV reflects on the broadest implications of my whole approach. These include the chances of regaining a more unified worldview than we at present have, and what contribution philosophy might make to that enterprise.

ENDNOTES

[1] In this I follow R. H. Popkin *The History of Scepticism from Erasmus to Descartes* (1964).
[2] In this very brief sketch, I ignore the later tradition of phenomenology, which may also be seen as seeking a sure foundation for all knowledge in yet another way; namely by examining the pure structures of our thought, while "bracketing" the question of whether or how they relate to the world.

3 The most famous exponent is F. H. Bradley. His *magnum opus* is *Appearance and Reality* (1897). Yet I think a more impressive work is H. H. Joachim *Logical Studies* (1948). This is the posthumous publication of lectures given between 1927 and 1935, which were already a rearguard defence of a retreating tradition.

4 Bradley thought we could not achieve proper knowledge of the whole, so the nature of reality was beyond our comprehension. Hegel, as I read him, thought that we could and he did.

5 It also had ambivalent attitudes towards religion, sometimes seeing itself as religion's ally and sometimes as its successor.

6 Among many accounts of the revolution, a useful one is J. O. Urmson *Philosophical Analysis* (1956). For the impact of logical positivism, the *locus classicus* is A. J. Ayer *Language, Truth and Logic* (1946).

7 The outstanding example is Bertrand Russell's Logical Atomism. See his *Logic and Knowledge* (ed. R. C. Marsh) (1956). Russell's technical analyses were regarded as paradigms, but his concern with very abstract problems of metaphysics was often later seen as failing to grasp their source in linguistic confusion. Cf. Urmson *op. cit.*

8 See especially W. V. O. Quine *op. cit.*: D. Davidson *Inquiries into Truth and Interpretation* (1984).

9 With the former, T. S. Kuhn *The Structure of Scientific Revolutions* has stimulated a voluminous debate. For hermeneutics, see particularly H.-G. Gadamer *op. cit.* and *Philosophical Hermeneutics* (1977). For general discussion, see R. J. Bernstein's admirable *Beyond Objectivism and Relativism* (1983). See too R. Rorty *Philosophy and The Mirror of Nature* (1980). For the debate outside philosophy, see R. E. Palmer *Hermeneutics* (1969); J. C. Weinsheimer *Gadamer's Hermeneutics* (1985). There are also important links with Lonergan's discussion of insight in the scholastic tradition; cf. Bernard J. F. Lonergan *Insight* (1958).

10 It was never clear whether simple ideas were sheer experience, or basic concepts somehow read off experience, but both were needed.

11 The criticism, though not the conclusion, is a central point made by Berkeley against Locke.

12 This view has often, though probably wrongly, been attributed to Kant. Historically, it comes after Berkeley's view, which I mention next.

13 This is often called an instrumental view of knowledge (e.g., Barry Barnes *Interests and the Growth of Knowledge* (1977), p.18). It must not be confused with the quite different notion within analytic philosophy of an instrumentalist theory of *truth*.

14 Cf. R. Rorty (1980).

15 Cf. R. Rorty (1980).

CHAPTER VIII

KNOWING AND UNDERSTANDING

1. Introduction

Analytic philosophy early developed an analysis of knowledge that I shall call the "standard account" of the concept. Today there are problems within this account which I discuss in Ch. IX, but I aim now only to relate it to my analysis of understanding. It treats knowledge as *justified true belief.* I know some statement "p" (for example, I know that Santiago is the capital of Chile) if and only if: (a) I believe that p; (b) I have proper justification for my belief; and (c) p is in fact true. The reasons for this seem straightforward. As for (a): if I know that Santiago is the capital of Chile, I must also believe that it is; but the converse is not true—I believe many things without knowing them. So knowledge seems to be a kind of belief. (b) If my belief is a mere unsupported hunch, then even if it is correct I surely do not really know it. (c) Even if I have good reasons for a false belief (I trust a normally reliable guide book, which by some error says that Montevideo is the capital), when I find my mistake I must admit that, while of course I believed it, I never really knew it. So "know" is objective, making a claim about how things are which must be withdrawn if they are not like that. "Believe" is subjective; that I believe p, though not of course p itself, is made true by the fact that I believe it.

I shall now argue that understanding *is* the most important type of knowledge, namely knowledge of structure and connections. This may not surprise non-philosophers, but is a challenging claim within my tradition. Any defence of it that was rigorous enough for professional philosophers would hardly be comprehensible to others, but I have presented a more detailed discussion elsewhere and now sketch some of its outlines.[1] Non-philosophers may either take this chapter as a simplified example of one form of analytic philosophy in action, or else they may simply grasp my basic point about the relation of understanding to knowledge. I shall claim that the standard account has two features which distort the relation of knowledge to understanding. First, though it usually acknowledges that there is practical as well as theoretical knowledge, it virtually ignores it. Second, its concentration on theoretical knowledge goes with an overwhelming emphasis on the *that*-clause ("I know that p"); whereas to understand understanding we must focus on other forms, particularly knowing/understanding *why* and *how*. I argue this by investigating the verbal forms of *know, believe* and *understand*.[2] But we shall find they give only clues, though valuable ones, to an answer. For the vital distinctions turn out to be semantic ones concerned with meaning, rather than syntactic ones concerned with grammar. Because of the amorphousness of word-meaning mentioned in Ch. II.7, analytic philosophy has met immense difficulty in finding expressions which "mean the same" as those being analyzed.[3] To avoid this, I introduce a notion that I applied implicitly in my less technical discussion of significance and importance in Ch. IV: the concept of *normal equivalence*. I shall say that two words or phrases are normally equivalent in a given context if substituting one for the other makes no difference to the normal meaning of the sentence.[4]

2. The Restriction of Knowledge to Knowing *That*

Undoubtedly a central paradigm of theoretical knowledge is found in the *that*-clause, as in:

(1) I know that Joe took his watch to the beach yesterday.

However there are also many others. I focus on two cases. First, there is knowing the significance of something, which can be expressed by various abstract nouns:

(2) She knows (the significance of the point/the need to strike a balance/the complexity of .../the difficulty .../the objections...).

The other case is the whole variety of what linguists call wh-forms;

(3) He knows ((a) why I came (b) how volcanoes operate (c) what she said (d) what an elephant weighs (e) where we are going (f) when I arrived... etc.).

In analytic philosophy, wh-forms are normally ignored. This practice is usually just taken for granted, but there is a syntactic point which might be seen as a defence of it. We can obtain the *wh*-forms that can follow *know* by deleting *that*, and replacing an element in the sentence by the appropriate conjunction. In (1), for *Joe* we can put *who*, to obtain "I know who took his watch..."; similarly with *when* for *yesterday* ("I know when Joe...") etc. So: (a) given the sentence we can construct the *wh*-forms; (b) the converse is not true, for *wh*-forms give less information (we cannot obtain "Joe took the watch" from "who took the watch"); (c) I cannot know any of the *wh*-forms unless I know the relevant fact; I can only know who took the watch if I know Joe did. But these verbal facts, I suggest, only show that syntactic points are inadequate guides to semantic ones for the cases in (3) actually conceal important distinctions. Consider *why*. Syntactically, it represents a *that...* *because* (to know why Joe took his watch to the beach is to know that he took it because ...). But, unlike such forms as *where* and *when*, this relates the *that-*

clause to the rest of our knowledge. To know why p is essentially to know the *explanation* of p, which may involve a large number of facts, structures and inferences. To emphasize grammatical parallels with other *wh*-forms here disguises the fact that to learn why p is essentially to *acquire understanding*, by articulating facts into a coherent structure. The same is often true of *how*. *How* may represent only a simple phrase ("How did Joe take his watch to the beach?—In his pocket"). But it can also ask for an explanation ("How—by what chemical process—does acid turn litmus paper red?"), and then it too involves relating p to other knowledge. Here grammatical similarities hide the crucial distinctions needed to relate the concepts of knowledge and understanding. It is a fine example of how a point which may seem insignificant from one standpoint is vital from another.

3. Knowing and Understanding

If we turn to the relation between knowledge and understanding, my analysis in Part A suggests the following. Understanding involves significant structure, while knowledge need not; there is not much structure involved in a simple fact like (1). Yet knowledge *may* involve significant structure, and when it does we might expect a close link with understanding. Comparing the verbal forms of *know* and *understand* strikingly, though not straightforwardly, confirms this hypothesis. Typically, when sufficient structure is involved the two words are normally equivalent. We may start by substituting *understand* for *know* in (2). If we say:

(4) She understands (the significance of the point/the need .../the complexity .../the difficulty .../the objections ...),

these are surely normally equivalent to (2). The *wh*-clauses of (3) are even more illuminating. Substituting in the first examples, we can say:

(5) He understands (a) why I came (b) how volcanoes operate.

In both these there is sufficient complexity of structure to allow *understand*. Leaving (c) "what she said", till Sec. 4, the point comes out particularly neatly in (d) "what an elephant weighs". We cannot say:

(*6) He understands what an elephant weighs—namely several tonnes fully grown.

But we could say:

(7) He understands what an elephant weighs—and that's why he wouldn't take Jumbo in the canoe.

For (*6) involves a sheer fact, and (7) a grasp of implications. Similarly, (3e) "where we are going" is normally a sheer fact, and does not allow *understand*. Yet with a specially significant destination, it may; taking a child to hospital, we might ask, "Does he understand where we are going?". Analogously, imagining an appropriately complex context for (3f) "when I arrived", might find a use for *understand*. As these cases bring out, we must move beyond syntactic structure to the semantic question of whether there is sufficient complexity. Too little structure in our knowledge, and the notion of understanding just does not get a grip; but when it does, it is normally equivalent to knowing.

However a complication arises with the central paradigm of the *that*-clause. Simple examples, like (1) seem sheer facts which, like "when I arrived", do not give rise to understanding. However we can say:

(8) I understand (that) Joe took his watch to the beach yesterday.

But this is a new sense of *understand*. It has special syntactic features;[5] and semantically it is subjective, for I may understand wrongly here. It usually indicates lack of confidence in my information, and what makes it inappropriate is too much information rather than too little complexity. If my neighbors are building a shed in front of my eyes, I can hardly say, "I understand you are building a shed". But I could say it to them elsewhere, if I had been told they were. This special sense of *understand* masks, but does not refute, the previous point, that simple *thats* give no more grip to understanding than simple *wheres* and *whens*. And since the test is semantic, not syntactic, the key word is "simple". Watching an amateur scientist, we might say:

(9) I suppose he understands that if he mixes chemical X and Y he'll get an explosion.

This is intellectual understanding, involving grasp of significant structure, and is normally equivalent to *know*. When we clear away the special sense, we see, as in other cases, that *that*-clauses also will support *understand* if and only if they speak of discerning structure.

4. Belief

The standard account makes knowledge a special case of belief, namely belief that is both justified and true. This is intuitively attractive, for surely knowledge does stand in some close relation to well founded beliefs. It is reinforced by how we withdraw knowledge claims if they turn out to be false, by retreating from "I know that p" to "At least I believed that p". Yet the verbal forms suggest the story must be more complex than this.[6] For if knowledge were a species of belief, we should expect the same variety of verbal forms for the latter, and they are not there. The most striking grammatical feature of *believe* is the poverty of its forms. Believing *that* is virtually coextensive with knowing *that*, so that corresponding to (1) we have:

(10) I believe (that) Joe took his watch to the beach yesterday.

Otherwise there is very little. There are virtually no parallels to (2) and (3). We cannot say:

> (*11) She believes (the significance of the point/the need .../the complexity of .../the difficulty .../the objections...),

nor, with one exception,

> (*12) He believes (why I came/how .../...where .../when ... /etc.).

The exception is the *what* in (3c) which I earlier postponed. Thus:

> (13) He believes what she said,

though not:

> (*14) He believes what an elephant weighs.

The criterion is that the *what*-clause must employ a verb such as *say*, which indicates an assertion.[7]

There are many problems here. First, in the few forms of *believe* other than believing *that*, we get changes of meaning that do not fit the standard account. To know what she said is to know that she said p; but to believe what she said is to believe that p. Here, far from *believe* being a weaker notion into which we can retreat if our knowledge claim is rejected, it is a stronger one: I may know what she said without believing it.[8] Still further issues arise,[9] including some concerning practical knowledge in Sec. 5. All this suggests that, though believing *that* is a weaker notion than knowing *that*, the standard account may be an oversimple picture of a more complex relation. I offer an alternative view in Ch. IX.

5. Practical Knowledge

I said in Sec. 1 that analytic philosophy acknowledges, but rarely examines, the existence of practical knowledge. Following Ryle, it usually distinguishes the two as knowing *that*, which is theoretical knowledge, and knowing *how*, which is practical knowledge or "know-how".[10] Thus knowing that Joe went to the beach is theoretical, but knowing how to get to the beach is practical. Yet this is quite inadequate. For:

> (15) We know how volcanoes operate

is a standard *wh*-clause of theoretical knowledge. Practical knowledge, if we had it, would be:

> (16) We know how to operate volcanoes.

The natural suggestion would be that the grammatical marker is not the *how*, but rather that theoretical knowledge has a finite verb (*operate*) and practical knowledge an infinitive (*to operate*). This is partly borne out by examining the range of *wh*-forms in (3), though we must alter the examples because with practical knowledge the subjects of the main and subordinate clauses must be the same. Omitting the first, we can say:

(17) He knows ...(b) how to operate volcanoes (c) what to say (d) what to weigh (e) where to go (f) when to arrive...

Only the *why* in (a) resists the construction, for it is odd to say:

(?18) He knows why to come.

So practical knowledge extends beyond the *how to*-form, and applies to other *wh*-+-infinitive constructions. But now we meet the problem that these need not represent practical knowledge. For practical knowledge seems to be the capacity to exercise a skill, as in:

(19) I know how to speak Spanish.

Yet *how to* can also apply to knowing the principles governing an activity, irrespective of capacities. A champion swimmer crippled by an accident still knows how to swim, but cannot do so; we are surely inclined to call this theoretical knowledge.[11] The distinction is again semantic, not syntactic. Speaking Spanish, as in (19), must be practical knowledge. Again,

(20) I know how to drive a car

seems ambiguous as between knowing the correct sequence of actions and being able to perform them, but the context may disambiguate it. If the organizer of volunteer fire fighters calls for four people who know how to drive a truck, we do not volunteer if we know only the former.

Relating these points to Secs. 3 and 4, in practical reasoning we find broadly the same relations between the verbal forms of *know, believe* and *understand* as in theoretical cases. As indicated in Ch. II.4, *believe* can apply to values, and so to practical reasoning, as well as to facts. But there are no more *wh*-forms in practical than in theoretical belief—not even in those that would correspond to (17). We cannot say:

(*21) He believes (how to operate.../what.../where.../when... etc.).

Virtually the only way we can express our beliefs about values and action is with a *that*-clause, as in:

(22) I believe (that) we ought to refuse.

This may have contributed to the view held by many philosophers that belief is a purely theoretical notion.

By contrast, practical knowledge and practical understanding are virtually co-extensive. For acting in accordance with values involves enough complexity to give a grip to that knowledge of structure which is understanding. So corresponding to (17) we have:

(23) He understands (..how to operate volcanoes /what../what../where../when.. /etc).[12]

Thus in practical as in theoretical contexts, the verbal forms of knowledge are closer to understanding than to believing.

There are problems here for moral philosophy. Philosophers take "ought" and "should" to belong to practical reason. Yet these have not only the apparently theoretical *that* and *why*, but also finite verbs rather than infinitives:

(24) I know (that we ought to refuse /why he should agree... /etc.).

To treat these as practical knowledge not only abandons the suggestion that infinitives, rather than finite verbs, are the mark of practical reason, but means that even knowing *that* need not be theoretical. The problem is particularly acute for defenders of the fact/value distinction. They typically hold that knowledge requires true belief; that value judgments are neither true nor false, and so cannot involve knowledge; and that *ought* and *should* express value judgments. So what is *know* doing in (24)? And if there were knowledge here, would it be theoretical or practical? I touch on this in Chapter XIII.5.

6. Final Implications

In arguing that understanding is one type of knowledge, a central implication is to reinforce the objectivity of understanding. Insofar as *understand* is normally equivalent to *know*, it is objective rather than subjective like *believe*. The view found in philosophy of social science, that *Verstehen*, or understanding, involves a mere subjective empathy, makes little contact with how we usually use the word. Indeed when we do express empathy we may well use *know*, in a sense very unlike epistemology's justified true belief, as in:

(25) I know what it's like to suffer like that.

Certainly, some uses of *understand*, such as the special sense in (8), are subjective.[13] This also occurs with the verbal noun or adjective. We say:

(26) Your understanding is quite mistaken,

and an understanding smile makes no claim about how the world is.[14] Yet the objectivity is dominant. A mistaken understanding means you do *not* understand, though a mistaken belief means you *do* believe. The nurse may wear an understanding smile, but whether she understands the patient's situation is a further matter.

We may now also see how an overwhelming focus on knowing *that* could lead to the neglect of understanding. Our theory of knowledge will need examples, so we start with simple ones, as in (1)—knowing that Joe took his watch to the beach. We proceed at once to ask what must be the case if we are to know it. *But our examples easily become our paradigms*, and they lack the structure to give rise to understanding. By focusing on simple cases, we

unwittingly treat knowledge as an atomistic collection of established facts. So
inevitably we assume we can understand what knowledge is, without understanding understanding. This has led to distortions, but I am not primarily
accusing philosophers of letting their theory influence their practice. For they
usually also know that the fundamental goal is not mere acquisition of facts,
but insight into structure. But such insight typically issues in claims to know
the *significance* of an assertion, or *how* to defend it, or *why* we should accept
it. It is the importance of these forms that is disguised by exclusive concentration on the *that*-form. Yet even simple examples in fact depend on complex
factors which they take for granted. *How* do we know Joe took his watch to
the beach? Because, as I argued in Ch. III.1, our evidence fits coherently into
our other knowledge. It is by the articulation of significant structure that we
justify our beliefs in even the simplest cases.

I have claimed that, where there is sufficient complexity, the link between
understand and *know* is so close that the two are normally equivalent.
Certainly we can often distinguish them if they are juxtaposed, by attaching
know more to sheer fact and *understand* to grasp of structure; as in the
teacher's complaint about a rote-learning class,

(27) They know it, but they don't understand it.

But still when they are *not* juxtaposed, they are normally equivalent.
Moreover sometimes I think we cannot make any contrast, and have as close a
synonymy as we are ever likely to get in natural language. Take chess, where
any knowledge requires some grasp of structure. Suppose we try to contrast
knowing and understanding that placing my rook here may lead to mate in
three moves. Perhaps, we may think, if I grasp the strategy, I not only know
but understand; if I merely accept what my friend has whispered to me, I know
but do not understand where to move. But surely the contrast will not work.
Even in the second case, I do understand where to move: I understand that this
is a permissible move which will lead, I am assured, to a mate. If I do not
understand this, then I do not even know enough about chess to know where
to move either; I at most know that, say, placing this object in that position
may have certain effects on certain people. The contrast in the second case is
not between *know* and *understand*, but between *where* and *why*. I both know
and understand where to move, but neither know nor understand why it will be
effective. I find no difference in meaning here.

In all this I have worked within the analytic tradition. Postponing deeper
challenges, such as whether both truth and knowledge are outmoded concepts
in a postmodernist age, I have assumed the standard account of knowledge as
justified true belief. I claim that discernment of structure, or understanding, is
not different from knowledge, but is in fact our most valuable knowledge.
Yet, finally, even if I am wrong, the importance of understanding remains. For
suppose understanding were, say, something extra to, and different from,

knowledge. That would not reduce the importance of making connections and obtaining insight; it would only show that epistemology could not be confined to theory of *knowledge*, but must also extend to theory of understanding. The implication is that we must graft the analysis of understanding into our theory of knowledge. But ultimately, we shall see, the graft tends to become the main trunk.

ENDNOTES

1 "Knowledge, Belief and Understanding" (1981).

2 When philosophers mention a word rather than using it, they put it in inverted commas. Linguists use italics for this purpose. In this chapter, to avoid a forest of inverted commas I use the linguists' device.

3 Thus W. P. Alston in *Philosophy of Language* (Prentice-Hall, 1964) Ch.2 was led to define sentence-synonymy in terms of similarity of illocutionary act potential, and word-synonymy in ways derived from that notion.

4 This is weaker than synonymy, for it allows that in other sentences or contexts substitution might change the meaning. Yet it is stronger than the formal notion of material equivalence, that two sentences merely have the same truth value. In particular, it is not logically transitive; w_1 may be normally equivalent to w_2, and w_2 to w_3, without w_1's being normally equivalent to w_3. Like most concepts it has blurred edges, but borderline cases can simply be noted as such. It is defined for normal meaning, but could be developed to apply to idiosyncratic speaker meaning.

5 E.g., it is grammatically parenthetical, able to change its place in the sentence easily ("Joe took his watch ..., I understand"); it lacks a negative (we cannot say "I don't understand Joe took ..."); etc.

6 Here I am in a complex mixture of agreement and disagreement with the penetrating discussion by Z. Vendler in *Res Cogitans* (1972). His arguments surely deserve more attention than they have received.

7 The distinction is semantic, and in particular is not the syntactic one between the relative *what* (= that which), and the non-relative one that Vendler calls a true *wh*-nominal (*op. cit.* pp. 94 *et seq.*). As he says, *what* is relative after *believe* and a wh-nominal after *know*. Thus "he knows what she said" and "he knows what she did" are both wh-nominals; but only the former can take *believes*, and even here it fundamentally alters the sense.

8 Subtleties cluster, for various reasons, round our talk about talk. Not only is "He believes what she said" stronger than "He knows what she said", but "He understood what she said" is quite different from both. Again, while knowing and understanding a language are often normally equivalent, I might understand Chinese though I could not speak it, but would hardly then be said to know it. And consider the striking ambiguity of "The verb was understood", as meaning either that it was comprehended, or that it was not expressed. Only the former uses the ordinary sense of *understand*.

9 *Wh*-forms can be grammatically reduced to *that*-forms, but there are no belief *wh*-forms to be reduced to believing *that*. So in retreating from knowledge claims in these cases we must retain and qualify the *know*. E.g., "I believed I knew (or: I thought I knew) (why /what/when)... etc."

10 G. Ryle *The Concept of Mind* (1949).

11 Peter Forrest has suggested to me that we might question the exhaustiveness of a simple theoretical/practical dichotomy—e.g., by saying that this is "imaginative" know-how.

12 Yet suppose I had acquired an ability—say, to wiggle my ears—without being able to explain how. I know how to, but do not understand how to. There is no discernment of structure—I can just do it.

13 Also *understand as* refers to believed rather than actual discernment: "He wrongly understood the argument as a threat to his position", though not "He wrongly knew ...".

14 But here the objectivity of *know* also fails. Besides an understanding smile we may give

a knowing wink, even though we do not really know.

CHAPTER IX

THE CONCEPT OF KNOWLEDGE

1. Problems with the Standard Account of Knowledge

In this Chapter I still work within the analytic tradition, before moving on to issues outside it. I focus on its standard account of knowledge as justified true belief, and develop my own view in relation to it. After Ch. VIII, I assume that knowledge of sufficiently complex structures amounts to understanding; but for convenience I still speak mostly of theoretical "knowing that", while assuming that what I say also applies in appropriate cases to understanding. Our problems concern the notion of justifying beliefs, which is so central to the standard account; for in the last few decades this has generated a literature of immense bulk and complexity.

Many issues in the debates turn on a distinction between externalist and internalist approaches. Externalist ones abstract from the standpoint of any particular person, whether actual or hypothetical, and so are taken to represent how the world is independently of what anyone may believe. By contrast, internalist ones involve a reference to a standpoint. Thus externalist analyses may assert that the justification of belief is at least partly independent of the information actually available to the knower, while internalist ones make it dependent on such information. Those who first developed the standard account of knowledge as justified true belief, took for granted an internalist view of justification and an externalist one of truth. The question of whether we were justified in claiming to know that p, was taken to depend on whether we had reasoned properly on the basis of the information available to us. But whether the knowledge claim was true or false, was independent of whatever we believed with whatever justification. Relying on a good guide book might justify me in claiming to know that Montevideo was the capital of Chile, but the truth of the matter was independent of my beliefs. Yet preserving these natural assumptions is not easy. For there are cases where A believes some statement "p", for reasons which justify a knowledge claim, and p is in fact true, yet we would not say A knows that p. So, it has seemed, if we keep an internalist view of justification and an externalist one of truth, then, while justified true belief may no doubt be a necessary condition for knowledge, it is not sufficient. The effort to plug the gap by finding what *is* sufficient for knowledge, has produced the complexity of contemporary discussions.

The debate has led to a questioning of each of the two assumptions of internalist justification and externalist truth. There are externalist analyses of justification, usually called reliabilist ones. They hold that a knowledge claim is justified only if it meets criteria which the claimant may not be in a position to fulfil, so that despite our most careful efforts we may make a claim which is not merely untrue but unjustified. Conversely, there are internalist analyses of truth, known as verificationist or warranted assertability ones. They say that calling p true *means only* that we have a proper internalist justification for believing it, and so are rationally warranted in asserting it. However the two assumptions of internalist justification and externalist truth seem to me entirely appropriate, and I shall argue they should be retained.

2. "Necessarily Normally"

Before developing my argument, I must introduce the notion of a connection which *necessarily normally* holds. Consider how we decide law cases by evidence. Witnesses sometimes get away with perjury. But if we came to believe that false witnesses could be routinely hired and rarely detected, we could no more regard our legal system as properly assigning liability, than did the ancient process of trial by ordeal. The practice might still remain for other reasons: it could give an official verdict on competing claims; the powerful might like to have "justice" under the control of the rich; and the rhetoric of impartial inquiry might linger on, like that of absolute monarchy in much British constitutional law. But the practice could not have its present rationale. So, though there is no conceptual necessity that witnesses speak the truth, there is a conditional necessity here. *If* we are to take legal processes to have their present point, *then* we must take the evidence of witnesses to be *normally* reliably assessable.[1]

The basic notion is that sometimes, though situation A can fail to have feature B, yet if this were the normal, rather than an unusual case, we would lose the *point* of a larger conceptual system in which A and B are embedded. Thus in Ch. II.3 I noted that intellectual understanding normally improves practical ability, and also that understanding normally involves the capacity to explain, but that in neither case does this always follow. Yet unless it normally did, we would not value understanding as we do. The point is often exemplified, if not recognized, elsewhere in philosophy. It has been argued as a reason for keeping promises that, though they are sometimes broken, yet regular breaking would subvert the whole point of making them. So promises are necessarily normally kept; when they are not—when, say, ceasefires are cynically agreed only because neither side wants to be seen as the aggressor— such cases reinforce the point by showing how quickly the value of promising is eroded. Again it has been said that, though we may conceal our inner feelings, yet behavior must normally provide criteria for mental states; for we could not intelligibly talk about these states unless their concealment, or the behavior without them, were the exception and not the rule. A final case is the "principle of charity", that when interpreting a new language we should make the maximum number of sentences come out true, thereby assuming that people necessarily normally tell the truth.[2]

The "necessarily normal" relation may seem a dubious one to many analytic philosophers, who often hold that connections must be either logically necessary (following from the meaning of words, or true in all possible worlds); nomically necessary (following from the laws of nature, or always true in the actual world); or else merely accidental. For here we have a sort of necessity that does not fit these patterns. Yet it must occur. Suppose that, in our imprecise ordinary language, we have a borderline case where a term is only dubiously applicable. If those cases should become common enough to be important paradigms, the whole meaning of the term will eventually change, because of the fluidity of language; but *unless* this happens, the cases will necessarily not be normal ones. It is a basic application of mutualism that, since the part may affect the whole, an expansion of one sub-system may not only be at the expense of others, but may transform a super-system in which it is embedded by causing it to lose its current point. But in cases where this transformation does *not* occur, the exceptions will necessarily be atypical.

Apart from the earlier philosophical examples, the notion directly applies to some current debates about knowledge. First, in considering justification philosophers have sometimes debated whether punters who could intuitively pick a horse and regularly succeed, would *know* that it would win. In my view, they would —not at first, but after enough success; for the acid test of a justification is that it works. But here we do not understand *why* it works. So *if* we are to keep our present belief that our knowledge gives us a reasonably coherent picture of the world, we must *necessarily normally* have a more comprehensible justification than the punters would. Second, philosophers have asked: does doubt destroy knowledge? Do unconfident examinees, who regularly get their answers right, really know them? I think so; but again these are necessarily not normal situations. To doubt p is not just to have a feeling, but to be disinclined to act as if p were true. If we doubt, we can usually test the matter. Neuroses apart, either success brings confidence, or else we set a higher standard and no longer regard the old reasons as justifying a claim to know. So confidence necessarily normally accompanies knowledge. These two cases have been debated because one side sees that we are right to claim knowledge here, and the other side sees that this could not be a normal situation. Both are right, for these are possible, but necessarily not normal, cases. However, besides these examples, I believe the notion is involved in the concept of knowledge in a much deeper way. For, I shall now argue, the justification required for making a knowledge claim is one which is *necessarily normally successful*; a concept which I abbreviate to NNS. This point needs qualifications which will emerge later, but first I set out the basic application of it.

3. A Parable About a Word Like "Know"

Consider a tribe called the Humans, who speak a language much like English. Humans believe they know many truths, with various sorts of justifications that are based on accumulated experience of what is reliable. They trust careful reasoning, and also appeal to such experiences as discovering something's color by looking at it in a good light; and they rely on coherence, believing that in general their types of justification reinforce each other. They grant these types may conflict, and do not think any of them infallible; but, they point out, unless they were NNS, normally though not always leading to truth, they would not be justifications. Justification depends on context in subtle ways that Humans rarely analyze, but they achieve much intuitive agreement. Thus they rely on identifying their friends by sight; but if they find out that Mary has an identical twin, the sighting might justify saying only that they had seen her or her sister. Justifications depend on how the world works, and so may have to change. If cloning became so common that many Humans came from indistinguishable batches, a sighting might be accepted only as a justification for saying they had seen a Mary-clone. Further, in assessing justifications Humans consider not only what information people had, but what they should have had. Just as their law attributes liability not only for malicious but also for negligent injury, so they think people should exercise reasonable care to look out for special circumstances.

Humans must rely on each other to achieve many of their goals, and so need reliable methods of passing on their stock of truths. The most important is to use sentences taken to express truths, called statements. A convention is that when people utter apparent statements, such as "I saw a giraffe on the lawn this morning", others may normally rely on their truth. To this there are subtle exceptions, which few Humans could make explicit: story telling; bargaining in their bazaars, where bluff is expected; and so on. Otherwise the rule is protected by powerful sanctions. Those who deliberately utter false statements are stigmatized as "liars", while those with no adequate justification are criticized as careless, or as rumor-mongers. Another convention, also governed by unanalyzed principles, is that what is uttered should normally be relevant to the context. It includes a rule of candor, that a statement should not merely be true, but should state as much as is relevant. Thus a Human is criticized for saying "I have two coins in my bag", if they also have three more; particularly if five are needed to buy the next round of drinks.

Humans have linguistic devices to facilitate these conventions. Phrases such as "I believe" are used to indicate that, though the utterers take statements to be true, they do not claim a NNS justification. Other devices emphasize that they do make this claim; the commonest is "I know", which not only claims that the utterance is true, but indicates that the utterer has a justification without saying what it is. Such statements can be passed on with special confidence. If Humans repeat information—"There was a giraffe on Joe's lawn this morning"—they take responsibility for its reliability, for now it is *their* statement. But, since the convention is that *any* statement should be reliable, they often do not check its reliability; that it comes from a normally reliable source is itself a NNS justification. Since that source would have been prepared to say they knew, a new utterer may say that the prior utterer knows—"Joe knows that there was a giraffe on his lawn" —even when Joe did not explicitly say he knew.

All this immensely helps the circulation of truths, but it requires a further rule. When NNS justifications certified by "I know" break down, as they occasionally do, the chain of "knows" must be obliterated. For if a statement turns out to be false, it always was false, so no one ever knew it to be true. Hence honest knowledge claims may have to be retrospectively withdrawn, though only rarely (necessarily not normally). Yet such withdrawals are not occasions for reproach. Rather, just as a jury in a Human trial must bring in a verdict of "guilty" if the evidence demands it, and they do their duty no less if in fact the evidence is undetectably perjured: so Humans with NNS justifications are often obliged by the rule of candor to say they know, even though their statements will occasionally turn out to be false.

The standards of justification depend partly on context. When Humans see their friend's sandals in the hut, they may properly say they know he has returned from his walk. A reasonable suspicion that this is an abnormal case (his enemies may have placed the sandals there to mislead them), would exclude the knowledge claim. But further, in more careful contexts such as giving evidence in a Human law court, they might well be told, even without taking this to be an abnormal case, that strictly they *assumed* he had returned. For circulating the stock of truths requires a trade-off between reliability and ease of passing on. In less exacting contexts the ease is the more prominent value, in more exacting ones the reliability. Yet, though some standards are more reliable than others, all of them are within the range of what is NNS, for here the trade-off is optimal. Less than this, and claims could not be accepted with sufficient confidence; more than this, and so little could be claimed that the circulation of truths would be restricted. This means that claims to know are sometimes mistaken, just as in Human trials wrong verdicts are sometimes reached; but the price is well worth paying.

4. Some Comments on the Parable

My parable emphasized passing on the stock of truths. Though "know" is used in contexts which do not pass on any truth ("We all know *that*!"), I focus on this case because it highlights how the tradition is appropriated by the individual. Justifications for knowledge are based on our society's accumulated experience, and so have unavoidable vagueness. If a society has survived, its accepted grounds cannot all be misleading, but some may well not be NNS. So they can be questioned, as when a few bold souls rejected the then current criteria for identifying witches; and if we find some ground is inadequate, we strengthen or abandon it. To justify is to give a reason, and, in the end, reasons must cohere with the rest of our knowledge. While some justifications, such as the punters' in Sec. 2, are less integrated than others, individual items of knowledge depend on the coherence of our overall understanding. Because of the mutualistic interaction between new information and older beliefs, justification involves *defeasible* reasons; that is, ones which hold *unless* some special case, which we may call a defeater, arises. Defeaters are themselves defeasible, and if they are defeated the previous justification is restored. Mary's having a twin is a defeater for our NNS visual identification; but if we find that the twin is, alas, now a paraplegic, our identification of a walking Mary is restored. Because of the unboundedness of understanding the list of defeaters is open ended, for we cannot foresee what might come to threaten a justification. But we have a criterion by which to judge new cases: would our justification be normally successful?

A central point in the parable is the distinction between claiming to know, and judging claims made by others. This corresponds to that between first- and third-person uses of "know", except that I can treat my *past* knowledge claims like other peoples'; not only "They think they know", but, retrospectively, "I thought I knew". Hence the relevant contrast is between *making* claims to know and *judging* others' or our own past ones. I call makers Ms and judges Js, and speak of M-claims and J-claims. The role of M and J depends on context: if M claims to know, J_1 may assess the claim and conclude "M knows", while J_2 may in turn assess J_1's assessment and conclude that J_1 (and M) do or do not know.

I can now set out some points that emerge from the parable. M- and J-claims contextually imply the following, in the sense that the claims would normally be out of order unless these conditions were met.

(1) M-claims (e.g. "I know that p") contextually imply:

(a) M believes that p, because

(b) M has justification for this.

(2) J-claims (e.g. "M knows that p") contextually imply:

(a) J believes that p, because

(b) J justifiably believes that M believes p because M has a justfication for this.

(3) Not only may knowledge claims be properly made under conditions (1) and (2), but candor often requires that they should be.

(4) A justification must be at least NNS.

(5) that a normally reliable person claims to know, is one type of NNS justfication for others. (So, in point (2), J has a NNS justification for p.)

(5) (a) In judging claims to know that p, if p is taken to be false, the claim is taken to be false.

(b) It may follow, however, from (3) that it would have been wrong not to make the claim.

Because of the flexibility and vagueness of ordinary language, (5)(a) may tidy up ordinary use, for perhaps truth is not always taken to be a necessary condition of knowledge. English does seem to allow sentences such as: "Medical knowledge in the eighteenth century was very imperfect, and included much that was false".[3] Moreover, it is a common rhetorical device to *claim* to know what is in fact dubious ("Everyone knows this is the only sensible course to take"). So some might argue we should drop (5(a)), and if we do so, virtually none of the usual philosophical problems arise. But I think careful speech supports (5)(a). Moreover, however we use "know", we need such linguistic means as points (1) to (5) for certifying truth claims. That need cannot be removed by any views on the meaning of "know" or any other word, though such views may disguise it or force its re-expression. Thus I offer points (1) to (5) as the *assertability conditions* of M- and J-claims, which indicate when we are entitled to say that we or someone else knows. I later discuss their relation to philosophical attempts to provide *truth* conditions for knowledge—that is, to establish all the conditions, and only those, under which a knowledge claim is true.

5. The Roles of "Believe", "Know" and "Understand"

In the parable, the *primary* speech act in theoretical contexts is the making of statements about how things are; other uses, such as deception, irony, etc., get their point by trading in various ways on this. For this practice to be successful, making a statement must contextually imply that we believe it, that we are justified in making it, and hence normally that it will be true. But this is the essence of the standard account of knowledge as justified true belief. *The points required for knowledge claims are already implicitly applicable to any ordinary utterance of statements.* Nor should this surprise us. For surely our knowledge is essentially those aspects of our belief system, insofar as they are true, for which we have NNS justification, and which with adequate articulation amount to understanding. So necessarily the normal case will be that statements made with sufficient care and intending to convey truth will express our knowledge.

Given this, the point of using "believe", "know" or "understand" is surely to place a specific emphasis on different aspects of what is already contextually implied. "Believe" basically makes reference to the utterer's belief system. We use it when we either lack full assurance or else cannot pin down any conscious justification, and so weaken the contextual implications of asserting p by saying that I (merely) believe it: "I believe we will see him at the party" because he said he would come, though he is not very reliable. "I believe that p" still contextually implies that p, by asserting that I believe it; but this implication disappears when, on finding an error, we retreat from "I know" to "(At least) I believed". Yet the word may also be used to affirm specially strongly: the Christian creeds begin, "I believe ...". These very different speech acts have in common only that they direct attention explicitly towards the beliefs we hold.

By contrast, "know" emphasizes more strongly our claim to have the justification which all normal utterance of statements requires. By underlining this claim, we give assurance that p. That is why knowledge claims can be passed on so confidently. "Understand" also claims truth, but emphasizes our grasp of significant structure. Because it, like "know", is objective, it can be used to give an assurance about how things are ("Trust me, I *do* understand how it works!"), but this is a less conspicuous use. For commonly we ourselves will want to understand, rather than just to know that someone else does, and for this we will need, not a mere assurance, but an explanation.

In Ch. VIII.4 we met a problem. A central feature of the standard account is that knowledge is a kind of belief; but if this is so, why does "know" have such features as the wh-clauses, which "believe" lacks? By treating both concepts as modifications of the basic act of making statements, I can put this problem aside.[4] I now relate my approach to some others. For convenience I still confine myself to "know", though adjustments to cover "believe" and "understand" could easily be made.

6. Justification and Truth: Internalism and Externalism

I said in Sec. 1 I would retain the natural assumptions that justification is an internalist concept, involving reference to the standpoint of the person making the claim; and that truth is an externalist one, asserting how things are independently of what we think. I discuss truth in Ch. XII, but now I defend my view of justification. I take justification to be something we must be able to achieve. If we make knowledge claims with reasonable care and on NNS grounds, then even if the situation was abnormal so that in fact the claims were wrong, surely we were justified in making them. This means that we were *without fault* in doing so; in fact we would have been at fault in *not* making them, if the rule of candor required it. This applies equally to M- and to J-claims, though in different ways since each judges from their own viewpoint. That point about justification is often overlooked here, but is familiar in the context of moral assessment. There we distinguish two questions. (1) Did people act properly in doing what they did, given the facts available to them? If so, they are not to blame, for they did what we ought to have done, if we had been in that situation with that information. (2) Do we, with *our* beliefs, endorse what they did as correct? If not, we may say the action was wrong, but not blameworthy, like the jury that properly reached an incorrect verdict because of undetectable perjury.[5] These are the contexts in which debate about justification is most at home.

Similarly, justification of knowledge claims concerns whether we properly claimed to know, while truth concerns whether the claim was or was not correct. So, as with morality, we have two questions here: (1) Was M right, in the circumstances, to claim to know; (2) Can J allow M's claim? Js should judge the *correctness* of the claim by their own information, for to say that M knows is to endorse the claim; but they should judge the propriety of *making* the claim by standing in M's shoes. In cases where M and J agree on what is a NNS justification, differences can arise only from different information. The whole practice of passing on truths assumes that J will normally grant that M knows that p;[6] but sometimes J's information indicates that p is false, and then J must say that M does not know.[7] Yet, if M had a NNS justification, J must acknowledge that M did just what anyone with their shared standards should have done, namely claimed to know.

To summarize: my approach depends on five interlocking points. (a) The necessity for a NNS justification gives "know" its importance in such social roles as passing on the stock of truths. (b) The sufficiency of such a justification allows us to use "know" without an impracticably high standard of justification. (c) The rule of candor often obliges us to say we know, though sometimes we will be wrong. (d) The distinction between M- and J-claims means that we assess others' claims in the light of our own knowledge, so we may have to deny claims which are properly made. (e) The notion of truth, when we treat knowledge as justified *true* belief, acknowledges in advance that, if we have gone wrong despite our justification, we must retrospectively agree that we never really knew.

7. The Gettier Problem

A large part of the complex debate in the analytic tradition arose from one
very short article, which presented what came to be called the "Gettier
problem".[8] This challenged the analysis of knowledge as justified true belief,
by showing there are cases where A believes that p, for reasons which justify
a knowledge claim, and p is in fact true, yet we do not say A knows that p.
Bill tells John he noticed Mary shopping yesterday. As Bill knows Mary well,
and is reliable, John reports that he (John) knows Mary was shopping yesterday. Mary was in fact shopping yesterday, but Bill did not see her; for,
unknown to Bill and John, Mary has an identical twin, whom Bill saw. Here
John believes something which is true, and has a NNS justification, but does
he know that Mary was shopping? If our linguistic intuitions petered out in
these situations, we could simply say that ordinary language is not made for
such complicated cases. But careful speakers agree that John does not know.
For the justification he relied on would have led him astray, but for the fact
that he accidentally happened to be right.

This is the heart of the Gettier problem, but discussions have usually
approached it as follows. The three elements in the standard account—belief,
justification and truth—had seemed sufficient conditions for knowledge; we
find they are not; so we must either make the justification condition sufficiently complex to cover the aberrant cases, or add a fourth condition. This has led
to enormous complexities, so that in one discussion the justification condition,
originally stated as "S is justified in believing that *p*", becomes an intricate
construction to cover counter-examples, which takes nearly three pages to
specify.[9] We may feel that a debate which reaches such an inelegant result
must have gone off the rails, but such feelings are fallible. As has been noted:

> When they first encountered it, most epistemologists were convinced that it must have
> a simple solution...[However] (A)t the present time, the Gettier problem has become
> mired in complexity and few philosophers now expect it to have a simple solution.[10]

Nevertheless I suggest we can satisfactorily explain it by distinguishing M-
and J-claims. Gettier cases assume that we are Js assessing an M-claim, and
that we have knowledge which M did not (for example, that Mary has an
identical twin). We have seen how J must sometimes acknowledge that M
properly claimed to know, while denying that M did in fact know, because J
has further information that p was false. The Gettier cases are a more
complex but analogous situation. M again claims to know, and J denies it on
the basis of further information. This time, however, p is in fact true, and J's
further information shows rather that M's NNS but defeasible justification is
in this case defeated. So J must say M does not know, though M properly
claimed to do so. In the present case, Mary's having an identical twin is a
defeater for a NNS visual identification. So Bill and John are justified in

claiming to know, but we, as Js, must say they do not. The principle cannot simply be mechanically applied, but I believe it covers even the subtlest cases.[11] The basic point is that justification has *multiple* standpoints. To ask "Is M justified in claiming to know that p?", is ambiguous; until we ask "From what standpoint—M's, J's, etc.—are we asking?", there may be no single answer. But this went unnoticed till Gettier's article, because necessarily in the normal case if one party is justified the other will be. However sometimes there is justification from M's standpoint but not from ours. If this is because our information defeats M's justification rather than the truth of p, we have Gettier cases. But we do not have a Gettier *problem*, for the cases are simply an application of the same principles.

8. Implications

The reason I could dissolve what has seemed so difficult a problem is that in Sec. 4 I gave only *assertability* conditions for knowledge claims. So reference to their truth dropped out of points (1) and (2); whether we are an M or a J, we make or assess knowledge claims on the basis of our justified beliefs (which, of course, we take to be true). Truth appeared only in (5)(a), as the point that such claims are retrospectively withdrawn if we decide they are false. Then the Gettier problem disappears. But discussions of knowledge usually look for *truth* conditions, which set out the conditions under which knowledge claims are true. Then we meet much deeper problems. For if we consider knowledge as justified true belief, we find there is a deep asymmetry between the truth requirement and the belief and justification ones.

We can try to justify our present beliefs by reflection or new evidence, but the notion of a truth condition may seem to require us to go beyond the justification to see if the belief is in fact true. This thought may be strengthened by the fact that often we *can* go beyond our *present* justification to get a better one, as when inference is surplanted by observation ("Don't assume the scratching is a mouse in the cupboard, look and see!"). Yet the thought is incoherent. Any attempt to go beyond "mere" justification to compare a belief to "the actual facts", could at most issue in a better justification for the belief. When we, as Ms, make a knowledge claim, we *take* our belief to be true, but a truth requirement, as something over and above a justification one, is as redundant as it is impossible to fulfil. It can apply only in other ways: when we, as Js, assess other peoples' claims or our own past ones; or as an acknowledgement that both M- and J-claims are liable to be retrospectively withdrawn. In these cases also we do not go beyond justification, but operate, as we must, within it. Similarly with an intelligendum, we can find structures that give understanding, and we can check in various ways to see if we have got them right. But there is no possible further act of going beyond our checking to see if they correspond to reality, for any such attempt would be only a further checking.

So how are assertability conditions related to truth? When a NNS justification misleads, as it inherently may, there is no knowledge, so points (1) and (2) in Sec. 4 are not enough. If knowledge needs truth as well as justification, and *if* the truth condition operates like the other two, then justifications must *carry the truth with them*, which NNS ones cannot do. Then we meet not only Gettier cases but other problems, and many paths diverge.[12] To eliminate the possibility of the error that defeats knowledge, some seek a justification that *could* not be wrong. This leads towards total skepticism; for if we insist on so strong a justification, there is little left that we can know. An alternative is to hold that a justification need only *in fact* guarantee truth—for example, that knowledge claims must be linked to reality in some causal way.[13]   These are "reliabilist" analyses, which make justification an externalist concept; they focus, not on M's efforts to reach the truth, but on what are taken to be the actual facts of the situation. They have many variants, which have spawned a massive literature, but my objection is that they make justification something that our best efforts may not be able to achieve. When a NNS justification breaks down, they hold, our proper use of available information does not justify a knowledge claim, even though we would have been wrong *not* to make it. This seems to me as mistaken as morally blaming someone for doing what on their information they ought to have done, and we can avoid it only by adopting an internalist position.

If we stick with internalist justification, we can try to avoid the tension by also adopting an internalist theory of truth. Such theories may start from the point that we take our beliefs to be true, and conclude that truth is whatever we are justified in believing. But I have foreshadowed that I shall reject this, for I believe that truth is an externalist notion that refers to how things are independently of what we believe. I combine an internalist view of justification with an externalist one of truth, simply because these seem to me the right analyses of these concepts, but this means I must face the full force of the tension between them. Focusing on assertability conditions for knowledge can bypass the problem, but we meet it if we try to ensure that assertability will guarantee truth. For then we must supplement points (1) and (2) in Sec. 4 by saying that, besides (a) belief and (b) justification, we further require that (c) the justification *has no undefeated defeater*; for only then can it carry the truth with it. But the list of defeaters is *open ended*, which is why Gettier counter-examples persistently appeared; and how could we find a closed set of conditions to cover this open list? For the whole notion of defeaters arises from an internalist approach to justification, which considers the information available to Ms. Yet speaking of one that *is in fact* undefeated (as opposed to one that

Js, with their information, *take to be* so) uses the externalist notion of what is the case whether or not anyone knows it.　So to extend the analysis from assertability to truth forces us from internalism to externalism.

I cannot avoid this tension, because from the beginning of my analysis in Part A I have taken knowledge and understanding to have a double aspect. On the one hand, their statements must be formulated by using the concepts of some belief system.　We can conceive of a purely hypothetical system that is not in fact anyone's, but not of statements outside any system.　Moreover, thought must have a standpoint, though again we can conceive of a purely hypothetical one.　So an externalist approach, which makes no reference to a belief system or standpoint, is a simplification of a more complex position.　It is a natural simplification, for we normally attend to the situation rather than to our beliefs.　Further, it is usually justified, for offering and accepting knowledge claims is necessarily normally acceptable to all standpoints involved. But it may sometimes be an oversimplification, as when it tempts us to externalist theories of justification.　Yet, on the other hand, I have also assumed throughout that claims to knowledge point beyond themselves, and purport to say how things are independently of what our belief systems or standpoints are.　The possible responses to this tension underlie many of the views, such as relativism and skepticism, that we shall meet in Ch. XI, but for me the central point is this.　If knowledge and understanding both need a standpoint, yet point to what is independent of it, must one aspect have priority, and if so which?　Do we construct our world from a standpoint, or do we discover what is independently there—or can we transcend this apparent contrast?　The general name for that problem is the conflict between idealism and realism, and I discuss it in Ch. XII.

ENDNOTES

1 "Normally" suggests reaching a standard - "the norm is that these claims are reliable"- rather than a sheer statistical likelihood.　It indicates that this is reliable except in non-standard situations.

2 In some situations they might not wish to tell outsiders the truth.　In fact I think the usual formulations of the "principle" are indefensible. See Ch. XI.2.

3 I borrow the example from J. Watkins *Science and Scepticism* (1984) p. 11.　But, as Peter Forrest has pointed out to me, we seem more willing to say that our *corpus* of knowledge may contain some falsehoods, than that a *specific statement* may be known though false.

4 One of the few places where this issue is taken seriously is in Vendler's underdiscussed *Res Cogitans* (1972).　I cannot here give his complex argument the attention it deserves.

5 More complex situations arise if we disagree not only with other people's information but with their *values*.　Do we say they should act on their, or on our, values?　Cf. my *Freewill and Determinism* pp. 185-191.

6 In abnormal cases, where Js have access to information unavailable to Ms, they could reject whole classes of M-claims.

7 It can work the other way.　With the unconfident examinee in Sec. 2, M does not claim

to know, but J says M knows.

8 E. Gettier "Is Justified True Belief Knowledge?" (1963). A thorough survey of the resulting complications, which brings out many of the subtleties I ignore, is R. K. Shope *The Analysis of Knowing* (1983).

9 Shope *op. cit.* pp. 3, 208-211.

10 J. L. Pollock *op. cit.* p. 9. Though my approach differs from his, I agree with his view that the problem "is basically a side issue" (*ibid*).

11 Thus my example has been an iterated one, where we as J_2s assess John as a J_1, who is assessing Bill as an M. Others turn on cases where defeaters are in turn defeated, etc.

12 A position rather like mine, since it involves something like NNS justifications and the retrospective withdrawal of knowledge-claims, is J. L. Austin's (1961). He, like I, emphasized how "know" gives an assurance that p; it is taking "a new plunge", "[giving] others my word... my authority for saying that 'S is P'" (*op. cit.* p. 67). However this led him to focus on parallels between "I know" and the performative utterance, "I promise", so that he may at least seem to say that "I know" does not state anything true or false, as "I promise" does not. But in my view, "I know" gives assurance *by* making and contextually implying statements in the way I indicated.

13 As a small selection from a vast literature, cf. D.M. Armstrong *Belief, Truth and Knowledge* (1973); G. Harman *Thought* (1973); H. Putnam, *Meaning and the Moral Sciences* (1978). I have not discussed the notion of knowledge as a "third world", independent both of the facts of the world and of people's beliefs. Cf. K. Popper *Objective Knowledge* (1972); I. Hacking *Why Does Language Matter to Philosophy?* (1975), pp.184 *et. seq.*

CHAPTER X

JUSTIFYING AND EXPANDING KNOWLEDGE

1. Resolving Issues

The previous two chapters were concerned with analyzing the concept of knowledge and relating it to understanding, but I now turn to the central issue of justifying, rather than merely analyzing, knowledge claims. Like most analytic philosophy, I still confine myself to theoretical knowledge, and postpone discussion of practical reason till Ch. XIII. I shall now develop my own view before relating it to others in Ch. XI, and I shall defend a cautious optimism about our capacity to extend rationally based knowledge. My starting point is this. Both in the search for knowledge and in the justification of it, we meet conflicts and doubts, whether explicit or implicit, vague or well formulated, posed by another or ourself. So *how far can we rationally resolve issues*? I first consider the ideal case where we are honestly trying to reach the truth, and then ask what relation this ideal may bear to actual practice. I focus on issues arising between people, and treat individual reflection as an internalization of a process that goes on when we debate with others.

With our own internal reasoning, we start from what we believe; but cogent debate between ourself and others must start from agreement. As with the gaining of information, discussion normally depends on a network of trust;[1] even when we select for criticism an aspect of what is said, we operate within a common framework of beliefs. This seems unavoidable. Even a conclusive argument shows only that *if* we accept its premises, *then* we cannot reject its conclusion. Essentially it raises the stakes by connecting one item to another, so that we must accept both or neither.[2] If we claim that it proves the conclusion, those who reject one of our premises may reply that we beg the question against them, and debate then shifts to whether the premiss can itself be justified. This contrasts with the foundationalist dream of a once-and-for-all justification of knowledge, which I rejected in Ch. VII. Foundationalism, in effect, claimed to base itself on special cases where the stakes were higher than any player could afford, so that there was no rational alternative to accepting the premiss. To those seeking an unshakeable base in Empiricist pure experience or Rationalist self-evident axioms, starting with mere agreement would seem a slovenly approach. How can it provide a basis for knowledge, when we may *both* be wrong? My reply will be that the important question is not whether we are wrong, but whether we can discover and rectify our errors, and we can do this without an infallible base.

How do we know we will have any initial agreement? A partial answer appeals to the notion of communication. Talk needs a common language; even with a chain of interpreters, this must be true of every link.[3]   To speak a language, we must agree on the application of most words. I have no *a priori* argument that we can communicate with every humanoid, sound-emitting organism we might meet, and how far our conceptual schemes might differ is an issue for Ch. XI.   But if we can communicate, we already have some agreement; and it must be relevant to our dispute, or we could not formulate that issue. But understanding is structured at many levels, and the fact we can formulate a disagreement hardly guarantees we can resolve it. So what can we appeal to? Here we may glimpse an important intuition in foundationalist starting points. Even if we abandon an Empiricist search for pure experience, examining things by our senses under good conditions is an immensely valuable source of data.   Similarly, even without self-evident Rationalist axioms, we may rely on the basic capacity which underlies logic to see, in simple cases, what follows from what. If I accept p, and also q, and later see that q implies that p is false, I must adjust my belief system. For until I do, I simply do not know what I believe.[4] The point comes out starkly when p has implications for action, as any belief may always do: am I to act as if p were true, or as if it were not? However, even if such insights into the process of justification are important, surely they do not go far enough. For, first, though they seem to me eminently defensible, I cannot show they are infallible. And, second, the very fact they are rarely denied shows they do not provide a framework sufficient to resolve actual issues.

To explore how we can move on from initial agreement, I distinguish three types of outcome to processes of rational discussion: (1) settling, (2) postponing or (3) transcending an issue. I call them *the three possible outcomes* of rational inquiry, though whether they are the only ones will be a later question. (1) By *settling* I refer to all cases where we agree on the answer. As examples, we may check beliefs by direct observation; trust an expert to be passing on the stock of truths, as when we accept a doctor's diagnosis of our disease; or find that, though we had thought we disagreed, because our initial standpoints differed, we can now reconcile our views. (2) *Postponing* an issue involves a meta-level of agreement. We see what evidence would settle it, but are unable to obtain it.[5] A test for a disease may yield ambiguous results, which we cannot at present resolve; or, in formal contexts, there may be doubt about whether a theorem can be proved, but not about what would count as a proof if we could find one. (3) We *transcend* an issue when we reformulate the discussion by agreeing that the original issue depends on another one, which might in turn be settled, postponed or again transcended. This reflects the unboundedness of understanding as we pass beyond earlier viewpoints, and it is what gives our search for coherence its dynamism. Transcendence does not resolve the original issue, but, as we saw in Ch. III, it can sometimes lead to greater depth of understanding.

In terms of the three possible outcomes, my cautious optimism claims that rational investigation can in principle either settle or postpone an issue, or else reach deeper understanding of it. But we must be aware of the difficulties in doing so. Essentially these involve the indispensable significance-judgments discussed in Ch. IV. Whether our data comes from observation, reasoning or trust in others, to make it coherent we must assess its significance. Such judgments may be as tractable as any others, but often they are not. Among other examples, we met in Ch. II.9 a clash between the notions of "social conditioning", and Gadamer's "Bildung", where the facts might seem agreed, yet a different overall interpretation is given; or there are cultural conflicts like the alleged Azande belief in witchcraft, mentioned in Ch. II.6. So unless we can find a framework of agreement from which to settle such vast differences, rational discussion will apply only to those cases where we happen to have enough in common to permit rational debate. So we meet our central problem. If we abandon foundationalism, as we surely must; and if large scale significance-judgments are unavoidable, as they surely are; then, unless we can debate them rationally, reason will fail us where we need it most. We must now see the depth of this problem before we can hope to resolve it.

2. The Threat of Vicious Circles

As an example to bring out the difficulties, consider again our Humans; assuming, implausibly enough, that they are like the Azande in their beliefs about witchcraft and natural phenomena, yet have a sophisticated grasp of philosophical issues. To introduce them to civilization, they are provided with a philosopher, Dr. Modernway. He is to show them by argument that his worldview is superior to theirs, and in particular that science gives better explanations than does witchcraft. Our information, the Humans tell him, is that scientific methods of farming and medicine are indeed more effective than witchcraft. But they have often left a rootless people, with a former culture destroyed and no clear grasp of a new one. Does this not show, they ask, that science is blind to an important Human value: namely that we can live in a sort of harmony with nature which the imported cultural package may obliterate? In reply Dr. Modernway, being also sophisticated, admits the danger of cultural disaster. The issue, he agrees, might seem open so long as we simply ask "Should we adopt a scientific worldview?". But we must distinguish between the *truth* of science, and its *impact* if adopted. Science is at least closer to the truth than witchcraft, even if its insensitive adoption might be disastrous.

Yet, the Humans reply, even if we accept the distinction, we still articulate the agreed facts differently. We see science as dangling material rewards, but destroying the social coherence that makes life worth living. For such a practice we already have an explanation: that "science" is a form of black magic. This, Dr. Modernway replies, still confuses truth with results; but now he meets three objections. First, the Humans ask, is there not within the Doctor's own tribe a clan called Pragmatists, who deny the very distinction between truth and results? "Yet", they continue, "suppose we concede your point. Consider, secondly, your own criteria for truth in science itself. These, you say, involve such items as 'accuracy, consistency, scope, simplicity, and fruitfulness' (Ch. III.3). Perhaps accuracy and consistency favor science. But as for scope, science ignores our harmony with nature; as for simplicity, our own viewpoint seems more elegant to us; and as for fruitfulness, your tradition has ignored the power of witchcraft. So your argument is hardly made out. However the crucial point is yet a third one: that on your own showing the list is *open-ended*. We hold that what gives meaning and purpose to life is probably true, and its opposite false. This criterion, we believe, is as plausible as any you list, and to us it tells decisively against science."

At this stage Dr. Modernway may feel, not very philosophically, that he just knows the Humans are wrong; even though they are too benighted to see it, and even though they point out that his arguments beg the question against them. But though the debate could certainly go on, how is the issue to be resolved? On such questions as whether antibiotics are more effective than spells, controlled investigations could presumably be made, but what would their significance be? If Western medicine proved superior, Humans could see that as the power of magic. If spells sometimes gave better results, then Dr. Modernway would conclude that the illnesses were psychosomatic, and so were more effectively cured by working within the patients' belief system, no matter how distorted it was. The problem lies not with the agreed, lower level facts, but with the higher level interpretation of their significance.

Yet we may still easily miss the depth of the problem, by thinking that facts are clear, and only large scale interpretation gives trouble. But since our basic experience verifies our knowledge only by relating it to our whole belief system, *any* fact involves implicit interpretation. If we have the concepts of a cat and a mat, that the cat is on the mat surely states a simple enough fact. And yet—you and I both see a cat on the mat, but suppose I believe all cats are incarnations of the divine (as you can see by noting how disdainfully they look at us mere mortals). We know what "the cat" refers to—there it is, sitting on the mat—yet the agreed reference is, at a deeper level, ambiguous. In one sense, we each see the same thing on the mat. But do we see a mere animal, which I take to be a divine incarnation; or do we see an incarnation, which you mistake for a mere animal? In another sense, we know what we see; you see an animal and I see an incarnation. But then how do we tell which of us sees correctly? Only, in each case, by deciding, if we can, which is the correct total belief system.[6] So clashes of interpretation may arise in any context,[7] and typically reflect rival standpoints that combine value judgments about how to act with theoretical beliefs about how things are. The threat to basing justification on agreement is that in such cases we might find we can neither settle the issue, nor even agree on what evidence would settle it. So we might find ourselves in a vicious circle that cannot be resolved, because we each speak out of our own presuppositions and beg the question against the other. This threat arises directly from my analysis of understanding, with its emphasis on significance-judgments. To meet it, we must explore what I called the third possible outcome of rational inquiry, namely transcendence.

3. Overcoming Vicious Circles

In facing complex disputes, we must in a sense go round in a circle, for the mutualism of understanding means we can only learn the relation between different beliefs by extensive exploration. We cannot just assess arguments and premises taken in isolation, but must come to understand the strategy behind them, by working ourselves into the standpoint from which they arise. So it is a familiar experience to philosophers, and no doubt to others, that our debates repeatedly bring us back in unexpected ways to what we had met before. In fact "circle" is too tidy a word for our tortuous path as we trace the overlapping relations between beliefs. Yet I suggest that the vicious circle is only *nearly* closed. It can in principle become a beneficent one, or a spiral where the circular movement also produces linear progress towards resolution.

Consider the previous examples. If the Humans reject modern science, what shall they say about its success? They might refuse to investigate it, saying they should not dabble in black magic; but that takes us beyond our present consideration of ideal cases. Or they might examine it, hoping to learn the spells and rituals which scientists employ. Yet if they come to understand how it works, they will meet the same rational pressures to reject witchcraft as our European forebears did. If, on the other hand, we have more to learn from their witchcraft than I have assumed, we could discover that too by appropriate investigation, once we were prepared to reconsider our original dismissal of it. As for my second example, what criteria do I have for something's being a divine incarnation? If I have none, how do I know that cats are? If I have some, however vague, then (a) they may be accepted for the sake of argument ("If *that's* what you mean by 'divine', then ..."). So we have a much more

tractable issue: do cats fit these criteria? (b) If, as here, they are not acceptable, you must say why not. Then we have a new dispute, and rational
argument can proceed. Thus suppose I say, as a last resort, that I need no
further proof: insightful people just *see* the feline divinity. Then would I allow
equal respect to those who claim to see the divinity of cockcroaches? Why is
not one untestable intuition as good as another? Such cross-examination is a
powerful weapon in the search for overall coherence.

What are the preconditions for this probing? First, by adequate delimitation
we must find a *sufficiently neutral vocabulary*, as my minimalist approach
tries to do. This is not an absolutely neutral one, such as Empiricist pure
experience would provide, but one which those particular parties accept as
stating their issue without begging the question. This already gives greater
insight, for we find out how much we have taken for granted by finding out
how others see things differently. Further, we may use this vocabulary to
clarify what the issues are. As with the defeaters of NNS justifications
discussed in Ch. IX, the list of difficulties is open-ended, but we have a principle by which to approach new cases: in this case, to develop a sufficiently
neutral vocabulary, and by using it, to agree on what is relevant. Our
differences may then become far more tractable.

In terms of the three possible outcomes of rational inquiry, if the debate does
not settle or agree to postpone the original issue, it will at least repeatedly
reformulate, and so transcend, it. In itself, that does not guarantee advance.
We do meet cases where all reformulation uncovers further rival interpretations, so our arguments still beg the question. We can set no limit to how long
this may last, so we might fear we will find impasses from which we could
never break out. These situations, we shall see, are emphasized by much
current pessimism about the power of reason, though they may occur not only
between individuals but also internally.[8]   Moreover, our capacity for
transcendence can be exploited to evade an issue by continually changing the
question. But if we are searching for truth, we can always use transcendence
to explore the assumptions that keep us apart. This leads to deeper insight,
even if it is only insight into why we differ. And increasing depth of understanding was what I offered as the third possible outcome.

What are the implications? Any optimism in this conclusion is a very cautious one. It does not say, for example, that we could always attain one of the
first two possibilites, and so either reach an agreed conclusion or postpone it
only for lack of information. For the third possibility of deeper understanding
does not guarantee eventual agreement, though it may keep alive the hope of
it. Moreover, this cautious optimism meets strong objections from opposite
directions: from those who think it too cautious or weak, and from those who
find it too optimistic. I discuss such views in Ch. XI, but I now foreshadow
some objections and my replies. It will, first, seem too weak to those who

embrace any truth or value as beyond question. They include far more than foundationalists, for this has been the attitude of most people at all times, including today. It may vary from rationally defended faith in some sacred authority, to the sheer acceptance of tradition. My position here is that I do not discuss, and so do not rule out, any of these specific views, and it is part of my argument that continuing differences about such matters may itself be valuable. But my argument does imply that even our most cherished assumptions might always be undercut by the unboundedness of future understanding.

Next, my position would also be seen as too weak by strong-minded critics of metaphysics. Positivism, for example, would give short shrift to the third possible outcome of greater depth. For, it would say, if we cannot see in principle how to settle or postpone a claim, which are my first two possibilites, the issue is meaningless. But I have suggested in Ch. VII.5 that all such attempts to end the inconclusiveness of debate become themselves at best one more inconclusive insight. Perhaps one insight here is that, in purely theoretical contexts (practical ones, we shall see, raise different problems), the more we found that after long and honest debate we could make no progress, the more we might suspect that we had equally legitimate viewpoints. That would count as one way of settling an issue, namely by dissolving an apparent conflict. Considered in this way, as a suggestion which may become attractive when a debate is deadlocked, the point may have value. But whatever we think of it, it plays no major part in my argument, and the ban against philosophical speculation is one I later reject.

There remain views that would find my cautious optimism too optimistic, including some that question the very notion of greater depth of understanding. Some of them have insights that I later discuss,[9] but above all they pose the question of how far the three possible rational outcomes actually apply in human reasoning. For light-hearted examples of Humans and divine cats give no hint of the pain of abandoning deeply held convictions, and do not ask what the limits of effective reasoning in human affairs may be. So this leads to the second major theme of this chapter: how does the ideal of a search for truth connect with the actual realities of our situation?

4. Constraints and Strategies

My sketch of how we can expand or justify understanding reflects the Socratic ideal in Western philosophy of following the wind of the argument wherever it blows—an ideal that is often called "dialogue". But dialogue is an abstraction from our total mental processes. Inquiry needs a standpoint, and I turn now to how standpoints may impede, rather than promote, the ideal. I noted in Ch. III the tensions between sub-systems within the personality, and also between the individual and the group. A basic contrast, reflected in the relation between depth psychology and sociology, distinguishes between the pressure of immediate family on the child, and that of class or society on the adult. These interact mutualistically, though much intellectual capital has been invested in arguing that one is more important than the other. Now I focus on the tension between two basic needs: first, the need to maintain both the core belief structures that protect our self-esteem, and also the social situations that give us security; and second, the need to adapt to new facts about the world. In broadly Freudian terms, this is the conflict between rationalization and the reality principle.

With large scale significance-judgments, a totally defensive attitude can maintain itself by allocating to given considerations whatever significance is needed. If belief in the divinity of cats means everything to me, I can always patch up my defence; even if only by claiming, not only that all insightful people will just see my point, but also that they will see the non-divinity of cockroaches. The real form of reasoning here is to take the conclusion, that cats are divine, as a fixed point, and then to adjust other beliefs to maintain it. Naturally this is rarely acknowledged, even internally, for it repudiates the reality principle and turns investigation into a sham. As we have seen, critical reasoning is powerful here, but reformulations may continue indefinitely without formal fallacies. We can only say that too extreme a resistance to new evidence involves a retreat from reality. By contrast, rational acceptance of the reality principle has an *openness* towards evidence which sees the truth as more important than defending our position.

Openness, however, can be very costly, and we rarely change deeply embedded views at first challenge. Even if we feel the force of the premises, and find no flaw in the logic, we are more likely to see the argument as a challenge to the known truth, and set out to uncover its hidden error. How can we break down this tendency? One point here is that openness is a moral virtue which we need if we are to reason well, so there is a direct link between theoretical and practical reasoning. But what I emphasize now is that we need a systematic exercise of our imagination. I mean here not merely having images or fantasizing for pleasure, but vividly bringing some situation before us in detail. In analytic philosophy, this process is rarely explored.[10] Philosophy of science accepts it as essential in the forming of hypotheses, but focuses on how they are tested rather than acquired. Reason and imagination, like reason and emotion, may even be contrasted.[11] Yet to make significance-judgments adequately and hence rationally, we need imagination. Strange though it sounds to those who confuse it with fantasy, imagination can be extremely taxing—as when, say, we make vivid to ourselves the wretched situation of an enemy, so as to strengthen our compassion. It is not a private activity immune to public assessment, for here too we need to express our views to others, and to listen to them in turn. Yet it differs from, say, scientific assessment in its mode of expression. For here is a proper role for rhetorical language, in evoking emotions which can influence our attitudes. Though rhetoric is a two-edged sword, easily used to reinforce prejudice rather than to outgrow it, still, just as I argued in Ch. VI that we need involvement beyond the intellect if we are to understand our deeper nature, so we need language to work on our imagination as well as (not instead of) our intellect if we are to test our attitudes. In each case, the disciplined control of evoked and acknowledged emotion makes vivid to ourselves situations which are not central in our previous experience.

I have spoken as if resistance to evidence, though understandable, was always undesirable, but the story is more complex. Though we must curb our easy tendency to believe, it seems we should not give up convictions too readily. For when a radical change is proposed, typically it cannot answer all the objections first offered. Investigating the sub-issues takes much time, during which its adherents must hold to it as a matter of faith and promise rather than because of clear intellectual advantage. In analytic philosophy, this has been discussed largely in philosophy of science. As one example, consider Copernicus and stellar parallax. If the earth did go in a huge orbit round the sun, while the stars were at various distances, the apparent relative positions of the stars should alter during the year. But no one could observe such parallax; the evidence here clearly favored the received Ptolemaic view. The new astronomers could only reply with a totally *ad hoc* defence: that the stars must be too far away for parallax to be observed, and so the universe must be vastly larger than there was any other reason to believe. This adjusts beliefs to defend a prior conclusion in just the way I earlier condemned. Similar avoiding, rather than answering, of counter-considerations can be found in virtually every great intellectual advance, and we can find no rules to discern where endorsement of an unproven belief degenerates into defensive obstinacy. The proper intellectual virtue is to hold a balance between defensiveness and recklessness, but the wisdom of any particular decision can at best be judged in hindsight.

I have emphasized how tradition and personal history shape individual belief, and so limit our flexibility. But we should also note the converse aspect of this mutualistic process, and ask how argument between individuals can affect the group. Rarely do we find that committed participants in an important debate radically change their views. But there are others, usually the majority, who are, by comparison, spectators rather than participants. What rational debate may do, if social conditions are right, is to *capture the uncommitted*, by showing that one side has more to be said for it than the other. In this way it may change the climate of opinion of the group as a whole. What seemed outlandish becomes a serious possibility, what was acceptable becomes obnoxious. It is of the nature of reasoned argument to appear an ineffectual force at any one time, but still to operate over a period to change group views.

5. Taking Issues Seriously

There is a further aspect of resolving issues. Since establishing beneficent circles is so time consuming a process, with any given claim we must decide whether to *take it seriously* as one that an honest and competent person might hold. This differs from taking an *issue* seriously, in the sense of thinking it important. For we might, say, take the issue of race relations seriously, and yet not take racist claims seriously because we think they stem from rationalization. Conversely, we might take a claim seriously (for example, hold that the Steady State theory is still a reputable astronomical hypothesis), without investigating the issue. I am now focusing, not on issues but on attitudes towards them, which reflect deeper than conscious beliefs. Our decisions here govern our allocation of time and effort, for when approaching issues we ignore what we do not take seriously. We may apply criteria, such as our estimate of the credibility of those who make the claim, but very often we just feel that the claim "makes sense" or "is nonsense".

Such attitudes are highly fallible. If large significance-judgments are always difficult to assess rationally, then *a fortiori* they are dubious here. Yet the massive, mostly unconscious support that we mobilize to support our core beliefs, means that such judgments are likely to seem obviously right. So arises a paradox: confidence in the rightness of the judgments is found in roughly equal proportion to the actual difficulty of justifying them without begging the question. The process occurs within both individuals and groups, though they vary widely in how much will be taken seriously. Sociologists speak of a group's "nihilating" those it does not take seriously, and this can have devastating effects on its victims.[12] But my concern is how far it limits our achievement of understanding.

Not taking views seriously may seem a paradigm of irrationality and intolerance. For it rejects dialogue by assuming it knows the answer, and blatantly begs the question against the other; moreover it is based on the most fallible of our judgments. Surely the sole defence for doing it is that we must. But that is sufficient. Among all the issues we might investigate, we must allocate our priorities; and in doing so, we cannot free ourselves from our nature as historical beings, embedded in what our tradition does or does not take seriously. So what is the implication for our rationality? If we give up the Enlightenment dream of a consciousness that is not historically conditioned, then, faced with the inevitability and yet fallibility of writing off many views, we can at least do so consciously, and with a realization of the risk. And though the practice no doubt restricts our facing, or even conceiving of, many issues, it need not stop us from making progress with those we face; for in debating them we take them seriously.

Writing views off may seem incompatible with following the wind of the argument, so perhaps some thinkers may honestly deny they ever do it. "Of course", they might say, "with today's knowledge explosion everyone must specialize, but I pass no judgment on debates outside my specialty." Yet to specialize in an area is to make at least an implicit significance-judgment about its importance. Moreover, a specialty delimits not just an area of study but also those who are taken seriously as its experts, while others with views on the subject are ignored. So I think we all do it, no matter what our commitment to openness. It is not, we feel, that we could not justify our position, but only that we cannot afford time to expose all mistakes. So, apart from how we react to outsiders who offer their views on our areas of expertise, even within our disciplines we may reject the views of others after an examination so cursory that we would justifiably protest if ours, in turn, were dismissed in this way. One example is how analytic philosophy has often ignored the Continental tradition. Yet here above all judgments should surely be provisional: "I believe I need not take this seriously, till someone makes a better case than I have seen." In now assessing the power of reason, I shall assume this is often the closest we can come to an impartial assessment.

6. The Potentiality of Reason

How far, then, can the ideal picture of resolving issues through dialogue actually apply in human affairs? What are the limits of human potentiality here? Strictly, my claim that we can overcome vicious circles is independent of the answer, for, whatever we conclude, that possibility would remain. But if it had no relevance to our actual situation, my argument would be a pointless exercise that need not be taken seriously. In answering the question, I first focus on the role of the group, which is central both in stifling and in encouraging reasoning. A group may spurn dialogue; either within itself because it enforces uniformity, or, as in wartime, between itself and another group. The resulting pressures may be almost impossible for its members to resist. Yet where, on the contrary, it encourages debate, it plays another role. However open-minded we are, we find ourselves attracted to or repelled by new views, as Copernicans and anti-Copernicans were; for our arguments manifest, at the same time as they test, our unconscious attitudes. But a group to which we all belong may, in effect, hedge its bets, as some take one view and some the other. Then, over time, it may converge on a solution, as rational argument captures the uncommitted. Such debate is fallible, for there are distorting influences such as superior resources or prestige; moreover, the common assumptions of the whole group may later be challenged. Yet it is our most valuable tool for testing rival standpoints. That different people emphasize different aspects of an issue and so form rival significance-judgments, is vital to the search for understanding. It is not merely in spite of, but by means of, our conflicts that we achieve our greatest advances.

Since openness to those we take seriously in dialogue can be costly, a central role may be played by *dialogical communities* where people will face new considerations, as opposed to groups where factions seek supremacy rather than truth. But such a community is an ideal notion, which can have many approximations. Debates marked by defensiveness and hostility may still make progress, if there is reason to reach agreement and a grudging acceptance of the reality principle. This applies both to theoretical cases, such as debates between rival schools within a discipline, and to practical ones where opposed interests reach a compromise. The lines between pure and quasi-dialogue, and total rejection of it, blur and shift. Dialogue is always precarious when our deep concerns are threatened, while conversely a skilled mediator may bring a tincture of openness to tense negotiating situations. So if effective reasoning is to flourish, one vital need is to create these communities that encourage rather than stifle it.[13] Another is to develop the theory and practice of conflict resolution. For this encourages opposed groups to form quasi-dialogical communities where issues may be resolved, and though designed for practical contexts it has application also to theoretical discussion. My argument underpins all such efforts by defending the possibility of what they aim to achieve. Where, as so often, appropriate communities are not available, the outlook is bleaker, but we are not totally bereft. For imagination can be, in effect, an individual's surrogate for such communities. We are free to exercise imaginative understanding about other views in any situation, but usually this is less effective than listening to their advocates. Conversely, we will not get far with the arduous process of dialogue, unless we listen to others with imaginative empathy. Imagination and dialogue are in no way substitutes, but reinforce each other. To ask about the potentiality of reason is above all to ask how effectively they can be jointly fostered.[14] I approach that question by asking, finally, how my whole argument applies to itself.

7. A Final Assessment

The question of the potentiality of reason is itself as difficult as any that reason can address. In principle it is a factual issue, applying both to both groups and individuals: how far may we expect sub-groups to moderate conflicts in the search for knowledge, and how great is the human capacity to take rival standpoints seriously? But our answers represent large-scale significance-judgments, and confidence in their rightness "is found in roughly equal proportion to the actual difficulty of justifying them without begging the question" (Sec. 5). For the confidence depends not just on reasoning, but also on the impact of those psychological and social influences which pessimists about reason emphasize. If rational discussion was influential in our early formative experience, we may grow up optimistic about its power; if that experience was shaped by the ruthless imposition of viewpoints, the thought that we, or society, might behave differently may seem naive. Then, as later experiences overlay early ones, we may rebel against, or compensate for, early patterns by reacting in opposite directions. And besides individual attitudes, the cultures in which we are embedded feel similar influences. The expansion of science encouraged Enlightenment optimism, while shattering experiences such as world wars produce disillusionment.

All this applies, of course, to my own views. Yet, while acknowledging the difficulties, I still maintain a cautious optimism about the power of reason. Pessimists may see my optimism as a naive relic of the Enlightenment, but I would emphasize the differences. By seeing us as historical beings embedded in our traditions, I reject the Enlightenment view of reason as timeless and ahistorical. I also reject its intellectualism, as discussed in Ch. VII, for emphasis on such things as dialogical communities implies involvement and an appropriate praxis. Pessimists and I rely on rival selective descriptions of human potentiality, governed by our judgments about the significance of relevant factors. The initial result might well be a paradigm case of a vicious circle, in which we each speak from initial presuppositions that the other does not accept. But my previous argument applies to this question of the potentiality of reason as much as to any other. If we genuinely set out to explore our presuppositions using a sufficiently neutral vocabulary, why could not the three possible outcomes apply again? Even if we could not settle the issue, could we not transcend initial differences to reach deeper understanding?

My view may still be rejected by those who hold that appeals to discussion are congenial to dominant groups in society because they mask the reality of social oppression. This reality, they hold, is to be met by confrontation rather than polite debate—whether the confrontation takes the form of polemics which refuse dialogue, or of meeting force with force. I approach this issue by a series of increasingly less minimalist points. First, my analysis in Part A is itself neutral about the power of reasoned debate. Next, I have argued in this Chapter that the search for understanding ideally leads towards three possible outcomes, and have now claimed that this applies to the question of the power of reason itself. But all this assumes the desirability of the process, and that is now the issue. Dialogue involves initial acceptance, no matter how powerfully it later transforms, and now we meet what I called in Ch. II.9 "the momentous choice of whether to accept, transform or reject our tradition". I do not fore-close that choice by saying debate is always appropriate. There is a continu-um of resistance to oppression that runs from the use of force, through hostile polemics, to negotiation that merges into quasi-dialogue; and what combina-tion is appropriate may be a difficult judgment. But I do judge that often there is real scope for the gradual effective impact of reasoned debate, and also that where this is practicable it is preferable to other processes. Many other views, including some we meet in Ch. XI, may still feel that in various ways I have begged the question against them by posing it in my own terms. Yet such objections are themselves new issues to which the three possible outcomes of inquiry apply; and however firmly protagonists retain their views, one side of the debate may progressively capture the uncommitted.

To summarize: the sprawling current debate about the possibility and reliability of knowledge largely turns on whether we can transcend our embeddedness in our culture. If we cannot, one side says, then ultimately "truth" would mean only what we are culturally conditioned to believe; and they see that alternative as both false and socially destructive. But, the other side replies, how *could* we get beyond this embeddedness, let alone know we had done so? So they become, with relief or reluctance, pessimists about the power of reason. Yet I claim *neither* to escape cultural embeddedness, *nor* to accept pessimism, but to transcend the issue by reposing it. If we are to com-municate at all, there must be agreement. In starting from that, we can formu-late issues that will lead to one of the three possible outcomes of rational inquiry. So we can expand our rationally tested knowledge. In calling it "knowledge", we imply it is true independently of our beliefs, so our truth-claims function to remind us that our best established beliefs might still be false. Yet the agreement we start from is culturally conditioned, and contains nothing that might not later be questioned. I replace the search for unshake-able foundations by the fact that we can communicate. We can do so, not only within our own cultures, but, with time and effort, between them. For cross-cultural understanding may never be complete, but it can be indefinitely expanded; and, like all conflicts, it gives opportunity for each side to expand its understanding.

In the ever-expanding network of what we call the knowledge explosion, some beliefs are accepted from our culture while others are carefully tested. Reliability is a matter of degree. Traditional beliefs may reasonably be accepted till we have cause to doubt them, while conversely even the strictest scientific procedures still depend on not-fully-questioned assumptions. But the mere possibility of being mistaken need not affect our knowledge, while if we meet an actual challenge we can explore it. So, though we have no guarantee for the truth of any belief, we can and do have ever-expanding knowledge. Above all, just as nothing can make us engage in dialogue or adopt an imaginative empathy towards other views, so nothing precludes us from doing so. These are attitudes we can adopt or refuse, and the experience resulting from our choice will in turn help to shape our belief in the potentiality of reason.

ENDNOTES

[1] Hence paranoics, who suspect everyone and so are locked out of the network, may argue acutely, and yet be immune to reason.

[2] In reasoning within a formal system, to raise the stakes would be to reject the system itself; and unless some actual flaw in it can be found, this can amount virtually to refusing to reason at all. However though my argument applies broadly to formal as well as non-formal reasoning, my emphasis is on the latter.

[3] I can ignore here how a chain of interpretations may progressively alter the nuances of successive languages.

[4] We might license inconsistency in isolated contexts, such as a game or a ritual, but they must necessarily normally be exceptions.

[5] I ignore formal but empty possibilities, such as that we would settle it if we agreed that one of us was wrong.

[6] In technical terms, my point is that whether "see" is taken as referentially transparent or opaque, the problem remains.

[7] Again, qualifications are needed about reasoning within formal systems.

[8] A famous internal case is when Hume confessed that "there are two principles which I cannot render consistent; nor is it in my power to renounce either of them". *Treatise of Human Nature* (1960 Repr.) p. 636. Yet even sympathetic Humean scholars have usually held that this showed the bankruptcy of his philosophy on the point.

[9] Apart from views discusses in Ch. X.5-7, there is also, with practical reason, the possibility of alternative life styles (Ch. XIII.7).

[10] An attack on what was taken to be the standard (Cartesian) view of images was launched in G. Ryle *op. cit.* It has been continued in complex and rather different ways by defenders of materialism. For a contrary view, cf. A. Hannay *Mental Images: a Defence* (1971). The far fewer discussions of imagination, as opposed to imaging, include E. J. Furlong *Imagination* (1961); M. Warnock *Imagination* (1976); E. Casey *Imagining: a Phenomenological Study* (1976). See also R. G. Collingwood *The Idea of History* (1946).

[11] For reason and emotion, cf. Ch. VI.4. For the undervaluation of imagination in theology, and an admirable effort to overcome it, cf. J. McIntyre *Faith Theology and Imagination* (1987). This also has in Ch. 5 a useful examination of philosophical views.

[12] P. Berger and T. Luckman *The Social Construction of Reality* (1946).

[13] R. J. Bernstein (1983), in a penetrating discussion which approaches the point from a different perspective, presents the need to foster such communities as ultimately his most important theme.

[14] Moreover, as conflict resolution may diminish the hostility of groups and thus make dialogue easier, so, at a more individual level, such practices as stilling the mind in meditation (Ch. VI.6) may produce an inner peace, by which individuals contribute in subtle ways to an outer one.

CHAPTER XI

OTHER DEBATES ABOUT KNOWLEDGE AND
UNDERSTANDING

1. Types of Objections

Many today would treat my cautious optimism about the power of reason as too optimistic. For there is a widespread and deep disillusionment with the whole Western intellectual tradition, which often extends to its culture, economics and government. I do not fully discuss these complex debates, but only define my views against what I judge to be the most relevant alternatives. For this purpose, I discuss three types of position: skepticism, or the denial that we have any knowledge; relativism, or the view that all truth is relative to a standpoint; and, finally, postmodernist views which reject the power of reason to justify any overall viewpoint.

Analytic philosophy discusses aspects of these views under the names of skepticism and relativism, but it formulates them in rather narrow and traditional ways. It has not yet extensively come to grips with more radical current critiques of our intellectual tradition.[1] Those critiques reflect the Enlightenment's rejection of appeals to traditional authority, but in other ways they present a systematic rejection of its values from a series of different but related standpoints. Examining views more pessimistic than mine will be the main thrust of this Chapter. But first I must turn to the opposite type of objection, which would see my cautious optimism as too pessimistic. One of the most influential of analytic philosophers, Donald Davidson, presents a viewpoint which starts from a position in many ways much like mine, but reaches in one respect a radically different conclusion. For I have left open the possibility that our belief system as a whole might undergo radical revision, but he sees that as an incoherent suggestion. I now discuss that issue.

2. How Far Might We Be Wrong?

Davidson claims that our overall belief system has nothing to fear in general, but only in detail, from future changes.[2] He defends a holism which differs from my mutualism only in my greater emphasis on how part influences whole, as well as *vice versa*.[3] Like me, he emphasizes that communication depends on agreement, yet that we are not unavoidably trapped in vicious circles. His approach is through philosophy of language, where he focuses on the notion of "radical translation"—the hypothetical situation where we are trying to make sense from scratch of a completely new language. Here he emphasizes the complex trade-offs in interpretation between language meaning, on the one hand, and our beliefs and desires on the other. "I'd like a beer" is a paradigm of an easily understood remark; in understanding it, you take me to have both a desire for beer, and beliefs about what it is like to drink it. But in both respects your judgment about what I mean depends on the rest of your knowledge. If you knew I was opposed to all alcohol, you might suspect that I meant by "beer" some non-alcoholic substitute, or else wonder whether my real desire was to disguise my beliefs. In starting from scratch to understand a language, we would be thrown back on working out meanings from what we take to be the speaker's beliefs and desires. We must initially assume these are similar to what ours would be, and proceed to guess about the meanings. All our hypotheses about beliefs, desires and meanings can modify each other, but they build up into a shared network of understanding which provides an ever more confident and effective pattern of communication.

With all this I have, in general, no quarrel, but I resist some of the implications that Davidson draws. The shared network, he claims, must extend to the sorts of things we take to exist—our "ontology"—and to the way we think of them: it must include "an ontology common to the two languages, with concepts that individuate the same objects".[4] But this is only possible if there is "widespread sharing of sentences held true"; and without this we could not communicate at all.[5] Even this echoes my point in Ch. X.1, that communication involves shared beliefs. But from this Davidson reaches the Principle of Charity, that most beliefs must be true, and that mostly people must be telling the truth. This is "not an option, but a condition of having a workable theory".[6] Skeptical or relativist doubts are incoherent. "[O]ur language—any language—[must] incorporate or depend upon a largely correct, shared, view of how things are".[7]

I later discuss skepticism and relativism, and whether most beliefs must be true,[8] but now I focus on this question: granted that to understand others we must start with agreement and extend it, *how much might the process change our present belief systems*, as sub-systems unforeseeably expand and erode? In particular, must there be, as a general background for communication, a shared ontology which individuates our familiar objects?   Consider here coming to understand the language of exotic beings. Suppose there was an information-processing being whose material base was an appropriate struc-ture of high speed fundamental particles. Given the power of the particles to penetrate matter, for this being the differences between our planet and the space surrounding it would be unimportant, even if it could make the distinction within its conceptual scheme. More relevant for it might be relations between what we would consider mere points in space. In considering its likely ontology, we might hypothesize that it would have a notion of persisting items, such as space-time points, which could have relations to other ones. If so, we could hope to understand the structure of its reasoning by analogy to our logic. Yet not only is this an initial hypothesis rather than an unchallengeable certainty, but the items to which its terms referred would not be our material objects and properties. Yet, though we would naturally first look for the sort of things which Davidson says we could not fail to find, we need not be bereft if they fail us. We might still find some starting point, though not of a normal intra-human sort. For example, we might be able to approach its belief system by finding isomorphic relations between its physics and ours. In expanding agreement, once we had begun to grasp the radical difference, we could do what we do now with difficult human communication: we could imagine as best we can what it would be like to be the other, and try to test the resulting hypotheses. After successful translation we would know how terms that referred to the world worked in its language, but why should this alter our own practice? We would have developed a new understanding of how we *might* speak, and of how it *did*; but in no ordinary sense would this involve a shared ontology.

One reply might be that in such a case we would really have a "shared ontology", namely the combination of our and its former ones, but that we chose for convenience to use different parts of it. Yet that defence seems a mere verbal manoeuvre; for the fact remains that, no matter how we described the situation, we could think about what exists in a radically new way. Our horizons would have been radically broadened. The central point is this. Though Davidson rejects foundationalism, and is an important voice in the debate about what is to replace it, he still seems to claim for certain fundamental features of our belief system the same sort of immunity to revision which foundationalism claimed for such favored cases as pure experience or axioms of reason. By contrast I hold that *whenever* we set limits to the threat of change, the unboundedness of our understanding may eventually undermine our stance.[9]

3. Skepticism

The emphasis on unboundedness raises the opposite, pessimistic challenge: if nothing is beyond future question, can we properly claim to reach any truth at all? A standard criticism of such views is that they are self-refuting: that they say something such that, if it were true, what they say would be either false or incoherent. As a simple example, if someone were so naive as to say they *knew* that we know nothing, they would be claiming to know something, which is what they say we cannot do. Though this criticism is not nearly as easy to establish as some of its exponents have believed, it will continually recur; for all pessimistic views must face the question of how they take their claims to apply to themselves.

I begin by considering skepticism. In ordinary speech, this word often refers to a science-based view that rejects all religious and paranormal beliefs, but in philosophical contexts it is the claim that we have no knowledge. Total skepticism denies we have any knowledge, while partial versions reject a given field such as moral knowledge. Even the total version may represent different things. In its Greek form it was a way of life; a praxis of training the mind to refrain from forming opinions, so as to achieve inner calm in a disturbed world. This could commend itself by the resulting peace of mind, while reasoning was needed only to rebut objections; so for some who practised it, the arguments for it may have been as secondary as those supporting their faith may be today for many religious believers. I doubt if modern discussions make this praxis any less defensible, but it was always a path for the few, and today is hardly a live option. Yet, as we saw in Ch. VII.1, skeptics did defend their view by arguments, such as questioning all criteria for certainty. So in analytic philosophy, which usually ignores praxis, skepticism functions as an intellectual challenge to the possibility of knowledge.

Skepticism has an internalist theory of justification and an externalist one of truth: justifications are based on our information, but truth is independent of what we believe. Thus far I agree. But skepticism claims that the gulf cannot be bridged, that no justification can be good enough.[10] For justification requires absolute certainty, where we could not be wrong; if we are wrong, we have no knowledge. Descartes posed the skeptical problem by asking if an evil demon might be systematically deceiving us into falsely believing that our perceptual experiences represent an external world.[11] The contemporary counterpart is the mad scientist, who keeps human brains alive in a vat, while stimulating their neural pathways to give them the experiences of ordinary life. The skeptical challenge can be dramatized as: how do you know you are not a brain in a vat?[12]

Replies to skepticism typically assert that it sets the criterion for knowledge too high: if we demand too stringent a justification, of course our beliefs cannot be "justified"; but this does not show they are not justified according to proper criteria. Moreover, it is argued, attempts to set criteria too high are self-refuting. For example, it is said that our whole belief system depends on reidentifying objects as the *same* ones that we met before, and that this presupposes the existence of a regularly operating independent physical world in which these objects exist. So in doubting such a world, the skeptic

> pretends to accept a conceptual scheme, but at the same time quietly rejects one of the conditions of its employment. Thus his doubts are unreal, not simply because they are logically irresoluble doubts, but because they amount to the rejection of the whole conceptual scheme within which alone such doubts make sense.[13]

Yet the impact of self-refutation arguments is not easy to assess. For not only are there possible reformulations of such terms as "justification" and "certainty", each of which needs discussion,[14] but the debate ultimately is not so much about how we speak as about how we rationally ought to. If we do not speak as skeptics recommend, that might be our carelessness, while if we did, that might only show we were overscrupulous.

Essentially, skeptics believe we are too casual in claiming to know, and so advocate a more stringent standard. They may invite us in various ways to raise our standard, or may simply assert as obvious that if we might be wrong, we do not really know. So one skeptic begins his argument by

> arbitrarily choosing something concerning an external world which might conceivably, we suppose, be *known*...e.g. that there are rocks

and continues

> Now, first, *if* someone, anyone, *knows* that there are rocks, then the person *can know* the following quite exotic thing: there is *no* evil scientist deceiving him [sic] into *falsely* believing that there are rocks.[15]

The argument then is that this "quite exotic thing" can*not* be known.

In asking whether this sets the criterion for knowledge too high, I return to my point in Ch. IX: that often if a practice (in this case making knowledge claims) is to achieve its goal, then a sub-routine (our justifications) must normally be successful; that our NNS justifications have an open ended list of defeaters, which cannot all be eliminated in advance; but that claims made with due care are justified, and that if there is in fact no defeater then we know. So knowledge claims are inherently, but necessarily not normally, liable to be retrospectively withdrawn, even though properly made; and this is the appropriate standard of care, because it facilitates the circulation of truths. I believe this provides a basis for answering skepticism. Yet to see it as in itself an answer would miss the depth of the problem. For just as people could reject our legal system by denying that we can discern the reliability of witnesses, so here skeptics could reply that NNS justifications are not enough.[16] If we might be wrong, they could insist, we do not really know, so we must eliminate all defeaters and show there is no evil scientist. Retrospective withdrawals, far from being an integral part of proper practice, show that the practice is wrong. Whether we *know* what we pass on is just the point; and unless we could remove all possible defeaters, we should not claim to know.[17]

This is an example of how we may seem to meet a vicious circle. The skeptic and I agree we cannot remove all defeaters in advance; but does this show that we should never claim to know, or that we should not let that fact deter us? We agree that relying on merely NNS justifications leads to occasional retrospective withdrawals of claims, but does that show they were improperly made? To break such deadlocks, we must reach deeper assumptions, so as to avoid begging the question. My argument now focuses on the *point* of claiming to know. If, as we both agree, we must risk being wrong if we are to pass on any information, the issue is whether we should engage in the total practice of properly-claiming-to-know-with-NNS-justifications-and-then-retrospectively-withdrawing-claims-when-occasionally-wrong.   I offer this as the optimal trade-off between reliability and ease of communication in circulating the stock of truths, so I deny that the mere *possibility* of error means we do not know. I see skepticism as being so frightened of being wrong that it rejects the whole practice, whereas the benefits of the practice in fact amply justify its risks. In this sketch of an argument, none of the steps are beyond challenge. Moreover, a skeptic could even conceivably concede it, and hence grant that "in practice" we should often *claim* to know, while still saying (but on what grounds?) that we never "really" know. Yet in the end, as indicated in Ch. X.4, we might increasingly suspect that such moves were merely attempts to defend a position at all costs.

A rejection of skepticism, however, gives no logical guarantee against discovering that we have been radically mistaken. It is conceivable that the whole natural order should cease to be reliable, and lapse into chaos. That would presumably mean the cessation of all human life and thought, but there could also be more limited cases. Suppose that the mad scientist has an assistant tending a row of brains in vats. After a while she learns, not just how to keep them in working order but how to interpret their thoughts. She finds that they all think they are assistants to the mad scientist, tending a row of brains in vats.[18] How could she *not* conclude that she too was probably a brain in a vat, so that virtually all her previous beliefs were mistaken? Here the cataclysmic new information still leaves her able to cast about for an explanation, but it combines with other beliefs to destroy the whole standpoint by which she judges reality. Yet I claim that such logical possibilities of dramatic error do not destroy knowledge, so we need not be concerned about them until we have some actual reason to take them seriously. That we have reliable knowledge conceivably might be false, but we have no reason to believe it is.

4. Relativism

Relativism is a vague word that philosophers apply in different ways.[19] I take its core to consist of these beliefs: that we must judge all things from the perspective of our own belief system; that there is no super-standpoint from which to judge between conflicting ones; and hence that ultimately no truth is objective in the sense used in Ch. IV.5, which is that a sincere belief might still be mistaken. Relativism can relate these beliefs to theories of truth and objectivity in various ways. Thus, while skepticism asserts an unbridgeable gap between internalist justification and externalist truth, and so denies that truth can be reached, relativism may remove the gap by an internalist view of truth which says that it is simply what we have reason to believe. Similarly, it may accept the subjectivist/objectivist contrast within belief systems, but not between them; it may say I can decide which of *my* beliefs may be wrong, but I cannot reject as mistaken those arising in a radically different system.

Today relativism is usually a more deeply felt and less purely intellectual position than skepticism, and its roots are complex. Our modern awareness of ourselves as historical beings easily leads, not only to a rejection of that absolute truth which the Enlightenment so confidently sought, but also to a belief that we are too embedded in our traditions to make objective critiques of them. This further attracts many people on moral grounds, as a basis for tolerance between opposing views. It also joins with viewpoints which suggest that hidden forces either operate in the individual unconscious so as to make overt reasoning a sham, or else, at the group level, manipulate the debate to serve vested interests. This may produce a feeling of powerlessness, which is reinforced by a sense that decisions in our large, impersonal societies are not open to input from ordinary people. So people conclude that reason is too weak to reach objective conclusions, at least on complex and emotional issues. If we happen to have enough initial agreement, we may be able to settle issues on which we disagree. But when differences are too great, there is ultimately no rational way of deciding them.

My own position accepts the first two points at the core of relativism—that we must judge from our own standpoint, and that there is no super-standpoint from which to judge others—but denies its conclusion, that there is no objective truth. For my argument in Ch. X was that, by starting from whatever agreement we have, we can reach one of the three possible outcomes of rational inquiry without needing any super-standpoint. So, like relativism, I adopt an internalist view that justification is always from a standpoint, and I have emphasized how our knowledge is historically conditioned. Relativism, however, insists on a stark choice: either we can establish objective truth once and for all, or we must reject the whole notion. But while I agree we cannot reach once-for-all truth, for we might always later transcend our best grounded beliefs, I still insist that an externalist view of truth, true or false independently of what we believe, is one we cannot abandon. I argue for this in Ch. XII, but I note now that it underlies my previous argument. Settling or postponing an issue, or reaching a deeper understanding of it, presupposes that we can come closer to a truth that we did not know before the inquiry. Certainly, relativism may point out that someone outside our circle of agreement might later reject our conclusion by challenging what we agree on. But then there is a new issue to investigate, where we can again make progress.

Many analytic philosophers take a much shorter way with relativism, by using the self-refutation objection. If all truth were relative to a standpoint, then that truth could itself hold only for relativists who accepted it; so a conflicting belief in objective truth would be equally true for those who accepted that. Relativism, this argument says, must take as its model for truth claims something like our expressions of preference or taste. If I prefer red wine and you prefer white, then, though we might be foolish enough to argue about it, there is really no question of who is correct; our tastes simply differ. Relativism must apply this model, not only to practical contexts of how to act, but also to beliefs about what is the case. But, whatever we think of it in prac-tical contexts (see Ch. XIII), in theoretical ones it is absurd. If we have incompatible beliefs, at least one of us must be wrong.

Even if this short refutation is cogent, however, it does not touch the main issue between myself and relativism, which is the potentiality of reason. There would be little point in showing truth cannot be relative to a standpoint, if large scale significance-judgments were too influenced by psychological or social forces to be resolved by rational means. Yet the self-refutation point is important. For when we ask how relativism applies to itself, we find it must resist a continual temptation to covertly suggest, without overtly saying, that it *is* the real truth, no matter what opponents believe. Yet insofar as it says this, it turns into another sort of pessimistic view. When it insists that we cannot validly judge between competing belief systems, it echoes the same point that criticalism applies to philosophical overviews—namely, that there is no effective decision procedure for judging between them. Thus while relativism says all truth is relative to a belief system, criticalism says explicitly what relativism is always tempted to claim: that the truth which holds for everyone, whether they recognize it or not, is that no coherent overview can be rationally obtained. I discuss that in Ch. XIV.

5. The Causal and the Justificatory Modes

I turn to a more specific view which, within the unfriendly climate of English-speaking philosophy, defiantly calls itself relativist. It has developed in what analytic philosophy sees as the relatively peripheral area of philosophy of social science, and it derives from the sociology of knowledge.[20] It focuses on the influences that cause us to think as we do, as opposed to the reasons we offer, so I shall call it the causal approach. Originally, sociology of knowledge, in emphasizing its status as a science, took science as the ideal type of reasoning, but now the causal approach applies itself as much to science as elsewhere. All reasoning, it argues, takes place in pursuit of interests, and so is to be causally explained. The traditional epistemological aim of justifying our beliefs should be replaced by causal, and particularly sociological, explanations of why we hold them.

However the notion of a causal explanation here needs explication. The Western philosophical tradition, including analytic philosophy, usually takes causes to be sufficient conditions for effects. To say that C causes E implies that *whenever* C occurs, E occurs. The great debate since Hume in the 18th century has been whether this is *all* that causation involves, or whether there is some further "necessary"connection between C and E. But in either case we know virtually no causes of our thought in this sense; we can rarely specify situations such that, when they occur, a specific result always follows. Rather, the causal approach looks to the social sciences to offer *causal factors*. These influence us but do not precisely determine the outcome, though they may provide a basis for statistical explanations of why people on the whole tend to behave in given ways. But still a central contrast with traditional epistemology remains. The causal approach, we may say, thinks *in the causal mode*. By contrast, epistemological assessments of knowledge claims think in an evaluative *justificatory* mode rather than a descriptive causal one. So, in taking scientific and other knowledge to be just one more cultural item for causal explanation, the causal approach extends into this new context the Enlightenment's belief in science, but rejects its optimistic faith in the potentiality of reason.

Critics of the causal approach again appeal to self-refutation. If, they say, our conclusions are the result of causal factors rather than rational reflection, then no belief can be justified. But this includes the belief that all beliefs are caused, so there could be nothing more to be said for the causal approach than for any other. That, however, is not my position. The causal mode can be separated from the relativism often used to support it, and in principle I find it complementary to the justificatory one. Broadly, the justificatory one aims to reach truth about the issue before us; the causal one asks why the issue arises, and why we are attracted to, or repelled by, different views. This applies both to ourselves and to others. In making up our minds we examine evidence and argument, and make significance-judgments about what coheres with other beliefs; that is the justificatory mode. But the question of why we find a given reason as impressive or unimpressive as we do, and hence why our significance-judgments may conflict with other people's, is typically a causal one, even when we answer it only with unsophisticated commonsense.[21] Seen in this light, the two modes are in general quite compatible.[22]

The modes reveal different aspects of reasoning. Even in as abstract a context as pure mathematics, we can ask causal mode questions: what social influences lie behind the formulation of the problem; or, did this person become a mathematician so as to retreat from the conflicts of life? Conversely, an argument put forward obviously from self-interest may still have to be evaluated to see if it makes a good point. The relevant question will be how these aspects fit together, and which makes the more illuminating point for our purposes. While reasoning in the justificatory mode, I may use the causal one to ask what motives might be influencing my conclusion ("Am I being swayed by my friendship with Joe?"). Conversely, if my causal mode judgment about others is that they will act rationally, I may reflect imaginatively on how they will reason so as to anticipate their decision. As a further example, I believe my present argument to be cogent, which is a judgment in the justificatory mode. But I also know it is a contribution to a debate, the outcome of which will probably be different from the expectations of all participants, including myself; and that is a causal mode awareness.

However, despite this general compatibility, some causal mode explanations do undermine the justifications they explain. This is when they expose a *hidden agenda* such as hypocrisy, rationalization or class interests. For even if, in principle, such arguments may still make a good point, awareness of their agenda may be valuable in picking out underlying significance-judgments on which they are based; and certainly, in tackling these most difficult of issues, we need all the illumination we can get. Yet with the causal approach, I often find both an official and an unofficial program. The official one is to trace the causal factors in beliefs; the unofficial one is that the only acceptable factors are those which bring out discreditable hidden agendas. It is hard-headed and "scientific" to expose pretensions to occupy a lofty plateau of reason untainted by base motives; but to suggest that a sheer love of truth could move anyone to embrace an unpalatable conclusion, would be unscientific naivety.

Against this I hold that causal mode explanations, if they are to cover all cases, must accept that the justificatory mode has an official, and sometimes an actual, interest in following the wind of the argument wherever it blows, and that this may operate as one causal factor among others in reaching our conclusions. Certainly the mutualistic interaction of our motives suggests it may never be found in its pure form, yet that it has some influence seems plausible for both individual and social reasons. Individually, a tendency to adopt the reality principle, to see things as they are, has survival value in adjusting to the world, and so presumably is built into our central nervous system. Socially, the tendency helps to adjust groups to change, and so may form one part of our socialization. I have presupposed this interest throughout Ch. X. If the causal approach should deny it, it must argue against it without begging the question. Otherwise it would show only that hidden agendas are not confined to its opponents.

Overall, the causal approach might endorse much of my analysis of understanding, but it will emphasize the role of hidden agendas, and might see my emphasis on truth-seeking as naive. What underlies this difference? We could certainly ask what causal factors lead us to our different conclusions, but, without speculating on that question here, we would also want to ask which of us was right; and that is an issue in the justificatory mode. Here I suspect that a basic difference relates to the rejection of the threefold syndrome of foundationalism, intellectualism and epistemological imperialism discussed in Ch. VII.4. The causal approach sees these as a disastrous package deal which must be replaced by sociology of knowledge, while I try to hold a balance. How might this incipient vicious circle become a beneficent one? We would agree, I think, that the causal and justificatory modes can each be applied to the other: that we can ask of justificatory claims "What interests led to their being propounded?", and of causal ones "How good is their reasoning?". But the causal approach insists that the causal mode has the last word: justification is just one more activity carried on to promote interests. In emphasizing our interest in reaching the truth, I assert, not the contrary claim that the justificatory mode has the last word, but rather that the last word depends on the context, and that each type of context is indispensable. That claim of mine is itself in the justificatory rather than the causal mode, and so must be tested by the processes indicated in Ch. X.

6. Postmodernism and Poststructuralism

Outside the analytic tradition, and still largely ignored by it, new developments have swept through the humanities and social sciences and are impinging on English-speaking philosophy. They still have no agreed name. The umbrella word is "postmodernism", but this relates to my position in more complex ways than I can examine here.[23] When one excellent discussion sets out "to explore how theories might be written in postmodern voices— nonauthoritarian, open-ended, and process-oriented",[24] I hope I might be included. But the word also covers many views that reflect in different ways what I called in Sec. 1 a "disillusionment with the whole Western... tradition..., its culture, economics and government", which would reject at least some of my position. In picking out relevant threads, I focus on the more specific, but still varied, set of views called poststructuralism; though some important voices would refuse the name, either because they are defining themselves against others or because they resist all labels on principle. Contributors to the debates now come from many backgrounds,[25] but poststructuralism began as a French reaction to the structuralism found in the

linguistics of Saussure and the anthropology of Levi-Strauss.   In particular,
Foucault has had great influence in the social sciences and Derrida in literary
studies;[26] and though their own conflict has tended to blind the followers of
each to the merits of the other, I can select the points I need without trying to
assess their respective importance.

One relevant feature is a focus on neglected aspects of language. Rather
than seeing it as the communication of explicit information, or examining its
rational structure as logicians do, poststructuralism is sensitive in powerful
new ways to how things are said, why they are not said, and what is taken for
granted. Foucault showed how social institutions—the hospital, the mental
asylum, the prison, or our sexual *mores*—represent "discursive formations" or
discourses, which present us with what we take to be facts, and so shape our
understanding of ourselves and others. They forge a mutualistic link between
knowledge and power. Power is normally asserted, not by direct enforcement
but by acceptance of authoritative discourses—children doing what their
parents say, lay people taking the word of professionals, or just a general
social acceptance of ruling groups.   Conversely, what we take to be
knowledge is shaped by the powerful discourses in our tradition. Together
with this emphasis on the knowledge-power relation goes an insistence, both
on the variety of discourses and also on how they constitute and reinforce our
social roles, so that our personalities are constructed piecemeal out of the
conflicting pressures that discourses place upon us.

Another central element, also with many variations, is the practice of
deconstructing texts.   This derives from Derrida, and focuses on how texts
contain conflicting discourses. It scans a text to see how images, style or
metaphors unconsciously reflect underlying assumptions that may conflict with
its explicit message. As a simple example, a text might assert in a didactic and
authoritative way the value of thinking for ourselves, so that its style presents
an implicit conflict with its explicit theme.   In a more specific sense,
deconstruction looks for how texts employ binary oppositions, such as light
and darkness. These contrasts are value-laden: the first term is privileged,
overtly or covertly, as a norm for controlling our thought, while the second is,
in varying ways, a denial or opposition or absence of the first.[27] After locating
such oppositions, deconstruction may ask how the text appears if we invert the
valuation.[28]   It may use other devices too, such as exploiting puns or
apparently irrelevant verbal similarities to suggest how a given text might
point in many directions. But always it insists that texts can be read in an
indefinite number of ways, and have no pre-given, "real" meaning for exegesis
to discover. We give a meaning to a text by our reading, and our reading
becomes another text for others to read, like a hall of mirrors that all reflect
each other.[29] Moreover, though this view centers on reading texts, it may be
generalized.   Texts, it holds, may be written or spoken, as may be their

readings. So any intelligendum may be seen as a "text", and all texts are deconstructable. Often deconstruction becomes the paradigmatic search for understanding.

The two themes of deconstruction and the knowledge-power relation have some common applications across the many strands of poststructuralism. One is a suspicion of any metadiscourse or overall viewpoint, which relates sub-discourses to each other and offers a general foundation for understanding. For a metadiscourse may be expected to present allegedly universal principles in ways that support the dominance of some powerful group; so it will both illustrate the knowledge-power link, and also suppress other voices in ways that make it eminently deconstructable. A more specific application of this notion is a critique of "humanism", by which is meant the Enlightenment belief in an essential or ideal human nature, which we might discern by philosophical reflection and then realize in our lives. The apparently universal ideal of "the man of reason", it insists, was in fact used to sanctify the power of a dominant class and sex.[30] The "man" was a privileged member of a binary opposition, against which women, the lower classes of Europe and the "savages" outside it, were measured and found wanting. In rejecting this or any other "essential" humanity, poststructuralism emphasizes that we as individuals are a collection of conflicting discourses, and also that those discourses are shaped by the power relations of the groups in which we are embedded.

To compare these poststructuralist themes to analytic philosophy brings out the complexity in each tradition. If we start from the syndrome of foundationalism, intellectualism and philosophical imperialism, each tradition rejects such foundationalist views as Empiricist appeals to the certainty of sense-data or Rationalist ones to indubitable axioms. With intellectualism, which is the attitude of the spectator rather than the participant, the dividing line cuts across poststructuralism rather than between the two. Much post-structuralism, particularly in literary studies, seems as purely intellectualist as anything in the analytic tradition, but its applications in the social sciences often emphasize the unity of thought and practice in praxis. The third strand in the syndrome is the epistemological imperialism which sees philosophy as adjudicating knowledge claims and assigning disciplines their proper role. Again both traditions reject this, but with difference emphases. Whereas the analytic one often compares philosophy unfavorably to science, poststruc-turalism may devalue both philosophy and science in contrast to the capacity of literature to exhibit the human condition in ways the pedantry of reason cannot capture. But its exponents vary from those who see it as the end of philosophy as we have known it, to those who see only a useful new weapon in our age-long assault on the problems of the human condition. So in both traditions, the relation of philosophy to other disciplines remains an open question, where varying answers are found.

Besides this syndrome, a different dimension of comparison concerns the contrast between constructivism and criticalism. This too cuts across the traditions. Analytic philosophy, as I noted in Ch. VII.2, has moved away from its original criticalism; and the poststructuralist suspicion of metadiscourses, though very different in ethos and starting point, is also ambiguous. In social analyses, a sense of hidden agendas beneath the surface of discourse may point towards such "masters of suspicion" as Marx and Freud. Yet not only are some of their 19th century beliefs outdated, but their arguments aim to support metadiscourses of the coming of communism or the truth of psycho-analysis. So while some poststructuralists, though deconstructing them, are still inspired by their critiques, others treat them like any other constructivist thinker. For those who abandon both Marx and Freud, the master of suspicion most likely to be their guide is Nietzsche. But, as we shall now see, there are also other complex issues in the criticalist/constructivist debate within post-structuralism.

7. Reason, Freedom and Creativity

In relating poststructuralism to my own views, the issues are not easy to pin down. If poststructuralism sees an individual as a collection of discourses, I also noted in Ch. II.8 the quasi-independence of sub-systems in our belief system. If it claims that no reading is finally authoritative, I too have empha-sized the unboundedness of understanding. If it fears that metadiscourses distort phenomena, I agreed in Ch. V.6 that in non-formal transcendence there are always costs as well as benefits. Further, its sensitivity to hidden agendas echoes my point in Ch. VI that we should not restrict reasoning to the detached intellect.[31] Yet there are surely differences, so where do they lie?

I approach an answer by raising a final form of the self-refutation problem: how does poststructuralism apply to itself? When it deconstructs, or explores the knowledge-power link, what conclusions follow? Here we find a tension between what is, in effect, a constructivist strand, however cautious, and a criticalist one. The first one sets out to expose the pretensions of metadiscour-ses as a way of reaching better understanding. It searches out hidden agendas in the belief that if we see what influences us, we can act more effectively. Rejecting Enlightenment humanism and becoming aware of inner discourses lets us, as individuals, reshape ourselves without conforming to socially imposed ideals. At the social level, awareness of the knowledge-power link offers some hope of controlling it. Hence its critiques are undertaken so as to work towards a better overview. The second strand applies its principles to itself more ruthlessly. Metadiscourses, it holds, should be not merely treated with suspicion, but eliminated. *Any* claim to achieve an overview, even an allegedly post-Enlightenment one, offers one reading as correct, privileges one set of terms as a norm, and so imposes only a spurious and deconstructable unity. With the individual, we must reject as illusory the concept of a free and creative person who is responsible for their actions, and who might therefore have a real impact on their situation. A person, like a text, is a set of discourses without a real unity. In literature, authors have no special insight into their texts, and appeal to their intentions is irrelevant. In social action, individuals reflect the struggle for power between dominant groups or their rivals. Only by exposing all ideals of intellectual, personal or social progress as distortions nourished by the humanist dream, can we escape the eternal frustration of failing to achieve them, and the strife which comes from attempts to impose them. The tension between these strands cuts across the varied forms of poststructuralism. Thus a large set of feminist, neo-Marxist and neo-Freudian views, with great differences among themselves, are on the constructivist side of the line, while Foucault and Derrida, despite their differences, are on the other side. As I see both constructivism and criticalism as coherent views, I take neither approach to be simply self-refuting, but in turning to a final assessment I must consider each separately.

The constructivist strand appeals to many who feel nihilated by oppressive social structures. In unmasking ideologies, they find discourse analysis or deconstruction an invaluable tool. When dominant social groups dismiss their insights, this reinforces their awareness of the knowledge-power link, and leads them to see themselves as the suppressed part of a binary opposition—whether female oppressed by male, colored by white, or poor by wealthy. Yet, though such viewpoints vary in their beliefs about improving the human condition, they share a basic hope of doing so that resists a pessimistic, criticalist rejection of all attempts at overall understanding. For these constructivist views I have great sympathy, and there is much room to integrate their specific arguments with my general position. My critical comment is, however, that often I find them so firmly focused on their own starting point of feminism, class conflict or racism, that they are blind to each other's insights, not to mention those from elsewhere. Still we have gained from them, I believe, much insight into ourselves and our social structures, and I hope for more to come, but I do not expect from any of them the key to all our problems. For—as many of them might agree—I see us as at bottom mysteries to ourselves, who can endlessly illuminate but never exhaust either our personal or our social being. In both respects, the unboundedness of understanding will have the last word.

If we turn to the criticalist strand in poststructuralism, my suspicion of overconfident answers might seem to echo Foucault, who, as I read him, would not develop his unmasking of hidden agendas into a systematic overview.[32] For him, when we deconstruct we are left only with innumerable, unpredictable aspects of the knowledge-power relation. But again I differ, and in Ch. XIV I suggest a different balance between overconfidence and pessimism. I agree that all overviews will be flawed, that they will have a potential to nihilate marginal social groups, and that they will inevitably seem to us more permanent than they can be. Yet I shall still claim that they may be, not only worthwhile, but our greatest intellectual achievements.

This requires me, finally, to define myself against another position which is found in Derrida: that rival readings are *undecidable*, in the sense that none can be allowed to foreclose understanding by overriding others. Rather, we need new concepts, called "undecidables", which present standpoints that retain the tensions.[33] Opponents often see this as a relativist claim that reason is impotent to arrive at truth. I read it rather as projecting a finely balanced vision that is deeply serious, though often expressed in irony, or in wordplay that exhibits multiple meanings. Unlike relativism, it treats some readings as better than others; otherwise it could itself be no better than any alternative. But it invites us to see how we and our texts are prey to ineradicable tensions which will always undermine our syntheses and metadiscourses.[34]

This approach might treat my defence of reason in Ch. X as favoring one member of a binary opposition. It might deconstruct that valuation to obtain a new reading which shows the importance of the non-rational, and then try to capture the tension by some new undecidable. But anti-rational readings can themselves be deconstructed, by finding in them a reliance on logical connections in their challenge to reason. So when all the texts have been deconstructed, including the poststructuralist ones, what are we to make of the notion of undecidability? It relates to my concept of polarization in Ch. II.8, that, whether in society or within ourself, attitudes never completely vanquish their rivals. Though I stressed how views provoke their opposites, while the search for binary oppositions looks for polarizations so embedded that they govern our accepted thought, these two emphases can be complementary. Yet we still differ. Is this because undecidability presents some fourth alternative to my three possible outcomes of rational inquiry? Well, presumably by reasoning in good faith we could reach agreement about what issues can be settled or properly postponed, which are the first two possibilities. What of the third one, increasing depth? Since this needs a metadiscourse to relate sub-discourses into an overview, some poststructuralism may reject depth as such, especially as claims to deeper insight are prominent in what it deconstructs. But would the search for undecidables take that path, or would it claim that deeper insight consists precisely in acknowledging undecidability? Perhaps it would look here for another undecidable—some concept that neither denies increasing depth nor abolishes the original conflicts, and so neither is nor is not in any simple sense a fourth possible outcome. But whatever reply were made, what emerges, I suggest, is that undecidability can be given two emphases. Does it point to the *futility* of metadiscourses or overviews, since they can all be deconstructed; or does it only *warn* us that, however valuable they may be, they too may eventually need deconstruction?[35] I endorse the second alternative, as would many poststructuralists; but others will insist on the first alternative, that all synthesis is futile. Here my cautious optimism about the power of reason confronts more than the criticalist rejection of overviews. For the reasoning I have advocated is a free and creative act, however embedded it may be in its social context, so my claims for it also challenge any anti-humanist rejection of individual freedom and creativity.[36]

I find explanatory importance in freedom and creativity because I see the relation between us and our tradition as a mutualistic one, in which we, as parts, really affect the whole just as we are affected by it. So I hold that our choices make a difference, that we can exercise our freedom creatively, and that we are responsible for the outcome. In developing our personalities, we may at least partly integrate the conflicting discourses of our inner voices.[37] In literature, I see the creativity of authors as a genuine dimension to be explored, though their texts also reflect their social situation. So when I look at such great poststructuralists as Foucault or Derrida, I do not see *merely* a play of impersonal forces producing texts whose sources are irrelevant. I *also* see brilliant minds, whose insights might be profound or perverse, but who have freely and creatively transformed their received tradition.[38] This underlies my cautious optimism about the potentiality of reason, and here I and anti-humanism extrapolate from different cases. I focus on conclusions jointly reached through dialogue; it emphasizes rivalry between groups, and the difficulty of frank communication. So we lay our bets differently, and neither bet is certain. If traditional cultures are to decay in a world linked only superficially by a universal technology, many may fill the void by a criticalist rejection of any overview. Others also, who can neither rise to the challenge of change nor bear the loss of meaning, may resort to fundamentalist reaffirmations of traditional values, preferring familiar conflicts with known enemies to the unforeseeable outcome of dialogue. Yet neither of these outcomes is inevitable. Against them I assert my cautious faith in the power of free and creative dialogue to extend understanding, and even perhaps to achieve a new overview of our human condition.

ENDNOTES

[1] As examples of efforts to bridge the gulf, cf. R. Rorty and R. J. Bernstein *op. cit.*

[2] D. Davidson *Inquiries into Truth and Interpretation* (1984), especially "On the Very Idea of a Conceptual Scheme", pp. 183-198. I have been greatly helped by discussion with Jeff Malpas, but he would probably reject my conclusions.

3 There are other issues I cannot discuss here. Davidson combines holism with a view of meaning and reference based on Tarski's theory of truth. That theory was developed for - and in Tarski's view was confined to - formal languages which restrict holism, and I see tensions between these two elements in the program. Davidson also holds that translation and meaning are indeterminate, since innumerable interpretive schemes will always satisfy all the data. While this is formally compatible with my analysis of understanding, I would take actual rival interpretations to be conflicting claims, which we can proceed to debate as in Ch. X.

4 P. 192.

5 P. 197. In fact, he holds, we would not even have grounds for believing that what might look like linguistic behavior was really *language* at all. For translation is at the heart of Tarski's theory of truth, which he believes is needed for all language. See pp. 194-195.

6 P. 197.

7 P. 199.

8 Davidson cites various thinkers - Whorf, Kuhn, Putnam, Quine, Bergson and Feyerabend - whom he takes to have unacceptably "relativist" views (pp. 184, 187-8, 190). Yet, though they use some language I would reject, most seem to me closer to my position than to "relativism". Since my interpretation of them is nearer to what Davidson and I take to be the truth, should not the Principle of Charity favor it?

9 As for the Principle of Charity, it does seem that (subject to the skepticism discussed in Sec. 3), most beliefs must have a sufficient element of truth to apply to the world with broad success. Cf. my remarks about NNS justifications in Ch. XI.4, and about correspondence theories of truth in Ch. XII.2. But this is much less than the Principle usually claims.

10 For reasons of space I cannot separately discuss Humean skepticism about inductive reasoning. I would argue that knowledge of the external world - even a belief in continuing material objects - is so dependent on accepting the regularities we find in nature, that skepticism about induction collapses into total skepticism. So, though it richly deserves separate treatment, I believe that the general thrust of my argument applies also to it.

11 Descartes *Meditation I*, in Anscombe and Geach *op. cit.*

12 Strictly, to speak of a mad scientist presupposes an external physical world which includes scientists, and Descartes' argument challenges even that. But the distinction does not matter for my purposes.

13 P. F. Strawson *Individuals* (1959), p. 34.

14 Thus one ingenious argument is found in P. Unger *Ignorance* (1975). He distinguishes between relative terms, and absolute ones which "purport to denote, an absolute limit" (p. 55). The latter, he argues, may strictly speaking have no application; and he takes "certain" to be one such term. I disagree with his linguistic intuitions. "Certain" seems to have both a subjective and an objective use. The first, fallible sense ("I was certain we had sugar in the cupboard, but obviously I was wrong"), is irrelevant. In the second, relevant, objective sense (typically "It is certain", rather than "I am certain"), at least one proper use is surely to say that something is certain if we have a good NNS justification.

15 Unger *op. cit.*, p. 7.

16 I have found particularly insightful here B. Stroud *The Significance of Philosophical Scepticism* (1984).

17 In terms of Strawson's argument, this form of skepticism does not seem to violate our conceptual scheme. Yet, as Unger's example shows, it can be extended to doubting the existence of anything in the external world.

18 The example is not my own invention, but I do not know where in the large literature it first appeared.

19 Davidson, for example, takes relativism to be the claim that there are totally incommensurable conceptual schemes, which he equates to the claim that there are totally untranslatable languages. As for his conclusions, cf. fn.8. But for my purpose of relating current views to my own, I need not discuss how far our definitions may differ.

20 See, e.g., D Bloor *Knowledge and Social Imagery* (1976); Barry Barnes *T. S. Kuhn and Social Science* (1982), and *Interests and the Growth of Knowledge* (1977).

21 In some formalized contexts there is no room for balancing imponderable factors, and

the remaining causal question may only be why we are willing to think rationally here. Perhaps this difference has contributed to the earlier view that scientific reasoning escapes causal explanation.

22 The strongest resistance to treating these two modes as compatible may come from a libertarian fear of a threat to freewill. Yet surely the fear is misplaced (cf. my *Freewill and Determinism, passim*; "Would Freewill Make Social Science Impossible?" (1983). *Inter alia*, libertarianism conflicts only with explanations which take causes to be sufficient conditions, so that actions could not be otherwise. It can agree that causal factors *influence*, without determining, our choices, and that a clearer understanding of such influences would enhance, rather than threaten, our freedom.

23 Cf. M. A. Rose *The Post-Modern and the Post-Industrial* (1991).

24 Jane Flax *Thinking Fragments* (1990) p.3.

25 For analytic philosophy, cf. fn.1. The important contribution of Habermas comes from his background in the Frankfurt School.

26 An extensive bibliography of Foucault, and also a useful introduction to his thought, can be found in M. Cousins and A. Hussain *Michel Foucault* (1984). For a bibliography of Derrida, as well as some penetrating discussion, cf. C. Norris *Derrida* (1987). I am also indebted to Norris's numerous other books. Throughout Secs. 6 and 7 I have benefited from comments from Alan Roughley and Bill McDonald. I have also found generally helpful Q. Skinner *The Return of Grand Theory in the Social Sciences* (1985).

27 This notion goes back at least to Nietzsche. It also owes much to earlier French structuralism, but that placed less emphasis on the hierarchy of values in the oppositions. I do not believe all oppositions are binary rather than many-sided conflicts, but we can always *make* them so. For of, say, three positions X, Y and Z, either we can treat them sequentially, as a conflict between X and Y, and then a further one between them and Z; or we can focus on X, and group Y and Z as not-X. In either case we then get a binary opposition.

28 Poststructuralism finds in Plato and elsewhere a value-laden hierarchy that thought is superior to the spoken word, and word to written speech, because the latter two are at greater distances from the privileged category of mind. In making the written text central, it subverts this hierarchy. This is an example of a threefold contrast reduced to a binary one.

29 There are complex relations to Davidson's argument in Sec. 2. For he holds a similar-sounding view of the indeterminacy of translation and meaning, from which he draws radically different conclusions.

30 Cf. G. Lloyd *The Man of Reason* (1984).

31 The deeper question in Ch. VI, of whether we should transcend not merely the detached intellect but intellectual understanding itself, may pose as great a challenge to poststructuralism as to other Western philosophy.

32 Foucault would have challenged many of my historical generalizations, such as those in Ch. VII.1. To avoid discussion I can only say here that, while these points are important, I do not think they are central to my position.

33 Cf. J. Derrida *Positions* (trans. A. Bass) (1981).

34 The impact of this process is not easy to convey, for it needs a skill of minute textual examination as lengthy and rigorous as any traditional philosophical argumentation. But I am impressed by many of its insights - not only in Derrida himself, but, e.g., in much of Norris's argument in such books as *The Deconstructive Turn* (1983).

35 Might we need another undecidable to reflect the tension between these two readings of undecidability? And might an infinite regress then open up? For the individual, I think not. Each of us must in the end accept one reading or the other, even if we acknowledge costs and benefits in each choice; otherwise, we are not achieving undecidability, but are simply unable to make up our minds. But the group may hedge its bets, in the sense that each alternative remains a living option.

36 The contrast is more difficult to pin down than it may seem. To open one dimension of complexity, anti-humanist views often deny that there are any strictly uncaused events, but say that if there were any they would be sheer chance. Within alternative views, the question of uncaused events divides compatibilist from libertarian defences of freedom.

Compatibilists see explanations of human activity as involving new levels of *significance*, but not a break in the causal chain. Libertarians say that human freedom requires such a break, which represents the place where creative choice breaks into the natural order. See my *Freewill and Determinism, passim*. Another issue that arises here concerns the relation of the individual to the group. See Ch. XIII.9.

[37] I would add that, apart from the value of depth psychology, I believe that the practice of stilling the mind (Ch. VI.6) permits a process of integration among sub-systems of the mind that is profoundly beneficial.

[38] For how these two standpoints are compatible, see Ch. XIII.9.

CHAPTER XII

OUR CONTACT WITH REALITY

1. The Realist-Idealist Tension

My explorations have focused on the scope and reliability of knowledge, but other, less direct implications are also important. Above all, there is the ancient philosophical question of the relation of thought to reality. To non-philosophers the situation usually seems so obvious that they wonder what the fuss is about. We are born into a world which existed long before we did and will continue after we die; we perceive it through our senses, reflect on it in our reasoning, and so acquire understanding. Yet that conviction conceals a central problem which arises with both perception and reasoning. With perception, since our senses are highly selective in what they convey, how do we know what the world is really like independent of them? With reasoning, how far are intelligenda presented to us by the world, and how far are they constructed by the mind? In general: how well does our belief system represent reality?[1] We could avoid this in Part A, because such words as "understanding" and "knowledge" assert, both that we have achieved a certain sort of mental state, and also that this is how things are; for if the mental state does not represent how things are, we have misunderstood or do not know. But now we must examine the relation between the mental state and the reality.

My answer starts from the distinction between externalist theories that present something as independent of what we think, and internalist ones that involve reference to an actual or hypothetical consciousness. For example, externalist ones will see an intelligendum as an existing state of affairs, that becomes an intelligendum because we are concerned with it. We come to understand it through many processes. These include reflection that articulates it, observation that brings new information, praxis that applies knowledge in action, and also those occasions where we consciously attempt to let reality speak to us rather than to fit it into the concepts we already have. For convenience, I call all these our "investigations" of reality. The externalist point is that, however varied these may be, there is always a gap between investigation and fact; our beliefs might not correspond to reality. By contrast, an internalist approach will see an intelligendum as an issue we pose. If it concerns the external world, then that is simply one of its features, which marks it off from such other intelligenda as trying to understand our dreams.

When we have adequately articulated the relevant information, we understand. The gap between coherence and fact disappears, except as the reminder that new information might later force us to re-examine what we thought we knew.

Inevitably we take these two standpoints as items to be fitted into a wider picture, and ask which gives the deeper view of the human situation. Then we meet an enduring conflict between two positions, each with many forms, that are traditionally called realism and idealism. At the heart of realism is an emphasis arising from the externalist standpoint: that, no matter how coherent our articulation, we may always ask whether it represents how things really are. At the heart of idealism is an internalist emphasis: that, as noted in Ch. IX.8, we can never get outside our investigations to see how the world independently is. "At the heart of" is the key phrase in each case. It is not that realist views just *are* externalist ones, or idealist ones internalist; rather any plausible answer must come to terms with both these emphases. But the difficulty of doing so is immense.[2] Idealism and realism are often defined as contradictories, such that one must be true and the other false: idealism as the claim that reality is mind-dependent, and realism as the denial, that it is mind-independent.[3] This then produces a baffling conflict. "You claim," the idealist says, "that reality is independent of us, but *what are its features*? You can only find an answer by your investigations, which depend on your belief system. If you pretend to speak of a feature that reality has independently of your beliefs, then either you smuggle in a hidden reference to them by taking for granted basic concepts (such as cause and effect), or you talk nonsense. For though we can try to stand outside our *present* standpoint, the notion of standing outside *any* standpoint is as incoherent as jumping out of our skins. All talk about reality is from a standpoint, so reality is mind-dependent." — "You refer", the realist retorts, "to 'talk about reality'. But all talk, including yours, must use a public language referring to our shared world, and this is essential to investigation. All investigation presupposes an independent world, which has the features we investigate. Reality is mind-independent."

To define the issue so that one alternative must be true is, I believe, a fine example of so posing a problem that it becomes virtually insoluble. The externalist emphasis that even the most coherent articulation might be wrong, and the internalist one that we can never get outside our belief system to test it against reality, seem to me platitudes which, far from being incompatible, are certainly true. As I have rejected foundationalism, I do not say they are unquestionable, but they are my starting point until they are challenged. I cannot justify them by appeal to something more fundamental, for I do not know what that would be. Rather than defending them, I aim to articulate an answer that does justice to both, and to consider some implications. But first I must comment on two basic concepts involved in the discussion—truth and reality.

2. Truth

Some concepts are under tension like an earthquake fault line, pulled in different directions by realist and idealist forces. Thus in Ch. IX I took justification to be an internalist concept that relates knowledge claims to the information available to the claimant, but I noted that reliabilist analyses would make it an externalist one. I also suggested the opposite about truth: that it is an externalist concept, though some analyses make it an internalist one. Now we must examine truth more carefully. To say a statement or belief is true, surely seems to say that it represents what is the case, independently of what anyone thinks about the matter. Hence it was almost unquestioned till the 19th century that a true statement corresponds to the facts. Then, with Hegel and the Absolute Idealists, came the objection that "correspondence" suggests, incoherently, we can get outside our belief systems to compare them to the world. Further, in allowing that the most coherent set of beliefs might be false, it creates a gap between our investigations and reality that we cannot even in principle bridge; for any attempt to bridge it would be only a further investigation. So this plays into the hands of skeptics, who can then say we should not claim to know because we might be completely wrong. To avoid all this, it was argued, we must say that calling a belief true means only that it does and will cohere with our past and future ones. So coherence, which captures our *criteria for judging* statements to be true, becomes a definition of what it *means to say* they are.

Today the explicit focus within analytic philosophy has shifted. Current debates about truth are highly technical, with complex roots in earlier 20th century discussions.[4] But now I need define my position only against certain views within the general idealist family, where the emphasis is on verification. We must, they argue, *learn* to apply "true"; but we can do so only from experience; hence the meaning must be some relation we can identify *within* experience, rather than one between all possible experience and something else; so all that is left for "true" to mean is some relation between appropriate beliefs. My objection is that such arguments underestimate our capacity to understand possibilities as well as actualities. By abstracting from a situation, we may start with what we experience, and then eliminate features till we end with something still intelligible, that could not be verified in experience. In the present case, we start with the experience of finding we were wrong. We abstract from it the concept of possibly-being-wrong-despite-good-evidence-for-our-belief. We can extend that concept to cases where we will never in fact find out we are wrong, and finally extend it still further to contemplate the possibility of cases where we *could* not find it out. Such cases are unverifiable, but the concept seems quite comprehensible.

In my view, this reduces verificationism to an onus of proof: "If you could not even in principle say how you would verify it, has your claim any meaning at all?". And in some cases, by tracing out the process of abstraction, I think we can discharge the onus. But verificationists might reply that I have only traced out a temptation to slip from sense to nonsense. So our conflicting intuitions already raise the threat of a vicious circle, where we argue from mutually unacceptable premises. Even apart from this, my argument would only show we can *form* such a notion, not that we have any use for it. Why should we need to take account of this possibility? One reason is that an externalist notion of truth enters into our internalist concept of justification as a regulative ideal; as a commitment that if better evidence should turn up, we will say our belief never was true. The realist extends this point to ask: "Surely it still *makes sense* to suppose that even our best evidence might lead us astray?". To that the verificationist replies: "Not if we could never discover it". So again we have the threat of a question-begging vicious circle. In discussing specific cases, the result may go either way: verificationists may concede that we can see how to decide a given case, or realists agree that it really has no truth conditions.[5] Yet the general question remains about our belief system as a whole: might we conceivably be wrong, even if we could never discover the fact? Here intuitions may still be in flat contrast.

Now we meet a further claim, that at the ideal limit we transcend the externalist-internalist distinction itself. For suppose we imagine an ideal scientific theory or, in general, an ideal state of knowledge. In such a case, no gap between investigation and fact could arise, or else the theory would not be ideal. Here, though only here, it is said, verifiability and truth must merge.[6] Yet though I too hope to transcend the realist-idealist tension, I am not convinced by this argument. For are we or are we not to suppose we can *know* our understanding is ideal? To know it, we would need a God's-eye view of the universe. Yet in rejecting foundationalism we deny that any elements of our knowledge are infallible, so we must *a fortiori* deny we could know we were in such an overall state. Any use of "true" based on that assumption would make little contact with how we actually use the word. The alternative is that our theory merely is *in fact* ideal, that it will meet all challenges though we do not know this in advance. That seems an intelligible conjecture. But then we should still take seriously the possibility that our investigations might have missed the truth, so we would need the distinction between justified belief and truth. Thus this dissolving of the tension seems to me in the end either useless or false: useless if it speaks of what we could not get, false if it speaks of what we could.

In short, the realist platitude that the world is as it is independently of what we know about it, surely extends even to what we *could* not know about it. Though as with all complex significance-judgments there is no logical bludgeon to crush any view, I believe that idealist views truncate the meaning of truth. The externalist concept seems the one we actually have; I have sketched how we can form it by abstraction, and have indicated why we need it, so I endorse it as correct.[7]

  The general notion of a realist or externalist theory of truth has, however, often been confused with the more specific one of a correspondence theory. For surely if "The cat is on the mat" is true, that is because it corresponds to the fact that it is on the mat. Yet, even putting aside the idealist objection that we cannot get outside our belief system to compare it to reality, there are overwhelming objections to any such simple theory. One type arises from considering statements other than simple indicative ones. Suppose it to be true that if we had offered the cat some fish it would have left the mat; to what fact does that correspond? Must we acknowledge hypothetical, general, negative, etc., facts to which such truths correspond?[8] That certainly weakens the initial appeal of the theory. But a more relevant objection is a second type, found both in neo-Hegelianism and in analytic philosophy of science. Consider how we modify and transcend conceptual sub-systems. Words can express many beliefs, and carry a heavier load of meaning than is needed for any one of them, so we get problems of how far we "mean the same thing" when our words are enmeshed in overlapping structures.   19th century chemists developed much knowledge through the false Daltonian theory of atoms as basic, unsplittable constituents of matter. When they correctly identified combinations of atoms, surely they uttered truths? Then did they know the facts to which their statements corresponded, or what their terms referred to? If we say "No", we must acknowledge that we, too, probably do not know what we refer to; for it is overwhelmingly likely that our current scientific notions will also eventually be revised. But if we say "Yes", we must say that they (and by analogy we) could state truths, though their beliefs about what those truths corresponded to were radically mistaken. Such problems also arise in other contexts. Whenever we have an effective praxis but no adequate theory, we may believe our sentences express truths, without being equally sure what their terms refer to. Or again, when language is used in poetry or religion, it may often be agreed that something true is being said, but the question of what the statements actually correspond to, and how far they are metaphorical, may be just the issue.

  In short, the model for correspondence is how a simple indicative statement relates to the world. One type of difficulty arises because we use language for so much more than this, and another type from our continual transcendence of belief structures. I suggest that, in delimited contexts where we take our conceptual framework for granted, the structure of our language is seen as the structure of the facts in the world, and it is often harmless to say, at least with indicative sentences, that the one corresponds to the other. But in other contexts this cannot apply, either because the structure is more complex, as with non-indicatives, or because the framework is itself under question. Thus the truth of a statement may sometimes be partly independent of precisely what its terms correspond to in reality. Even if a more sophisticated correspondence theory might meet these difficulties, it would remain only one specific version of an externalist theory. So, though I have endorsed externalism, I can remain neutral about correspondence.

3. Reality

Another concept on the fault line between realism and idealism is that of reality. Though it, like truth, is often used by philosophers, unlike truth it is rarely examined in the analytic tradition. There has been some inconclusive discussion of its role in ordinary language, but here I only outline some points for which I have argued elsewhere.[9] "Reality" is used untechnically to refer to whatever exists ("Reality impinges on the retina of the eye in the form of light rays which..."), and here it endorses the realist platitude of an independent world. But as soon as we reflect, philosophical problems lie beneath the surface. Does reality have features apart from those our nervous system presents? If so, how do we know it does? Or is it, perhaps, an unknown somewhat, forever inaccessible behind the information filtered through our nervous system? When philosophers ask such questions about "the nature of reality", their concept seems to have a more complex meaning. Here we easily build into it features which reflect our own philosophical views, but we must resist that temptation. For unless opponents mean the same thing by the word, even though they offer different accounts of what reality is, they can hardly hope to avoid vicious circles. We need a sufficiently neutral vocabulary: in this case, an analysis of what philosophers mean by "reality", which will not beg questions about what they take its nature to be.

Now we meet the classic hermeneutic problem of mutualistically interpreting a word by its context, while the context consists of all other uses of the word. We must be true to the textual material, which is the whole corpus of philosophical writing about reality, while still being prepared to overrule some remarks as misuses. The result is, I believe, that sometimes, particularly when writers focus on ontology, or theories of what exists, "reality" may mean simply "what exists". But typically it has a further element: it means "*what exists, as rightly conceived*".[10] It is in this sense that philosophers debate the nature of reality, by which they mean the correct overall conception of what exists. This applies both to constructivist and to criticalist views. Constructivism aims to present overviews that conceive reality rightly. For criticalism, the right conception is the metathesis that overviews are beyond our grasp.

My present concern, however, is that in the realist-idealist dispute these meanings of "reality" may produce confusion. "What there is", which we find in untechnical contexts and sometimes in ontology, is an externalist concept, and so may initially attract realists. "What exists, as rightly conceived" makes reference to an actual or hypothetical understanding, and so is internalist. In my view the second concept is philosophically more basic, and I shall use it from now on. But it need not favor idealism. For realists may accept it, but say that we rightly conceive what exists when we see that it is independent of our conception of it.

I have examined some externalist and internalist analyses of concepts that cluster round the fault line between realism and idealism. I take justification to be an internalist notion, despite reliabilist analyses, and truth to be an externalist one, despite verificationist ones. Reality has, I think, two uses, but the more important one makes an internalist reference to our conception of the world. While I have not examined the complexity of current debates, their persistence manifests, I believe, an underlying issue. What attracts philosophers to different answers is often the hope of vindicating realism or idealism. But the hope is always dashed, for no matter what answer we give to specific issues, the clash reappears in new forms. This is the problem I now face.

4. The Nature of the Debate

As a first step, we must ask what *sort* of debate the realist-idealist one is, and what sort of answer we can expect. Issues like this arise when we employ concepts at the limits of their applicability, rather than in usual contexts. Just as we often ask whether a particular belief is justified, but a skeptic pushes this question to the limit and asks whether *any* of our beliefs are *ever* justified: so here we often ask whether our beliefs properly represent how things are, but now we are asking whether *as a whole* they match reality. Any answer to such a limit question must involve, I believe, what we might broadly call an analogy, or model, or metaphor; I use "model" to cover them all. Essentially, we take a structure found in one area of our thought, and use it as a guide in articulating a broader intelligendum. In itself, this is only one example of a common pattern; it also applies, for example, to the forming of scientific hypotheses. For in general, if we transcend an intelligendum by taking some aspect of its form and making it the subject matter of new reflection, the form must be there, however previously unnoticed; and how else could our understanding expand? But in the case of limit notions, I shall speak of the chosen models as *master-models*. Their special feature is that we take something *within* experience as a clue to answering a question about experience *as a whole*. For example, the skeptical model is the need for due care in reasoning, which it uses as a master-model by extending it to the limit case in such a way that no knowledge is possible.

Here we meet a new point about the constructivist-criticalist debate. We might first think that, while constructivism must use a master-model to produce an overview, criticalism will reject all appeal to such models as extending reason beyond its proper bounds. Many criticalist arguments do appear to do so, but the position is more complex. Criticalism, in saying there is no adequate decision procedure for judging between overviews, is as much a claim about our thought as a whole, as are constructivist attempts to provide them; so it, too, needs a master-model. Certainly an alternative strategy would be to present no argument that overviews are impossible, but merely to allege specific objections to those actually offered. We may do this without implying any view about the limits of thought as such, and so without using a master-model. But then we can hardly show we have considered and rejected every relevant candidate, let alone those that might arise in the future. Further, the more success we claim, the more we invite the question *why* overviews all fail; and unless we refuse to answer that question at all, our explanation must involve some criticalist master-model that applies to all limit questions. In fact, I believe, all significant criticalist views do use master-models. The most basic one is when we hold that some accepted pattern of explanation only provides answers to questions that are themselves wrongly posed; as when some 17th century Europeans began to reject astrology because it explained how our destinies were linked to the stars, when they no longer believed they were. Here we reject a whole *type* of explanation, by denying what it presupposes. If we apply this to limit questions as such, and say that all their answers are only pseudo-explanations, then it becomes a criticalist master-model. In Chapter XIV I assess the strength of this sort of argument.

Meanwhile, qualifications are necessary. First, I do not say that an answer to a limit question can have only one master-model. But I believe that in fact we can often detect one key principle, and that isolating it for examination may be a useful element in our overall assessment. Next, I do not suggest that constructivist or criticalist master-models need be consciously held by those who apply them. Even our most rigorous thought reflects assumptions that we have absorbed from our culture, so a pattern that seems to link together much in our knowledge may be used to answer limit questions without explicitly treating it as a guiding principle. Hence, finally, the attempt to identify the model that a thinker has used is a difficult critical enterprise, which may be illuminating, but may also mislead. For example, the claim that Western epistemology is modelled on the role of spectator rather than participant provokes intense debate about whether it is an insight or a distortion.

Now, however, I aim, not to identify the master-models of others, but to offer one of my own. Applying the previous discussion to the realist-idealist debate, the implication is that, whether we aim at the victory of one of them, at rejecting the problem as an intellectual confusion, or—as I do—at resolving what I take to be a fundamental tension in our thought, the argument will rest on a model. We are not dealing in mere metaphors, though all models involve an extension which may initially be metaphorical. The choice is not between metaphor and literal, or even between live and dead metaphor; it is between a conscious model which we can try to control, and an unconscious one which will implicitly control our thought. I shall introduce, and try to control, what I see as the best master-model for overcoming the realist-idealist tension, and for understanding the relation of thought to reality.

5. The Aspect Model

I noted in Ch. II.7(a) that multiple sub-systems of understanding present different aspects of intelligenda. "Aspect" is the key word here. It is originally a visual term, meaning a perspective from which we see something: from this aspect, the square table appears as a rhombus. But it is now mostly used as a very dead metaphor. In its usual meaning, an aspect of a given item is *the significance that it has within a sub-system of our understanding*, so the notion floats, with sub- and super-systems and aspects. In the sense in which mutualism is an interaction between whole and part, an aspect is part of a whole. But in a narrower sense "part" contrasts with "aspect"; here a part is what can in principle be detached, like a leg of the table, while aspects, such as the condition of the table, can only be conceptually distinguished.

The concept of an aspect is neglected in analytic philosophy,[11] but as a floating term it enters into my argument in many ways . I have emphasized that all reasoning is from a standpoint, and in a broader sense any standpoint represents only one aspect of a situation. Again, I noted in Ch. III.4 how styles of criticism function more as complementary insights than as rival theories, and this is because they capture aspects of a work of art which do not exhaust its total reality. "Aspect" may also provide a neutral vocabulary for debating various issues; for example, the debate about the primacy of individual or of group may be posed by asking which aspect of individual-group interaction is the more significant. Again, the word reminds us that there are aspects of our understanding of which we are not conscious. The notion also relates praxis to understanding. Successful activity shows that our standpoint has some appropriate relation to reality; but still we may, say, make successful predictions with what turns out to be a false theory. So success does not show the theory is true as formulated, but shows it captures some aspect of reality. Finally, the aspectual nature of understanding underlies my whole argument in Ch. X. To pose an issue is to conceive a situation under an aspect that presents a problem; objections to our views come from those who see different aspects of the situation; to resolve the issue is to reconcile those aspects; and by assuming that conflicting views may each capture aspects of reality, we may slowly turn vicious circles into beneficent ones. As a general formula: inquiry reveals the aspect of reality that corresponds to our question. What we find depends on what we look for, though normally it would be there whether we looked for it or not.

I now take this notion of an aspect as it functions *within* ordinary thought, as a master-model for understanding the realist-idealist debate about relation between thought and reality *as a whole*. First, if we take "aspect" where it is at home, before we use it as a model, it captures both the externalist and the internalist platitudes that underlie realism and idealism. It has an externalist dimension, both in the original visual sense and in the usual non-visual one, because we see aspects of what exists independently of us. It is the table itself, and not our experience of it, that is in good condition, etc. Yet an aspect of anything, being the significance it has within a sub-system of understanding, is an internalist notion that implies an actual or hypothetical consciousness. So it also reminds us that we cannot get outside our belief system to compare it to reality. Now let us take this notion of an aspect as a master-model for the limit question of the relation of thought to reality. As we continually examine different aspects of a given intelligendum, or as disciplines present their own aspect of a phenomenon: so, I suggest, our total belief system should be seen as presenting to us an aspect of reality, as compared to other aspects which might be grasped by other people, by ourselves if our consciousness should radically change, or by non-human beings. Since we know only a small part of what we could in principle know, I can summarize the claim in a formula: we know *an aspect of a part of reality*. One implication is that what we investigate is really there; so I reject those theories mentioned in Ch. VII.3, which doubt whether our senses give us true contact with reality. Again, aspects can be illusory; so though a statement claims to present an aspect of an independently existing reality, I agree, as in my treatment of skepticism, that our whole belief system might conceivably be wrong. But my reply has been that unless some actual mad-scientist case arises, we need not take seriously the mere logical possibility of a gap between the coherence by which we judge truth and the truth itself, apart from our normal corrections. A final implication is that there may be aspects of reality forever hidden from us, because our minds are incapable of grasping them. I accept that this, too, reflects the nature of reality and the limits of understanding.

In all these ways, the externalist and the internalist platitudes, which are at the heart of realism and idealism, are preserved. Yet I noted in Sec. 1 that realism and idealism are often defined as contradictories, so I may be asked which of them I ultimately accept. My reply is what we must always say if we have so transcended an intelligendum that we can no longer work within it: that its terms are ambiguous. Reality—what there is, as rightly conceived—is mind-independent, as realists say, in the sense that it has existed long before us, it will outlast us, and its features do not in general depend on our being aware of them. It is mind-dependent, as idealists say, in the sense that a right conception of it (including the aspects of it that realists emphasize) can only reflect the capacities of our belief system. Realists make a first-order point about how our concept of reality applies to the world: namely, that the world does not depend on our knowing it. Idealists make a second-order point about the concept itself: that any concept, including this one, can only have the content which our belief system gives it. It is mixing the orders which produces confusion. So if I am asked: "Does reality have the features we attribute to it?", my reply is: "Yes. For, apart from mistakes, what we know is an aspect of it. But what other aspects it may have I do not know. And if you ask me what it is like independently of all aspects under which we might grasp it, you must give a sense to that question before I can answer it."[12]

In general, we can conceive reality only through a belief system, but one belief in any normal system is that reality is independent of us. This is what the platitudes safeguard. As with the form-matter distinction, reality and belief system are linked concepts where each requires the other. Reality is not an formless somewhat, nor does our belief system impose pure form on unstructured matter. If realists so emphasize the mind-independence of reality that they forget the idealist point, they seem to say our understanding of the world is not structured by the selectivity of our senses and belief systems. If idealists present their second-order point as a first-order one about what exists, they seem to say the world is so mind-dependent that it would not exist without minds. By using the aspect model, and keeping first- and second-order remarks distinct, I believe we can avoid such unfortunate suggestions, while doing full justice to the basic insights of both realism and idealism.

Finally: some forms of idealism, usually with either Hegelian or Eastern roots, may be seen as insisting, as I do, that we cannot conceive reality independently of an aspect, and that the notion of an aspect carries an implicit reference to a consciousness. Then, accepting the externalist platitude that the world exists independently of us, they conclude that, though reality is as independent of *human* consciousness as realists claim, it presupposes an *absolute* consciousness. On this consciousness all finite things depend, our consciousnesses are aspects of it, and it includes and transcends all aspects. This claim has affinities, as well as tensions, with traditional Western religious ones, where God is at least like such an absolute consciousness. But I can take a minimalist position here. In my argument, the notion of an aspect presupposes only a *hypothetical*, not an actual, consciousness. We could consistently hold, either that our consciousness is indeed an aspect of a divine one, or that it is an unplanned by-product of an evolutionary process, or else adopt some other alternative. However vital an issue this may be for attempts at constructing an overview, for the purpose of transcending the conflict between realism and idealism we can leave it aside.

ENDNOTES

[1] So such issues arise as whether the world really consist of material objects, as our conceptual scheme indicates, and whether they have all their qualities or only the primary ones, etc.

[2] The closest parallel to my own view that I have seen is W. M. Urban's underdiscussed book *Beyond Realism and Idealism* (1949).

[3] I confine myself to assertions that *physical* reality is mind-independent, and ignore, e.g., Platonist views that ideas are independently existing entities which are non-mental, though also non-physical.

[4] Early Positivism claimed that truth the notion for formal systems, which, he claimed, captured the correspondence intuition. (A. Tarski "The Semantic Conception of Truth" (1944), reprinted in H. Feigl and W. Sellars *Readings in Philosophical Analysis* (1949) pp. 52-84.) If, he showed, we take a statement p, and give it a name "p" (which can be the same words as the sentence, but in quotation marks), we can define truth by saying that "p" is true if and only if p: "snow is white" is true if and only if snow is white. This has led to programs of truth conditional semantics that aim to explicate the concept of meaning in terms of reference and of Tarskian truth. I bypass not only these complex debates, but also the redundancy theory. The latter avoids the problems of externalist theories by claiming that the use of "true" lies not in relating sentences to the world, but within language—e.g., by endorsing what is said when we say "That's true". Because I am committed to externalism, I cannot take this path.

[5] Thus it seems that some counterfactuals have no truth conditions, so the issue of what these conditions are turns out not properly to arise.

[6] This view was presented by the previously staunch realist Putnam. See "Realism and Reason" in H. Putnam *Meaning and the Moral Sciences* (1978). His reluctant following of what seemed to him of the wind of the argument has provoked a bitter reaction from those who felt betrayed by the change.

[7] I have defined my view against standard coherence ones, but S. Blackburn *Spreading the Word* (1984) has suggested (pp. 249-250) that a coherence (or neo-coherence?) theory might allow for these points. I would have no objection. The more that non-realist and realist approaches tended to converge on the view expressed in Sec. 4, the better.

[8] The *locus classicus* for this sort of issue is Bertrand Russell's lectures on Logical Atomism. See R. C. Marsh (ed.) *op. cit.*

[9] See my "The Concept of Reality" *Aust. Jnl. Philos.* (vol. 64, 1986, 158-169), which also contains further references to the scanty literature. I now place rather more emphasis on the "what exists" analysis of reality.

[10] "The Concept of Reality", *passim*. Actually that formula could, I think, be caught in an even shorter one: reality is *how things are*. That there are these things is "what exists", and how they hang together is the right conception of them.

[11] N. Rescher *Cognitive Systematization* (1979) has a brief discussion on pp. 23-26, but many issues remain.

[12] I do not discuss here whether any context could give it a sense.

CHAPTER XIII

PRACTICAL REASON: FACTS, VALUES AND TRUTH

1. Practical Reason

I now turn to an issue I have often foreshadowed: the nature of practical reason. The line between practice and theory is drawn in various places: Ryle's concept of knowing *how* and knowing *that* (Ch. VIII.5) is very different from a casuist's elaboration of a moral system, and both differ again from what is often said about "values" when they are contrasted to "facts"; yet all these may be called practical as opposed to theoretical contexts. I believe there is no one right distinction, since what is vital for one standpoint may be unimportant for another. But while we may choose where to draw the line, we must draw it rightly for our purpose, and also be alert for unexamined assumptions. For my purpose of examining how we can expand rational agreement, the important difference lies in the project: theoretical reasoning asks what is the case, practical reasoning asks what to do.[1] I bypass complex philosophical debates, and focus on just two themes: first, the scope of practical reason, in the sense of asking how effective reason can be in practical matters; and, second, the relation of practical reasoning to the concept of truth. As elsewhere, I focus centrally on my own philosophical tradition.

During this century, analytic philosophy has undergone radical changes in its attitudes to my two themes. It has focused overwhelmingly on ethics or moral philosophy, which is by no means the whole of practical reason, but is the vital part for our purposes.[2] The first analytic philosophers did not doubt that moral judgments, like ordinary statements of fact, were either true or false, but they faced two problems. First, they insisted that such judgments are *overriding*, in the sense of saying what we should do despite all other considerations. We might balance caution against risk, or one aspect of self-interest against another; but if such matters came into conflict with moral obligation, then even to ask how to balance the two was already a crucial mistake. So, it seemed, any reasoning that tried to justify moral judgments by appealing to benefits which might come to us from keeping them, was totally confused. The second point was that, unlike ordinary statements, the truth of such judgments could not be established by sensory observation. If we scrutinized every detail of a knife going in to a victim's body, we still could not in this way see the wrongness of the act. Both points suggested that morality could not be

supported by other sorts of reasoning or evidence. So, since these philosophers had strong moral convictions that seemed to them clearly correct, their
conclusion was ethical intuitionism: that moral judgments depend simply on
the fact that on reflection "we" find we have these convictions.[3]   Morality
deals with "non-natural" facts that can be grasped only by an act of intellectual
intuition, as opposed to the natural facts that observation can establish.[4]
Moral philosophy must establish this point, must report what the intuitions
were, and must battle our perpetual temptation to confuse morality with something else. There was little else for it to do.

Later, however, the Positivist impact on analytic philosophy produced a
radical challenge. What if appeals to intuition gave different results? An
intuitionist could only assert that rival views were blind to the truth. But,
Positivism insisted, truth claims are appropriate only when we can see in
principle how issues might be resolved. Appeals to intuition are no answer.
Moral judgments, they concluded, are unverifiable not because they report
special facts, but because they do not report facts at all. For there is a basic
distinction between facts and values. We cannot legitimately derive evaluative
conclusions from factual premises, or obtain "ought's" from "is's".

At this point, the two sides agreed on the limitations of practical reasoning,
but differed over whether there was moral truth and knowledge. Intuitionism
said: "We can give no reasons for moral judgments, we just know them to be
true". Positivism said: "There is nothing true to be known here, so we can
give no reasons for moral judgments". As Positivist trends prevailed,
discussion centered on what moral judgments were, given that they did not
state facts. With the two key terms of "good" and "ought", did "good" merely
express our sense of approval, or was "ought" merely a disguised imperative
that told us what to do; and if not, what were they? But later analytic
philosophy came to doubt precisely the earlier conclusion that moral reasoning
was so limited. For surely it was not all mere rhetoric or irrational persuasion?
So typically today we find what are often called "good reasons" approaches.
These say in various ways that we can give better reasons for some moral
views than for others, even though moral judgments do not state non-natural
facts, and are not, strictly speaking, either true or false.[5]

This is my background in discussing the two themes of the scope of practical
reason and its relation to truth. I assume that, however varied the contexts in
which we use moral judgments, they are a part of practical reason, and that
their basic point lies in guiding our actions. I shall agree that practical reason
has a larger role than Positivist or intuitionist views allowed, though I accept
that moral judgments cannot in any strict sense be true or false. So the crucial
question is: what is left for reason to appeal to, in debating these or any other
issues of practical reason? Here my two themes impact strongly on each
other. I begin with the point that Positivism brought into analytic philosophy,

but which was itself borrowed from earlier discussions elsewhere: the distinction between facts and values.

2. Fact, Value and Understanding

In Enlightenment thought, one thread held, like the first analytic intuitionists, that reason could grasp universal foundations in morals as elsewhere. "We hold these truths to be self-evident", the American Declaration of Independence could proclaim, and the truths in question were moral ones. But another thread, namely the admiration for science as a paradigm of reliable knowledge, led in a different direction. Science, which meant the natural sciences, seemed to establish facts which were independent of individual bias or cultural background, and so were free from contaminating evaluations. The second thread easily suggests that the discovery of facts is one thing, and the holding of values is another. So it led, through complex developments, to the view that there was a sharp dichotomy between facts and values.

The fact/value dichotomy is one way to approach the distinction between theoretical and practical reasoning: facts belong to the theoretical side, while our practice reflects our values. It is related to the distinction made in Ch. IV.4 between statements and evaluations, where "statement" extends from simple reports of observations to complex hypothetical potentialities, and "evaluations" covers wishes, goals, obligations, etc. But we must be alert to where the differences lie. The theoretical/practical distinction rests on whether we are reasoning about what is the case or what to do; the statement /evaluation one is basically a linguistic classification in terms of the type of utterance; and the fact/value one expresses the conviction that we can distinguish sheer facts—particularly scientific ones—from pure values.

In analytic moral philosophy, the third, fact/value distinction was closely examined and found to be more difficult than it might seem. For statements in ordinary language commonly carry an evaluative as well as a factual component; for example, "He is an honest man" seems both to state that he tends to behave in certain ways, and also to evaluate the tendency favorably. At best, the distinction seemed to be a logical skeleton often disguised beneath the softer flesh of ordinary language. Outside philosophy, the distinction was widely accepted, and led to the belief that the social sciences should be value-free: they could explain the *fact that* people hold certain values, but should not judge the values themselves. Yet how was this principle to be applied? Clearly, social scientists accepted the values presupposed by all scientific inquiry, such as the obligation to report results honestly; and also, like any scientist, they had to evaluate their evidence. Certainly, one thing they meant was that their work should be free from *other* values, such as partisan bias;

but, if they really stuck to factual inquiries, how could they defend their choice of "good" scientific values over "bad" biassed ones? Conversely, critics could correctly point out that social science can never be value free, for all inquiry at least presupposes the values that make it worth undertaking. But when does this become a criticism? Only, perhaps, if it unmasks a hidden agenda of other values, such as a disguised and undue support of the current social order. For such reasons, there is intense debate today over the fact/value dichotomy. And though valuable points may have been made by using that terminology, my own approach, in common with many others today, forces us to rethink it.

Take first the concept of a fact. All observation and inquiry is made from a standpoint, and the facts we discover will, like our standpoint, represent only an aspect of reality. Calling something a fact, like calling a statement true, claims that this is how things are independently of our beliefs; but still it is at best one aspect of how things are, though if the standpoint is taken for granted we may believe we simply see what is there. Adopting a standpoint involves an evaluation of reality, whether conscious or unconscious. Fact and evaluation are complementary notions rather than a sharp dichotomy. Articulation, whether theoretical or practical, must focus on what is relevant if its selective description is to be illuminating; and to do so it must evaluate the situation. This applies as much to scientific inquiries as to others. To approach a situation from the standpoint of a relevant science is to evaluate it in a highly specific way. Further, the scientific standpoint requires its own values, such as the need to report data correctly and to control for bias and wishful thinking. Scientific explanation ranks among the greatest of our cultural achievements; but its skill lies precisely in the evaluation of a situation, which gives the relevant insight. Moreover, the scientific standpoint is as embedded in its culture as any other, so the question of what cultural conditions gave rise to it and support it, is a legitimate and important one. If, as the Enlightenment thought, science is particularly free of distorting evaluations, and so is uniquely placed to correct our prejudices, that is not because it is free from values, but because it has, and at its best applies, an appropriate set of them.

On the other side of the fact/value dichotomy, value judgments have often been the intellectual poor relation, the suppressed other of a binary opposite. Though moral philosophers and others have examined their nature in various contexts, for many science-based views they have seemed a sort of puzzling, though doubtless indispensable, non-fact. This was how Positivism could hold that reasoning was essentially restricted to theoretical contexts, and hence that the scope of practical reason was so limited. Yet, though we speak of values in so many contexts that we can give no neat definition, I suggest they are essentially what *assigns a priority*. By doing so, they give significance to a situation, and so are relevant to action—whether in the conduct of theoretical inquiry or in our decisions about what to do. Thus values, too, presuppose a

standpoint that makes facts significant. If facts state how things are, values give them significance—in each case, from a standpoint.[6]

In short, fact, value, standpoint and significance are a package deal: no fact except as it appears from a standpoint; no value unlinked to a standpoint that relates it to facts; no standpoint that is not a theoretical-practical mixture which makes facts significant. In our reasoning, the central distinction is not between facts and values, but between what is and is not at issue. Debates start from agreement, which is the overlap in standpoints. This includes both what we take as facts, and the shared values by which we give them significance. Sometimes it might be tempting to describe certain conflicts —such as the contrast mentioned in Ch. II.9 between the attitudes of Gadamer and much sociology towards social conditioning—as cases where the parties simply assign opposite values to agreed facts. But even these are really contrasting standpoints, with enough agreement to accept some facts, but enough difference to give them opposite significance. Whether the issues are factual or evaluative, what we meet are complex vicious circles, that might eventually become beneficent ones. To examine this, let us look at both the similarities of, and the differences between, theoretical and practical reason.

3. Theoretical and Practical Reason: Similarities

In considering the power of theoretical and practical reason respectively, the difference lies in the project: whether we reason about what is the case or about what to do. This cannot coincide with the fact/value contrast. For, since all inquiry involves significance-judgments, we have not only practical values about what we should do, but also theoretical or intellectual ones governing the investigation of how things are, such as the desirability of facing the truth. In fact, as we found with the causal and justificatory modes, theoretical and practical reasoning each provide standpoints from which the other can be assessed. The social sciences may ask the theoretical question of why we hold given values; but reasoning is also something we do, and we may examine the values involved in doing it. My approach treats theory-making as one sort of practice, namely that of reasoning about what is the case. In doing so, it focuses on the underlying fact is that we are beings who must live in the world. Even our perception selects information in ways that developed because of their survival value, and our brains have evolved so we can use this information to live. If we acquire, as one of our values, the theoretical goal of understanding how things are, this is still guided by selection of what is significant for that purpose.

If we focus in this way on reasoning as an activity that we undertake, some basic similarities between theoretical and practical reasoning at once emerge.

Theoretical articulation works towards coherence by seeing the significance of one element for others. We start from accepted beliefs, and when we meet differences we may hope to move through vicious circles to beneficent ones. This effortlessly carries over to practical cases. The overlapping standpoints from which we start contain shared values as well as factual beliefs. In discussing whether democracy can properly restrict some sorts of speech, neither the worth of freedom nor the need to preserve order are normally in dispute; in debating abortion, both freedom of choice and the sanctity of human life are agreed values. Conflicts articulate the values differently: how to draw the line in reconciling freedom and order, whether a fetus attracts the status of a living human. The parallels extend further. In practical as well as theoretical contexts, reason can be creative. Gandhi's program of non-violent confrontation transcended what had seemed exclusive alternatives of violent rebellion or acceptance of political injustice; and though it later produced its own problems, that also parallels the growth of new theoretical issues. Between cultures, the parameters of debate may differ more radically than they normally do within a community, but that again is true in theoretical cases. Our beliefs about the nature of the world may differ from those of pre-scientific societies more than do our moral ones.

Besides the point that all reasoning starts from, and depends upon, agreement, something else also underlies these similarities. It is that understanding is many-levelled. In theoretical contexts, information is structured into increasingly abstract levels of facts and generalizations; in practical ones, immediate desires are similarly structured into higher-level objectives and principles of action. Our reasoning largely concerns the relations between levels, as we adjust relevant considerations. It is in the many-levelled complexity of the process of articulation that we find the parallels between theoretical and practical reason.

4. Theoretical and Practical Reason: Differences

After the similarities, I turn to the differences. First, emotion is often more prominent in practical reasoning, because precious values are more often threatened. When emotion replaces rational discussion, this easily suggests that value judgments are *nothing but* expressions of emotion.[7] But this is a confusion. Emotional attitudes are not confined to practical issues, and pure mathematicians may defend their viewpoint as stubbornly as the most bigoted moralist. Conversely, some people can reason calmly about matters very dear to their hearts. Certainly this is so difficult an attitude that, to those who feel their values under threat, this whole discussion of the scope of practical reasoning may seem remote and academic. But still, whether emotion eliminates reason is a fact about the reasoner, not about the type of reasoning.

A second difference concerns one of the three possible outcomes of rational inquiry, namely the postponing of an issue when we have no adequate grounds to decide it. Even in theoretical cases this is a sophisticated attitude, and many people accept the flimsiest evidence rather than leaving a question open. But with practical reason there is a further point. Refraining from forming a belief is not a belief; but refraining from acting is, in an important sense, an action, for it competes with potential decisions to act differently. Hence we must often act on less evidence than would rationally justify a belief.[8] Yet this is itself a rational principle, and does not mark a great distinction in the scope of reason.

Next, in practical contexts we meet issues where, though very basic principles may be generally acceptable, there is no calculus to resolve them. A crucial case is conflict between narrower and wider loyalties. Surely parents owe their children more concern than they do to strangers? Yet if they should help the destitute only after all legitimate family desires are fully met, they will never help them. How should we strike the balance? Or if the overall purposes of groups are in dispute—say, where a cultural minority seeks independence—mere agreement on the desirability of freedom and of order cannot itself generate a satisfactory solution. With such cases, my point at this stage is only that we should neither suggest, as some existentialists do, that all cases are like this, nor claim, like some systems of casuistry, that we can solve them by applying cut-and-dried moral principles. There are agonizing cases for any sensitive moral standpoint, but not all cases are equally difficult.

All this, however, only leads up to what I have foreshadowed as the second theme for this Chapter: the relation of practical reason to truth. Theoretical investigation in principle aims at reaching the truth about an independently existing reality. But practical reasoning centers on what to do, and so on the articulation of desires, principles and obligations. No matter how important the parallels and interactions between the two, this is a radical difference. If my goals conflict with yours, we might negotiate an acceptable settlement; we might even call it a true reconciliation. But this is not what theoretical reason means by truth, for it does not claim to state how things are *independently* of our beliefs. So if there is no appeal to belief-independent truth, what can reason aim at? We meet a crucial question: is the distinction between statements, which are true or false, and evaluations, which are not, in the end more important for the purpose of understanding understanding, than is the theoretical/practical one which is based on our project in reasoning?

5. Truth and Objectivity

In discussing this issue, I start from the concept of objectivity outlined in

Ch. IV.5: objective claims are where a sincere belief may still be mistaken, while others are subjective. I said there that, while "true" is an objective notion, it is strongly tied to statements about how things are; but by distinguishing it from objectivity, we can leave open whether utterances other than statements can be objective. This point is central to the "good reasons" approaches to ethics mentioned in Sec. 1. For in this way we can accept the view that value judgments, including moral ones, are not statements that are literally true or false, and still leave open the question of their objectivity.[9]

This approach has complex implications for my earlier discussion of knowledge. I said in Ch. VIII.5 that "analytic philosophy acknowledges, but rarely examines, the existence of practical knowledge". Yet if we treat knowledge as justified true belief, and if value judgments are neither true nor false, there can be no practical knowledge. One way to approach the problem would be to note that we do in fact speak of beliefs as including value judgments as well as facts.[10] If we accept this, we could try to develop a concept of practical understanding and knowledge as justified *objective* practical beliefs, that would parallel justified *true* theoretical beliefs, and the two might then be integrated into a coherent overall analysis of both types. But there are other possible approaches, and a large and technical discussion would be needed. For present purposes, the crucial question is simply whether value judgments can be objective. If they can, the further question of whether and how we should speak of practical knowledge is one I can leave aside.

So are moral judgments objective? Can they be mistaken, rather than being merely the assertion of convictions, or the issuing of instructions, with which we may happen to agree or disagree? Here I first note a significant parallel between the logic of such words as "true" and "real" in theoretical contexts, and "good" and "ought" in practical ones. They float in a particular way; they have, we may say, specific content or matter, but transcendent form. They have specific content, in the sense that we take some statements to be true, some goals good, etc. But they also have a formal element, that depends on our capacity to transcend. We build into them the possibility of being applied *in the same sense* to new things, and no longer to some of the old ones; for we know in advance that, if we were to change our values or factual beliefs, we would call the new ones good or true respectively. An externalist analysis of truth may grant we can apply the word only on internalist grounds, but builds into it the possibility of our being wrong about how things are. The parallel point with "good" is that any proposed content, such as a moral principle or belief, cannot be identified with goodness. For if we were later to reject it by articulating our beliefs in another way, we would say that we no longer accepted it as good.[11] Similarly with "ought", we need it because our levels of values restrict, as well as create, possibilities of action. If we merely followed immediate desires, we would not need oughts; but when we have stable higher-level priorities that are not up for revision with every passing whim, we say we ought to do what they indicate. So "ought", too, has specific content but also a built-in possibility of revision; if our values altered, it would apply in the same sense to different commitments.

These parallels indicate that we talk as if there were objectivity in practical as well as theoretical contexts, for in each case the logical grammar allows the possibility that our present beliefs may be mistaken. But we could explain this in terms of the many levels of understanding. If we are to articulate evaluations at different levels, as we surely must, we need language that allows correction of lower-level ones, irrespective of whether there is any *ultimate* objectivity. So the fact that our language is structured to suggest objectivity, is still compatible with the view that in the end we have no rational way to choose between moral positions. Whether we call that possibility moral relativism, or skepticism, or ultimate subjectivity, it may seem to arise in practical contexts in a way we can avoid in theoretical ones.[12]

6. The Dispensability of Theories

For those trying to answer this challenge, a natural strategy is to look for an adequate overall theory of practical reason. For if we can find one, we may hope in principle to answer disagreements by appealing to it, while if we cannot, the value of practical reasoning seems threatened. As the crucial questions concern our ultimate, overriding values, what we need, it may seem, is an overall theory to justify morality and explain why we should act morally. This is what we typically find in good reasons approaches to ethics. Attempted answers, I believe, fall into families, though specific views may have mixed ancestry.[13] One family, which includes intuitionism, says that even asking why we should be moral already makes the key mistake. For it assumes we must show how morality would *pay* us, and hence wrongly tries to base it on self-interest. Another family appeals to the basic principle underlying both theoretical and practical reasoning, that like cases should be treated alike. This leads us to ask what criteria of likeness are relevant to our articulation. Its thrust in moral contexts is to challenge our temptation to make exceptions in our own favor. To seek my own advantage while admitting that, if all others sought theirs, then society, and I with it, would collapse, is seen as a completely irrational case of wanting to eat my cake and have it too. So morality is seen as the voice of reason, the only reasonable way to behave. A third family looks to the satisfaction of our wants. It aims to balance them so as to maximize some goal, which is usually taken to be the greatest happiness of all concerned. Finally, a fourth family appeals to the notion of self-understanding. If, it says, we can penetrate to our own deepest and perhaps unconscious *needs*, rather than our mere wants, we will find that only a certain type of living in harmony with ourselves and others will truly allow us to flourish.[14]

Each of the four families claims to present the underlying justification of morality. Behind them lies the recurring drive to articulate all knowledge into a whole, which also appears in constructivist metaphysics. Their merits and defects, and their criticisms of each other, form the staple diet of much moral philosophy, and have produced valuable insights. But my concern is that discussion often proceeds on the assumption that if we cannot find an ultimate moral principle, we are left with subjectivity. Yet that assumption essentially parallels the foundationalism which, in theoretical contexts, says we can know nothing unless we can find an unshakeable base. I rejected this in theoretical contexts, and I now do so in practical ones. For here as elsewhere, we must start from agreement and expand it. As a suggested starting point, morality, whatever else it might be, enables us to live together; and however little we can delimit in advance its possible forms, its rules must make group life possible. As examples—not as my own moral theory—we may expect it to endorse whatever a society takes to be central cases both of reliability, such as truth-telling and promise-keeping, and also of concern for others.[15] We may also expect that specific forms of reliability and concern will often reflect different circumstances which make one rule more appropriate for that society than for another.[16] We may expect that, as justifications for knowledge may be wrongly believed to be NNS, so evaluations may be accepted that seem functionally inappropriate; particularly when they represent ossified values that once were functional. But here we may reasonably anticipate that further dialogue could lead to significant advance. Insofar as conflicts are open to discussion, we may expect to find an inherent tension. On the one hand, there will be efforts to sweep away outmoded rules; on the other hand, there will be claims that current enthusiasms may be blind to the experience of former generations, and hence that we should be sensitive to our tradition's accumulated wisdom.[17] Such debates reveal a typically mutualistic situation: rules prescribe conduct in individual cases, but an intolerable result may lead us to question the rule. Principles like reliability and concern may be accepted because they underlie specific rules, yet they in turn may suggest that some accepted rules are aberrations.[18]

We can make such investigations without either accepting any of the four families of approaches, or finding a view which transcends them; and in doing so, we avoid problems which otherwise arise in both theoretical and practical contexts. We naturally seek a coherent overall viewpoint. But since, as we saw in Ch. V.6, with non-formal generalizations there are always losses as well as gains, attempts to produce an overall theory breed polarization, and we commonly find rival views that cannot permanently vanquish each other. With the four families of approaches to morality, probably we can best reach deeper understanding by taking them all into account, for I suspect they all reflect aspects of careful moral thought. As one possible starting point, they all broadly endorse the general principles of reliability and concern; for if they did not, the mutualistic interaction between initial data and reflection would disqualify them as serious theories. From such starting points, we can take the very fact that each of the families appeals to some philosophers more than others, as a valuable resource in attempts to transcend current understanding. Thus in practical as in theoretical contexts we may hope to reject doubts about reason in the same sort of way. We no more need a universally applicable moral theory than an unshakeable theoretical foundation. It is enough in each case that we can continue to articulate better, and even where we cannot solve a dispute, we can at least hope to transcend it to reach deeper insight.

7. Further Problems

To say we may "hope to reject" doubts about practical reason is not yet to say we can succeed. Now and in Sec. 8 I examine other challenges to its scope, involving a running comparison with theoretical reason. One type of challenge arises with the cases mentioned in Sec. 4, where we may be torn between conflicting moral concerns with no calculus to reconcile them. Two points may be made here. First, these dilemmas bring out an important aspect of practical reasoning: that, over and above the specific reasons we give, our acts manifest at a deeper level what sort of person we are. In particular, even those who agree on general principles may have different styles, or types of approach. One, for example, may give more weight to broader loyalties and another to family interests; or one may be more interventionist, while another emphasises letting others work out problems for themselves. We may debate the rival merits of different styles, but also we may often accept them as expressing a desirable diversity among human beings. To suggest there is a calculus to resolve such cases denies the real difficulties involved. Yet, though this is a limit to the scope of reasoning, it is not confined to practical contexts. In, say, the theoretical calculation of probabilities, we also often meet cases where no formal reasoning is available, and where the opinion of competent judges differs. Here too, their views express deeper aspects of their whole belief system than is expressed by their overt reasons. The second point, also noted in Sec. 4, is that the occurrence of undecidable cases does not mean that all cases are undecidable. As, in theoretical contexts, a doubt presupposes what is assumed in formulating it, so moral dilemmas presuppose a background of accepted principles. Only when we accept each alternative as having weight, do we have a problem. So, while such cases limit reasoning, to

make them ground for a *general* subjectivity is to extend a genuine
bewilderment arising from agonizing cases into a rejection of the very
background that gives rise to the bewilderment.

Another type of challenge arises from radically contrasting evaluations.
This may occur either between societies with divergent moral codes, or within
a pluralist one which experiences conflicts of gender, race or class. Honest
views conflict here, because the situation into which we are born so strongly
shapes our experience and beliefs. Deeper insights do not alter this: typically
we have secular, Christian or Muslim insights—or feminist, colored or prole-
tarian ones—even if we can glimpse convergences and develop them by
dialogue. Such cases bring out how far a way of life is so mutualistically
entwined within itself, that attempts to isolate and change a part of it, whether
coming from within or imposed from outside, have endless implications that
we cannot hope to foresee. Debates repeatedly beg the question by formulating the issue in ways the other cannot accept, and the resulting vicious circles
may often seem insurmountable. Moreover, the preconditions of debate, such
as a willingness to admit the possibility of being wrong, and a tolerance that
accepts the viewpoint of others, may not only be more difficult to achieve in
moral contexts, but may be rejected in principle. So there are powerful limits
to dialogue here. Yet still, insofar as we can achieve it, we may expect to find
initial agreement on such values as reliability and concern, and may hope to
make progress here as elsewhere.

Yet a further challenge arises if we consider how two sub-groups in a
society, A and B, may reach agreement at the expense of a third sub-group, C.
Here A and B might be factions within a dominant class, while C is the
majority of the society; or else C might be some minority, which is being
disregarded and thereby nihilated by the majority. In either case, A's and B's
agreement may only lead to more effective oppression of C. This could be so,
even if A and B reached agreement through a genuine, open dialogue, for even
this need not reveal their joint blindness to the interests of C. The parallel
point with theoretical reason is that, while A and B can only start from what
they hold in common, C might challenge an assumption they both shared. But
there is also a fundamental difference. In the theoretical case, C can claim to
be heard, because, ideally at least, all parties agree that they are aiming at a
truth which is independent of what they believe. But if this does not apply in
practical contexts, why *should* A and B, who have settled their differences
satisfactorily, take any notice of C? We meet again the problem: if we have
no guiding concept of believer-independent truth, how could we ground any
ultimate objectivity?

It is tempting to reply that *everyone's* interests should *always* count in the
same way in practical reasoning, but that is too sweeping to be plausible. We
all do and must discriminate in various ways. We do not hold that young

children should be given the vote, that convicted criminals are entitled to their liberty, that we should tell the truth to enemies in wartime. No doubt *appropriate* interests should not be ignored, but A and B will offer reasons for why the ignoring of C's interests is appropriate. If, say, C is a minority group nihilated by a majority that does not take it seriously, reasons will be given why its claims are absurd. Or if C is a majority deprived of political rights, A and B may say Cs are inherently incapable of governing themselves, and so must be ruled by the competent As and Bs. We might strongly suspect that these are rationalizations, which are really believed just *because* they imply that C's interests may be ignored. But how is this to be shown?

Here we may deploy that cross-examination by critical reason which I used in Ch. X.3 against the claim that cats were divine but cockroaches were not. This is powerful in practical as well as theoretical cases, particularly against the universal temptation to make exceptions in our own favor, by allowing in our own case what we would condemn in others. Yet so long as we operate with the picture of a stark contrast between facts and values, there are limits to the power of this weapon. It can only appeal to consistency, so a consistent set of values, however irrational or revolting, seems immune to criticism.[19] An A or B, for example, might agree that *if* they had, unfortunately, been a C, they too would deserve to be ruled. But a more powerful answer emerges when we remember that debate is between standpoints, which are an interlocking tangle of factual and evaluative claims. Thus the claim that C lacks the capacity to govern is a factual one, which could in principle be assessed by evidence. To adopt this justification implies that if the factual claim were false, there would no longer be a valid reason for denying C full rights. Even an appeal to a God-given right to rule must be based on, say, the exegesis of a revealed text; and, as we saw in Ch. XI.6, it is extremely questionable that any text has only one true interpretation. In considering the implications of such probing, we must distinguish between the causal mode question of its actual impact, and the justificatory mode question of its logical cogency. The actual causal impact would no doubt be more likely to produce fury, scorn and violence than any change of attitude. But this applies not only to practical but to theoretical contexts, where rational debate may also often be rejected. As for the justification question, the ineffectiveness, far from challenging logical cogency, is strong evidence of it. For a refusal to investigate, or to accept, counter-considerations is a good indication that a sound argument is threatening a treasured rationalization.

8. An Overall Assessment

The previous discussion raises deeper issues. My approach to theoretical reason in Ch. X focused on its form, rather than its content. While I claimed there must *be* shared content, namely the agreement from which we start, the argument was independent of what that agreement was. But this, it may seem, only works if all parties accept appeals to an externalist notion of believer-independent truth. If this does not hold for practical reason—if here there is no "truth" to work towards—then when, for example, we are trying to show that one whole way of life is better than another, or to persuade A and B to consider C's interests, we shall need some other fulcrum for the argument. And what could this be but some *content* about what was relevant to our reasoning? That content is what the four families of approaches to morality aim to provide. My earlier argument was that we need not fix on any one of them, but could start from whatever agreement we found about, say, the relevance of reliability and concern. But now the point is that we may need some more specific value content, rather than merely whatever we may have in common, to take the place of an appeal to believer-independent truth. Yet I argued, in Ch. XI.2 and elsewhere, that *no* content is beyond question. So, it may seem, practical reason suffers from a limitation that theoretical does not. Then subjectivist doubts may awake again. For if practical reason presupposes a content that theoretical reason may avoid, then, if we happen not to hold that content in common, there will be no fulcrum on which reasoning can rest.

In facing this issue, I return to the point that practical and theoretical standpoints can each assess the other. One side of this point is familiar in the social sciences: that theoretical reasoning can assess practical, by making causal mode assessments of why given values appeal to us. But the less familiar converse side is that practical reason can also ask deeper questions about theoretical thought than it can ask about itself. Consider two examples. First, with theoretical reasoning we can simply note, as in Ch. X.4, that it presupposes values such as openness to unpleasant truth. But in the practical context, we could be asked to justify these values, and then two points arise. The first, which is enough for my argument, is that theoretical reasoning, like practical, requires agreement on values. The second is that the parallel may extend further. If reasoning with others is something we do, the values needed to do it well might involve those, such as reliability and concern, that are needed to act well towards them in other ways. In other words, sound theoretical reasoning is an activity that requires certain virtues, just as much as moral reasoning may require accurate knowledge of facts. By now we have come so far from the original picture that facts but not values can be rationally assessed, that we acknowledge that even theoretical rational assessment must be justified by defending its values. So, though no doubt people may have scruples in one area of their lives and none in others, we might find it in the end rationally impossible to repudiate such values as reliability and concern in one of these contexts but not the other.[20]

As a second example, I noted in Ch. X.5 that in complex cases—and, we may now add, in practical as well as theoretical ones—movement towards consensus will not persuade everyone, but rather involves a process of capturing the uncommitted. This is a point in the causal mode, but is also relevant in the justificatory context of the proper roles of theory and practice. From the theoretical standpoint, the point is simply a fact. But evaluatively, it sounds embarrassingly like nihilating those who resist an emerging consensus by refusing to take them seriously—though the description is given from the standpoint of those doing the nihilating. Certainly this is how we may expect those affected to see it. So here too practical reason examines what theoretical reason takes for granted. Precisely what answer it should give would be a further question, but we must, I think, agree that the process of debate does have a painful, even ruthless, aspect for the losers. We can justify it only by agreeing on the value of free inquiry, which acknowledges in advance that this may be a possible outcome for any of us. Moreover we could learn from it, perhaps, the desirability of considering the feelings of opponents when we are fortunate enough to find ourselves on the winning side.

The general point in both examples is that both theoretical and practical contexts presuppose values, and the values may well have significant similarities. So we may sum up as follows. However important in many contexts may be the contrast between statements which claim to present the truth, and evaluations which do not; and however much the achievements of theoretical reason often seem to surpass practical ones; yet for understanding understanding, these points are not decisive. For both in theoretical and in practical contexts, we begin with standpoints which are theoretical-practical mixtures. These—including, of course, my own—spring from our cultural embeddedness. Further, since they manifest deeper attitudes behind our explicit reasoning, we may be led beyond purely intellectual understanding to situations where we can win insight only by accepting personal involvement. Unless we do so, we will each remain within our standpoints while our arguments politely or hostilely beg the question against each other. Yet in both theoretical and practical cases, involvement combined with disciplined reasoning may penetrate to deeper insight, and may struggle for a new balance between acceptance and criticism of tradition. Whether we can reach worthwhile results are will depend on much more than intellectual factors, but it is important to understand the process intellectually. I believe I have sketched a framework for doing so.[21]

Certainly, the sketch leaves many questions unanswered. Not only does it bypass numerous issues in moral philosophy, but objections to it will come from many sides. Yet my comments can be brief, for the issues are essentially those already arising in Chs. X and XI over theoretical reason. On one side, moral and religious conservatives will see me as eroding morality. For I claim it must *change* to meet new circumstances, while they look for unchangeable certainty; and I claim *we* can see how to change it, while they appeal to a revelation or other source beyond human revision. My reply was offered, in the theoretical context, in Ch. X.3. I acknowledge that such views may be argued with force and seriousness, and I do not endorse the Enlightenment attitude that acceptance of tradition as authoritative is irrational. But I have argued that new developments may challenge any standpoint, and that, when this happens, we can in the end no longer simply appeal to even the most venerable of our traditions. On the other side are the skeptical, relativist and postmodernist views discussed in Ch. XI, and again many former issues recur. For example, poststructuralists might suspect that I assume there is such a thing as an essential human nature, which could provide a standard by which to live. But though in fact I believe this may well be so, my argument leaves open the possibility that we might turn out to be equally well suited to radically different value structures. Further, while in practical even more than in theoretical contexts my cautious optimism goes further than they will accept, I also see the use of reason as a greater risk than the Enlightenment recognized. A risk to the individual, because it leads beyond intellectual understanding to what may be a painful journey of self-exploration. A risk to the group, because the rejection of traditional patterns may lead to a rootless and lost community. However I take these points, not as reasons for refusing the debate, but only as sounding a warning about its dangers.

So what is my final conclusion about the power of practical reason? The answer is not easy. The interlocking complexity of a way of life warns us to be cautious in passing facile judgments. Further, even if we gradually achieved a consensus on value structures appropriate to a new world culture, there would still remain for each person the choice of whether or not to accept it as good. Nor could we expect it to be permanent. For the unboundedness of understanding will have the last word; particularly if, as I believe, we remain mysteries to ourselves, who can endlessly illuminate but never exhaust either our practical or our theoretical understanding. So if I am asked what reasoning might achieve, I offer a cautiously optimistic faith that, in large part, we can objectively adjust our conflicts of interests, and so can develop a morality appropriate for our ever-changing circumstances. But if I am asked for stronger reasons than that faith can provide, I must resort to the second, and least satisfactory, of the three possible outcomes of rational inquiry: that we must postpone the answer because we do not know.

9. Individual and Group

In considering the nature of morality, a final set of issues concerns the relation between the individual and the group. Morality can be investigated from either standpoint; we may ask why a group needs a morality, or why an individual should obey it. For the group, at least one answer is clear;[22] though we may ask whether a rule really promotes a group's goals, people just cannot live together without guidelines for conduct. But from the individual stand-point, the case is different. If I ask "Why should I be moral?", the rules of my group are only one factor, however important, in deciding what to do. If others suffer when I break the rules, why is that a reason for me to keep them? This question arose at the beginning of the European tradition, when Greek culture first developed a sense of the individual as standing over against the community. Plato posed it by reference to the mythical ring of Gyges, which gave its wearer invisibility.[23] If you had the ring, and so were safe from discovery, would not the *rational* course be to take advantage of others?

The basic question here is: can the group's welfare be a rational motive for my action, even if I do not expect to benefit from it personally? This has been a recurring theme in debates between the four families of moral theories.[24] My argument suggests, though it does not presuppose, that it can be; that showing reliability and concern towards others is both possible and worthwhile, even if we do not benefit. Certainly I would expect that anwer from any soldier or fireman who has risked their lives for others, not to mention a host of lesser cases. Yet the justification of this view is not easy. Opponents may argue that the very notion of such altruism is incoherent, or else that it is a foolish or contemptible ideal. I cannot now give this ancient issue the attention it deserves, but I would reject these arguments.[25] Part of my reason for doing so emerges if we pass to what I must now discuss. This is the related, but much less discussed, question: is the individual or the group the more important concept for understanding our human situation? As I put it in Ch. II.9, "is a tradition ultimately only a way of talking about the beliefs of past and present individuals, or are our own beliefs only the manifestation of our tradition's self-understanding?".

One issue arising here concerns the rights of the individual against the group. Some extreme views speak as if a group had a consciousness of its own, superior to its members, and so encourage totalitarian claims that they can properly be subordinated to it.[26] But even if we reject a group conscious-ness, problems remain. The assertion of personal rights against the state or other groups originated in an Enlightenment emphasis on the value of the isolated individual, while the experience of living in today's impersonal societies may breed a counter-emphasis on the need for roots in a community. Yet surely if we ask *why* the rights of the individual should conflict with the need for community, we can see this as a false contrast that can be transcended. For each strengthens the other; we need the psychological assurance which flows from proper embeddedness in a tradition before we can easily accept others as individuals with diverse beliefs; yet their diversity, if contained within an overall agreement on basic values, can enrich our tradition.[27] Both in theoretical and in practical contexts, the mutualistic inter-action between individual and group ensures that our tradition is the deposit of past individuals' reflection, while our reflection is the growing point of tradition. If we see ourselves in this way, as embedded in the sub-traditions of so many valued groups—family, country and others—and if we then return to the ancient question of whether it is rational to consider these groups' good irrespective of our own benefit, then the onus of proof may seem reversed. The denial of altruism may look like an individualism which has forgotten its roots, while the affirmation of disinterested concern for the group may seem simply a sane recognition of our role within it.

The crucial question remains, however, of the extent and nature of our independence from tradition and the group.[28] Here we meet the poststructur-alist rejection of the explanatory force of freedom and creativity, which denies the power of the individual as against the group. We may first ask: is there a real contrast here? For I have emphasized how creativity is not within our power but must come to us, and that surely fits with the notion of impersonal forces. Are these just the "inside" and "outside" of the same phenomenon? Is creativity only our name for what it feels like to be the place where social forces play? I believe it is this, but not *just* this. For, first, creative work involves not merely inspiration that comes to us, but discipline. This is where creativity meets with freedom. We must wait on inspiration, but we can choose whether or not to shape it; and the shaping is a free, conscious activity. Second, freedom and creativity are linked to responsibility. We can nurture or disregard our creativity, as we can accept or neglect its discipline, and for those choices we are responsible. When we consider these points, something more than a mere difference of idiom between inside and outside emerges. If creativity only labelled our ignorance of what really moves us, then the disci-plining of it must also be nothing but an unknown play of forces within us. Talk of creativity, freedom or responsibility would be an outmoded relic of Enlightenment optimism. That view gives primacy to the "outside", while my emphasis on the significance of individuals—even though mutualistically influenced by their tradition—emphasizes the importance of the "inside".

My answer is that we need both inside and outside perspectives. For as with the causal mode and the justificatory mode, and as with theoretical and practical reasoning, here too we have different standpoints which can each assess the other. As an analogy, when we pass beyond intellectual understan-ding, we do not forgo critical reflection, but rather place it in a wider context as a manifestation of forces within us that are deeper than we know. So here also we may consciously learn to see our efforts as contributing to a broader tradition, where we must wrestle to formulate our own ideas, but where they may have an impact, for better or worse, quite other than we intended. To see ourselves in this light, I find, in no way detracts from our creative freedom or responsibility, but rather provides a better base for dialogue with the other voices we meet.

ENDNOTES

---

[1] I cannot show these categories to be logically exhaustive, but I shall not consider any cases which might fall outside them.

[2] I discussed aspects of this in more detail in my "Recent work in Ethical Naturalism" (1973).

[3] This was easily assimilated to the then current appeal to the ordinary meaning of words, for in each case the appeal was to "what we would say". The difference between the moral convictions of Oxbridge dons, and the conditions for speaking a common language, went largely unnoticed.

[4] The classic texts—with great differences between the first one and the latter two—are G. E. Moore *Principia Ethica* (1903); H. A. Pritchard *Moral Obligation ... Essays and Lectures* (repr, 1968); and W. D. Ross *The Right and the Good* (1930).

[5] The commonest form has been a renewed interest in the 19th century doctrine of Utilitarianism. The classic text is J. S. Mill *Utilitarianism*, where the innumerable editions include Everyman (1948). Utilitarianism sees morality as based in some way on what would produce the greatest happiness of the greatest number. It allows much room for the role of reasoning in calculating what would be the most beneficial act; though it has not always been clear how the view that we *should* seek the happiness of all is related to the claim that we are value-maximizers who *do* seek our own happiness. Debates about various forms of Utilitarianism, and objections to all forms of it, play a central part in current analytic moral philosophy. A more recent development has been an interest in applied ethics, the discussion of issues ranging from abortion to ecology.

[6] Those who seek absolute moral or religious values, may protest that I beg the question against them. But the notion of an absolute value can be formulated simply as one which overrides all others wherever it is relevant. Thus I do not foreclose their possibility, though whether we should seek them is a further issue.

[7] An example is the emotive theory of ethics in analytic philosophy.

[8] Descartes acknowledged this point before beginning his systematic doubt. See *Discourse*, Part III.

[9] See Blackburn (1984) Ch. 6. In general, "true" is a vaguer word than philosophers often realize. It is cognate with "trust" (cf. "a true friend"), and perhaps most broadly means simply "whatever will not let us down". Hence the fact that plain people often speak of moral truth may mean no more than that they accept moral objectivity.

[10] See the discussion of "belief system" in Ch. II.4, and particularly Ch. II fn.10.

[11] Philosophers may recognize here my own version of Moore's "naturalistic fallacy". See G. E. Moore (1903).

[12] As I have defined relativism by reference to truth, I cannot use the common phrase "moral relativism" for views that say truth is inapplicable. "Moral skepticism" might suggest the attitude of the Greek skeptics. So I shall speak of subjectivity.

[13] Thus both the first two approaches are prominent in Kant.

[14] Plato is the first great figure in this tradition. Today it gains support from depth psychology, and may have applications in theoretical as well as practical contexts. Lack of appropriate love and care at an infant stage may produce not only the psychotic who cannot relate to others in moral contexts, but also the paranoic who cannot extend to others the rational trust which is necessary to acquire theoretical information.

[15] The latter is the deeper of the two, since reliability expresses one form of concern. In that sense, "Love your neighbor as yourself", where "love" is a name for generalized

concern, has been presented as underlying all moral rules.

[16] Variations seem to arise largely in two areas. One is the extent and generality of obligation; whether it is conceived as a network of specific relations which ignore those outside, or as more universal in scope. The other is the perpetuation of the group over generations, which particularly involves regulation of property, of sexual mores and of family patterns.

[17] Cf., e.g., my *Freewill and Determinism* (1968) Ch. IX.

[18] Given the variety of moral codes, the pooling of expertise here between social scientists and philosophers is surely desirable, but unfortunately uncommon.

[19] Philosophical readers will recognize echoes of the debate about universalizability in ethics.

[20] This point distantly echoes the second of the families of approaches to ethics.

[21] I believe that, in this debate, philosophers who renounce imperialist pretensions may play a valuable role. For both their knowledge of the history of their discipline, and their expertise in debating complex issues, may give them an important voice in the debate.

[22] The *mores* of a group may not be of the type that philosophers would usually call moral ones, but that point can be ignored here.

[23] *Republic* Bk. II.

[24] For example, while Plato aimed to show it would be in our own deepest interests to be moral on all occasions, early analytic intuitionists held that even to ask how morality might pay us was already to make the crucial mistake.

[25] The first claim, that the concept is incoherent, is based on the point that even a sacrificial action is done because I *want* to do it. The standard reply is that, even if I do it because, in some sense, I want to, it does not follow that what I want is *my own good*. Wanting someone else's good is a quite coherent notion. For the second claim, that such actions are undesirable (foolish, contemptible, etc.), various reasons are offered, but again I would reject them. Strictly, the two claims are incompatible. If altruism is an incoherent, or logically impossible, concept, then examples of it cannot occur, and the question whether they would be undesirable does not arise. But quite often reasoners confuse the two, arguing both that altruism really cannot occur, and also that it does, but should not.

[26] For we must ask how we tell what its consciousness is, and the tempting answer is that some charismatic leader is the true Voice of the Group.

[27] However embeddedness is also an ambivalent phenomenon, which may make for intolerance and fanaticism.

[28] Many aspects of this debate might benefit from more cooperation between philosophy and other disciplines.

CHAPTER XIV

PROSPECTS FOR THE FUTURE

1. The Possibility of a Worldview

I turn now to what many will see as the central question arising from my whole argument: can we reasonably expect that our present fragmented culture might again be integrated by a coherent worldview?[1] Here we must begin with the recurring philosophical conflict between constructivism and criticalism.[2] Constructivist metaphysical systems present a framework, and often much detail, for a comprehensive worldview. They see this as the greatest service of philosophy to humanity, for without a vision the people perish. Criticalism finds this pretentious. Among modern forms of it, we saw how analytic philosophy treated metaphysics as verbal confusion or as the search for knowledge beyond possible empirical verification, while poststructuralism expects to uncover by deconstruction the voices that have been suppressed. But something deeper underlies these objections. Since we continually alter the meaning of words in innumerable contexts, why must we cease to speak sense when we do so in metaphysical ones? Why must we lapse into nonsense when we go beyond empirical verification? And why should we see deconstruction as more than a warning to be alert for what we suppress? When we ask this, criticalism appears as a remedy for what it *already* takes to be a disease. It asks, not "Is constructive metaphysics desirable?", but "Granted that it is not, why does it occur?". So beyond its reasons lie causal mode questions. Why did Absolute Idealism or Hegelianism lose their grip on a generation of philosophers, so analytic philosophy and Positivism reacted against them? Why did poststructuralist disillusionment with the European tradition arise when it did?

Such causal mode inquiries could show how a cultural situation encouraged metaphysical optimism or pessimism, though in each case individuals might go against the trend. But in a longer historical perspective, what emerges is a pattern of recurring polarization. If optimism or pessimism triumphs for a time, it tends to stimulate its opposite. In this sense of a tension that we can neither vanquish nor abandon, I echo the poststructuralist notion of undecidability. I accept that the generalizations needed for any worldview will have costs as well as benefits. They will not capture the significance of all phenomena, and so will leave suppressed voices to be recovered later. Yet I believe the costs of the process may be minimized in a way I indicate in Sec. 7, and that the benefits could be immense; so, in our actual situation today, my cautious optimism remains.   I cannot prove it is justified, but nor, I claim, can pessimism be established. We must reason as best we can; but the proof of each pudding will be in the eating, so in the end we must just wait and see. My present argument first focuses, as usual, on my analytic tradition, and then, after brief discussion of other views, offers my own approach.   A central theme will be the proper place of science in an overall worldview. For, as the first modern philosophers could only begin by grappling with their medieval heritage, so I must start with the impact on us of the growth of science.

2. The Impact of Science on Our Worldview

If we disregard previous anticipations, modern science is usually taken to begin with Copernicus' argument that the earth and planets revolve round the sun. Yet, momentous though the implications of that claim were, from the viewpoint of method rather than conclusion it was more an internal convulsion within the old view than a radical break with it. The crucial innovation in method was when Galileo asked a new type of question, which looked for mathematical relations between measurable quantities, and so led to our mathematico-experimental method. As science expanded, this method repeatedly took into account in later refinements what it first ignored. When initially applied to the movements of material objects, it ignored their color, smell and taste. Later it took account of these by scientific theories of color, etc. It extended to living phenomena through biochemistry, and to mental ones through psychology. Increasingly, nothing seemed beyond its scope.

To grasp the significance of the change, we must contrast it with what it replaced. In the medieval picture, with the earth in the center of the universe as the stage for the drama of humanity's fall and redemption, the believed facts about the nature of the universe seemed to make obvious the value of so living as to gain heaven. Any gap between fact and value would have seemed artificial. The increasing tide of scientific success washed away this worldview, and steadily overwhelmed the further barriers which philosophers and others erected. The Rationalist appeal to innate ideas, and even the Empiricist emphasis on experience, could leave some room for values by placing the reasoning, experiencing mind at the center of philosophy. But the nature of matter, which this mind scientifically investigated, became alien. Gradually the universe seemed indifferent to life and life itself a biochemical process. Values to guide our lives had no link with the facts that science discovered. No wonder we found a fact/value dichotomy!

The transformation in method was as great as in content. Medieval learning was exegesis, but was radically different to poststructuralist approaches. For it saw texts as *authoritative* documents, which could only have one correct interpretation. This applied both to Christian and to classical texts, such as Aristotle. Certainly, at the outset of scholastic philosophy, the discovery that the ancients had held different views on the problem of universals meant that it was necessary to decide that issue for oneself. Moreover the scope for differing interpretations was so great that probably few medieval thinkers felt unduly constrained by authority. Yet the appeal to it, particularly in questions about a worldview, was universal. That attitude was natural in its cultural context. Society had drastically declined, and was not expected to recover. This was stated in the texts themselves, which spoke of an expulsion from the Garden of Eden or a decline from a Golden Age, and it also echoed memories of the collapse of the Roman Empire. So truth lay in the past to be *re*covered, rather than in the future to be *dis*covered, and the way to recover it was to interpret what fragments had survived. Here lies the deepest difference between the medieval outlook and our own, that a new confidence came to contemplate acquiring more understanding than its ancestors. That confidence, beginning with the Renaissance and reflected in a different way in the Reformation, became the cultural air that the Enlightenment breathed.

Though this confidence informed all aspects of life, it was justified supremely by scientific achievement, so science acquired its immense prestige in our culture. In understanding this prestige, what matters is not so much how science did operate as how it was seen to operate by those exhilarated with its progress. For them, the mathematico-experimental method joined with the advancing technology of the 17th century. A prime example of technology was the watch, which was becoming so cheap that wealthy individuals could afford to own one. Both the technology and the science explained the behavior of material things by showing how their parts interacted, and they merged to suggest a picture of the universe as an intricate watch-like machine. So mechanism became a new master-model—a structure found in sub-systems of our thought, which was used as the basis of a super-system. Today "mechanism" has a range of senses, and in particular we must distinguish a broader from a stricter one. The broader, and metaphysically neutral, one applies to any explanation of a whole in terms of the interaction of its parts. So those drawing up a constitution might ask what voting mechanism to adopt —first-past-the-post, preferential, etc. But in a stricter sense, a mechanism is a material thing, like a watch. Using this as a master-model led to a *mechanistic worldview*. At first this co-existed with religious belief; for though we may understand a watch by seeing how its parts interact, we know it must have a watchmaker. So the dominant Enlightenment viewpoint accepted a Supreme Designer of the world-mechanism. But eventually, and particularly after the theory of evolution suggested how a random process of biological selection could produce adaptations that appeared to be purposeful, the need for the Designer dwindled.   So the mechanistic worldview tended towards materialism, the doctrine that only matter exists.   If life was a biochemical process, might not consciousness itself be only a process in the brain?

The modern form of this worldview has implications both within science and between science and other disciplines.   Within science, there are three points. First, the natural sciences, which deal with material things, are the standard by which others are judged.   Criteria for accepting disciplines as scientific involve asking whether their methods are sufficiently close to the natural sciences, and whether their results cohere with them.[3]   Second, if the causes of phenomena lie in the interaction of their parts, larger-scale phenomena must be the effects of smaller ones; and if these cannot be observed, they are postulated to exist at a smaller level than we can yet observe.   Repeatedly such postulates have later been vindicated, not only by their results, but also by developing new techniques, such as more powerful microscopes, which could observe what had already been assumed.   So, thirdly, the point applies not merely within but between sciences.   Since what we observe at a given level is the effect of smaller processes, the minutest causes must tell the ultimate story.   So in principle each science should reduce to the level below it: psychology should be explicable in terms of the physiology of the central nervous system, physiology by biochemistry, biochemistry by chemistry, and chemistry ultimately by the action of the smallest entities, which are those studied by physics.   Thus physics gives the final explanation of how things are.

The mechanistic worldview gives an elegant structure to human knowledge, and has achieved impressive successes, but it has always been under attack. Partly this comes from trying to work out the implications for science itself, for efforts to reduce larger- to smaller-scale phenomena produce great problems in philosophy of science.   But besides such technical issues, stronger opposition focuses on the implications for the relation between science and other disciplines.   For this worldview, as exponents note with eagerness or regret, downgrades the significance of such areas as religion, esthetics and the realm of values.   I shall also suggest that it downgrades more than its friends often realize.   Yet it can claim support from much of the expansion of scientific knowledge, and so easily seems the worldview which has the support of science.   The result is a widespread conflict between science-based views, and others such as humanities- or religion-based ones.   I believe this is the key issue out of the many we must face in examining the possibility of a viable worldview for our time.   I begin by considering a specific version of the mechanistic worldview that is current in analytic philosophy.

3. Analytic Materialism

I noted in Ch. VII.2 how analytic philosophy moved from an early humanities-based to a later science-based attitude, and also left behind its criticalist rejection of metaphysics. Today its science-based form has developed a view of the nature of a human being, which I call analytic materialism.[4] The arguments are as abstruse as any in philosophy, but the central thrust is as follows. The traditional view, which was reinforced at the beginning of modern philosophy by Descartes, spoke of our mind as distinct from our body, and treated it as an immaterial entity. Hence the question of the nature of a human being is still often called the mind-body problem. Analytic materialism challenges this view. It is an ontological doctrine, a claim about what things exist: that since science, which gives a true picture of the universe, deals only with the structure of matter, ultimately only material entities exist.[5] It treats the mind as nothing but the body's central nervous system, or, more briefly though less accurately, as nothing but the brain. So the mind is a material thing.

Arguments for this view aim to analyze our thought and experience entirely in terms which *could* apply to material entities. To do so, they use causal and functional concepts, which define a given mental state in terms of what it causes or is caused by, or else in terms of the function it plays in our thinking. As a simple example, they might describe the experience of being thirsty as being aware that something is going on in us which is, in appropriate circumstances, apt to make us drink. This allows the *possibility* that the "something" might be a brain process. Analytic materialism then applies the ancient principle of Ockham's Razor, that entities are not to be multiplied beyond necessity; for if we can explain by using a smaller number of types of entity, we achieve a more elegant result. So it argues that, if the experience *could* be a brain process, we should not also assume an immaterial, experiencing mind. The claim covers not only the experience central to Empiricism, but the reasoning so dear to Rationalism. Here it is reinforced by such developments as artificial intelligence, which produce functional concepts that can be applied both to human thought and to computers. This provides both inspiration for new philosophical analyses, and a general sense that materialism reflects the progress of science. The overall thesis is that consciousness is merely the monitoring by one part of the brain of other processes within the central nervous system.[6] Philosophy, by rebutting objections, can show that this might be the case; science will eventually show that it is.

Though there is much divergence within analytic materialism, it amounts overall to the most rigorous of all expressions of the mechanistic worldview. It crystallizes beliefs that many people hold, or perhaps inconsistently half-hold. Many within the analytic tradition reject it, but few defend a traditional mind-body dualism, and there is no consensus on an alternative. I shall now assess it in terms of my own approach.

4. Commonsense, Ontology and Significance

Because of its internal history, analytic philosophy has defended the dominance of scientific discourse in a rather idiosyncratic way. As its earlier appeal to commonsense and ordinary language later gave way to a science-based approach, it has primarily argued for the pre-eminence of science over commonsense, rather than over, say, the humanities or religion. Yet this rather specialized approach does provide, I believe, one way of getting to the heart of the issue. To the later science-based form of analytic philosophy, common-sense seemed, above all, smug; something that accepted tradition without scientific examination, and relied on experience without scientific control.[7] It is not, as its defenders assumed, an unchanging certainty to oppose to the absurdities of metaphysicians, for it absorbs scientific truth: one generation's demon possession is another's mental illness. But the absorbtion is confused, fragmentary, outdated and uncritical, and the resulting amalgam of truth and error must be reconstructed in the light of scientific discovery. When this approach did consider the humanities, which were a model for much Continen-tal philosophy, it often claimed they made no real progress because they did not use the scientific method, and so emphasized or exaggerated the contrasts noted in Ch. III.3–4. But above all, it saw the humanities as primarily concerned with human artifacts, from the documents of historians to works of art; and as these represented only a miniscule part of the whole universe, their concepts lacked the universal application of the natural sciences. After rejecting these alternatives, the justification of a science-based view seemed straightforward. Science is our most successful method of reasoning, and it alone applies universally to all phenomena; so its concepts should determine our worldview.

Yet this takes far too short a way with the issue. The mere success of science no more shows it should be central to our worldview, than a population explosion in one country shows there is no growth anywhere else; while the role its concepts should play is precisely the issue. Our answer depends heavily on our cultural tradition. Scholastic philosophers were no less acute than contemporary ones, but if they were transported to our day they might object that the "success" of science in destroying any picture of the universe in which we could feel at home, only illustrates the dangers of reason unguided by faith. In fact the medieval appeal to accepted texts and the modern one to science have two things in common. First, both carry authority in their culture, though for opposite reasons: the texts because of disbelief in our capacity to reach new truth, science because it demonstrates that capacity in its own area. Second, both claim universality in application. For the middle ages, everything was seen in the light of the divine purpose revealed in the texts; for the full-blown scientific outlook today, there may be much we cannot at present explain, but nothing that is scientifically inexplicable. So each easily seems in its culture the *obvious* way to settle issues;[8] though, as Ch. X.5 noted, this very obviousness makes it easy to beg the question. It is such vast rival significance-judgments as these that conflicting worldviews present.

The very fact that they present them reminds us that the scientific method cannot be used to establish the significance of science. Not that *all* questions of significance are beyond science, for in a delimited context we may, say, establish that a pattern in our data is statistically significant. But the overall assessment required for a worldview cannot be delimited in this way. We saw in Ch. III that even large-scale conflicts arising within science cannot be settled by the mathematico-experimental method, and those between worldviews are far more intractable. Rival views can always adjust to new evidence, though not always equally easily, and we cannot quantify the arguments mathematically so as to calculate their probability.[9] Yet here as elsewhere rational debate can slowly clarify the issues, and I now try to contribute to that process.

Analytic materialism approaches its worldview as an ontological question: "Are there immaterial entities, which cannot be fitted into the mechanistic worldview?". The central candidates, our minds, are then shaved off by Ockham's Razor. But, bypassing current technical debates,[10] I believe we should transcend this ontological formulation, for it distracts attention from the real issue. The key notions in my argument are those of an aspect and of significance; for sub-systems in our belief system represent aspects of reality, and a worldview aims to relate them into a coherent whole by allocating each one its appropriate significance. I assume for the sake of argument that all entities have a material aspect, and hence that the natural sciences apply universally, so I do not postulate any immaterial minds. But we have seen that, though what we find would normally be there whether we discovered it or not, inquiry reveals only the aspect of reality which corresponds to our question. So what we find also depends on what method we use. I now consider the implications of these points.

The natural sciences present an aspect of reality. Granted that this aspect applies universally to all reality, the question is how significant it should be for our worldview. Here we meet the resurrected ghost of the commonsense that analytic materialism buried. Even if its absorbtion of science is "confused, fragmentary, outdated and uncritical", it points to an indispensable notion. For it is, or at least includes, the amalgam of factual and evaluative beliefs, including our tacit knowledge, by which we *deal directly with our world, including other people*; though that amalgam also includes, for some people, various pieces of technical knowledge that we would not ordinarily include in commonsense. This amalgam cannot be dismissed as merely a pre-scientific view of the world, without the threat of a self-refutation argument. For science is something we do, and we need the amalgam to do it. Scientists need tacit knowledge to recognize laboratories, instruments and colleagues. They need the values which led them to science, motivate their research, and restrain them when they are tempted to distort or plagiarize results. And they must use the set of concepts that express relationships within society. To apply, for example, for a research grant involves a grasp of a whole economic, legal and administrative background. Without all this we would have no science.[11] So suppose we could be given a total description of a brain state at a given time. This would be a vast document of baffling complexity, but assume we could understand it in its own terms. To *respond* to it, we would have to translate it in terms of the amalgam—"He is calibrating the anemometer", "She would like to be kissed". The significance here flows the other way; we can use the scientific description only by reducing it the commonsense amalgam.[12] Some such amalgam of concepts, though not our present one, is indispensable. For we could live without science, as many societies have done, but we cannot live without dealing directly with our world.[13]

This does not show commonsense should be more significant than science for our worldview, but it does suggest the issue is more open than analytic materialism believes. That materialism, however, because of its ontological approach, takes the point lightly.[14] However indispensable the commonsense amalgam may be, it feels, any extra alleged entities can be philosophically rejected. The amalgam may be indispensable in practice, but that is an epistemological point about how we come to know. Natural science gives us the true ontology of what exists; what is epistemologically primary is ontologically secondary. Yet this begs the crucial question: how relevant should an ontological approach be in deciding our worldview? For whatever we say about ontology, the explanations of natural science are irrelevant to much of our knowledge. So we meet a vicious circle, where each view seems to answer the other: materialism admits the indispensability of the commonsense amalgam, but treats this as a purely epistemological point; the reply admits the universality of scientific explanation, but questions the implications. Here we enter the vast, continuing debate over whether we should modify the mechanistic worldview. It is immensely difficult for rival standpoints to feel the justificatory force of opposed arguments, and the causal mode question of which will eventually capture the uncommitted is undecided. But to take the debate further, I shall pass beyond this relatively restricted conflict between science and commonsense to note some other important factors in the debate.

5. Alternative Approaches

As we cannot use the scientific method to establish the significance of science, we must turn to more general forms of selective description. Since the humanities use such forms, we may ask: should they, rather than science, provide the model for articulating standpoints into a worldview? We also meet here such disciplines as depth psychology and Marxism, which call themselves scientific but cannot use mathematico-experimental methods. Then we find again the problems discussed in the latter part of Ch. XI, and reach a dividing line which still, though decreasingly, tends to separate Continental from English-speaking philosophy. Such views as these relate more easily to our direct dealing with the world, and so conflict less with the commonsense amalgam. Also they, like I, emphasize the importance of aspects of our knowledge not captured by the mathematico-experimental method. But still I find in them no satisfactory answer.

Putting aside postmodernist rejections of all constructive worldviews, we find two broad types of approach. The first type, including Freudianism and Marxism, gains its power essentially from pointing to hidden agendas. It usually calls itself materialist and scientific, but it uses these words differently from the analytic tradition. Thus for Marxism, "materialism" means that the material means of production, as opposed to ideas, are the real motive force in social change; while for each of them, "scientific" means an acceptance of a mechanistic worldview rather than adherence to the mathematico-experimental method. However I can bypass the many conflicts between these views and analytic materialism. For I need only repeat, as in Ch. XI.7, that I find among hidden agenda views many insights, but no fully acceptable worldview. The second type of approach are humanities-based ones, that make no claim to be scientific. They are exemplified by Gadamer's hermeneutic theory, which also reflects aspects of Hegelianism and phenomenology. His penetrating analysis of understanding in the humanities complements and often reinforces my own. Yet despite his sense of the power of tradition, I find little recognition of the power of social forces or of hidden agendas. Moreover, I find a defensive fear of science, which he sees as the prime dehumanizing element in modern culture. Since we do not easily understand what we distrust, it is not surprising that his analysis of humanities-based understanding uses as a foil a picture of how scientists work which is sometimes a virtual caricature.

What does emerge amid all the conflicts is a convergence between views developed largely in isolation. If Gadamer's insights unduly deprecate science, a converse point applies to the analytic tradition. Some of its best work is in philosophy of science; but it fails to ask how far its insights are confined to science, and how far they apply to good reasoning as such. When we do ask such questions, I believe we can see that many approaches converge on what I have tried to present: a general analysis of understanding, which applies equally to the humanities, the sciences and the commonsense from which both arise; an exploration of the need to go beyond intellectual understanding; and an awareness of both the limits and the power of reason. From such a vantage point, we could relate and then distinguish the various forms of understanding, and so transcend both the uncritical admiration of science in science-based views, and the overcritical suspicion of it in many other ones. That might equip us, not only for deciding if a coherent worldview is possible today, but for the much greater goal of trying to develop one. As the next step, I shall look at the relation of the mechanistic worldview to modern science itself.

6. Science and the Mechanistic Worldview

I claimed in Sec. 4 that the mechanistic worldview, which sees the smallest entities as giving the ultimate explanation, does not capture the significance of the commonsense amalgam. I now suggest it is no longer adequate even within science itself. Current patterns of scientific explanation, though still using the mathematico-experimental method, are changing rapidly. Here we may start with a suggestion made some decades ago;[15] that science is moving from a first stage of "problems of organized simplicity", through a second one of "problems of disorganized complexity", to current "problems of organized complexity". The first stage of Newtonian physics and early chemistry, dealt with problems involving only very few variables, such as the movement of the planets round the sun. A second stage came with the development of statistics, whereby science could handle immensely complex phenomena. Unlike the first stage, the variables used did not consider individual entities, but reflected only large-scale patterns. A third stage of organized complexity considers the *organization* of wholes which have very many variables. Science has thereby extended to deal with functional relations, from information theory to ecology. As in the second stage, the micro-entities involved are not individually considered, but here the specific types of relationships are crucial.

Though no simple schema reflects the full complexity of scientific development, this captures much of how science transcends earlier successes by taking into account what its previous approaches had put aside. New levels of explanation do not negate older ones. An ecosystem *is* a set of material entities, but it is not *just* that; what is more significant for scientific understanding is the structure of the relationships within the set. The implications are best seen in such fields as information theory and artificial intelligence. Much theorizing here applies in principle either to brains or to computers.

Though these are both composed of material micro-entities, they have a totally different chemistry, which the theory ignores. In fact the theory would apply to any entity, including a immaterial one if there be such, which had a structure that could be conceived as processing information. I now argue that this shift presents a basic challenge to the whole mechanistic worldview.

In Sec. 2 I distinguished a broader and a stricter sense of "mechanism". In the broader sense, information theory deals with mechanisms of passing information, for it considers how parts interact to produce the result. But the master-model for a mechanistic worldview uses a stricter sense, where a mechanism is a material entity like a watch. This is what gives rise to the picture that each science is to be explained in terms of the micro-level below it, so that the whole is understood in terms of its parts, and physics gives the final explanation of how things are. But in a science like information theory, a part is defined in terms of the whole; the part is anything—no matter what its material content, and not even necessarily a material thing at all—which is picked out by the fact that it plays a given role in a larger process.[16] Certainly in many contexts, from ecology to designing computers, the actual material features of the part are relevant to understanding the whole. For scientists, wisely ignoring the philosophical implications of their work, use whatever type of explanation best suits their purpose. But this only reinforces the point that, in the investigation of organized complexity, the one-way street of reducing the whole to its parts is replaced by a two-way explanatory traffic.

At the beginning of my analysis of understanding in Ch. II.2, I noted that it seemed to have two forms: connecting parts to form a whole, and distinguishing them within one. But I went on to bring out that the typical, though not universal, form of understanding was mutualistic, where whole and part influence each other. The master-model of the mechanistic worldview takes as its basis one special form of the distinguishing aspect, namely the relation of material parts within a whole. This reflects a highly successful historical marriage of technology with the problems of organized simplicity; and it may, in a modified form, apply to the problems of disorganized complexity.[17] But the problems of organized complexity are essentially mutualistic, for here whole and part are understood in terms of each other.

For analytic materialism, these changes create a largely unrecognized tension. Developments in organized complexity, such as artificial intelligence, provide its sense of being in the van of scientific progress. But its search for a minimal ontology is nurtured by the mechanistic worldview, which aims to show that the smallest items, as required for physics, are ultimately all that exist.[18] Now these two factors are pulling apart *as a picture of scientific explanation itself*. So increasingly, not merely when we compare scientific to other knowledge but within science also, the mutualistic approach of organized complexity, that significance may flow from whole to part as well as *vice versa*, challenges the mechanistic assumption that the significant explanation is always how the parts determine the whole. We see here the unboundedness of understanding, whereby new developments impact back on the framework that gave rise to them. A great earlier example was the origin of science itself, when exciting but arcane developments in what was then called "natural philosophy" gradually came to transform the whole medieval vision. Now this seems to be happening to the mechanistic worldview which that earlier revolution produced. If so, analytic materialism must eventually choose which of these elements—the organized complexity or the mechanistic worldview—is the more significant for it, and that would involve a deep reappraisal. But for my approach there is no problem. Unlike many humanities-based views, I do not fear science as a dehumanizing force, but echo materialism's admiration of it both as a praxis and as an intellectual achievement. What I deny is what both these standpoints assume: that successfully relating mental phenomena to material ones would show that "the mind is nothing but the brain". Rather, it would only forge another, and most exciting, link between the many aspects of our knowledge that we must integrate into a worldview.

In the complex debates arising here, I see two key issues. The more technical one for professional philosophers is the relevance of analytic materialism's initial ontological assumption. Should we, as it asserts, decide our worldview merely by asking what candidate requires the smallest number of types of entities; or is that only one relevant question among others?[19] Here I claim that at least the conflict must be fought on the ground I have marked out. For my argument focuses on the need for (and the immense difficulty of) large scale significance-judgments; and if that is correct, materialists must argue that an ontological approach is the proper way to bring out the *significance* of different bodies of knowledge for a worldview. Underlying this debate is a less technical but more important issue: whether the prestige of science has pre-empted its significance for our worldview, as the prestige of authoritative texts seems to us to have done for the middle ages. My approach suggests it has. For if what we discover about reality depends on what questions we ask, then scientific method can be only one type of question-and-answer. It is particularly powerful where it applies, but the key issue is how to integrate its answers with others; and there, as we have seen, the scientific method cannot be used. I offer some further suggestions.

7. Avoiding Reductionism

Any master-model involves a significance-judgment which articulates our thought. In delimited contexts like the search for elegance within science, such achievements as the reduction of chemical to physical phenomena may be an unquestioned advance. But the wider the context the more contentious the judgment, and at the broadest level of seeking a whole worldview, whether we have the right master-model is the central issue. I focus now on how we apply such models. When some aspect of our experience makes a deep enough impact on us to serve as a model, the temptation is always to apply it in a *reductionist* way. The notion of a reduction has received much technical discussion, but I can bypass it simply by saying that it is the claim that something is *really nothing but* some other thing. Here "really" means, as in Ch. XII.3, "what there is, as rightly conceived". So the mechanistic worldview says that what exists is really nothing but the particles of physics. More specific reductions include biological ones that explain human motivation in terms of territorial imperatives or selfish genes; psychological ones that treat it as a conflict between a sexual drive and a death instinct; and social ones that accept only such hidden agendas as class struggles. But since non-formal generalizations have costs as well as benefits, such single-minded approaches breed polarization. Opponents object that they do not preserve the significance of what they reduce. We cannot completely avoid this situation, but we should be sensitive to it. For a worldview must have a master-model, but it need not apply it reductively.

With a worldview, a central, and partly unavoidable, danger is that our embeddedness in our tradition will blind us to aspects of reality which our culture downgrades. Hence in applying a master-model we should aim to be alert to counter-evidence, so as not to bury clues that may lie at the borders of our accustomed thinking. In itself this, like Ockham's Razor, is a simply a maxim of good reasoning, and one often expressed within science itself, but it has a specific function as a counter to oversweeping reductions. I suggest we should replace the "nothing-but" of reductionism with a "yes-but": "*Yes*, this discourse has its point in this context, *but* how does it fit into the wider picture"? We may still entirely reject some discourses, such as the stock examples of witchcraft and astrology in Ch. III.8, but we acknowledge that in such cases the burden of proof is on us to show why. In this way we might apply a master-model with the sensitivity that the criticalist opponents of intellectual constructions rightly complain is so often lacking.

This is much more easily said than done. The ideal of giving each subsystem its due before incorporating it into the whole is one that Hegel and the Absolute Idealists explicitly endorsed, but their systems are often seen as supreme examples of forcing phenomena into a pre-determined scheme. However several points may help. First, we should try to remember, even in the enthusiasm of intellectual construction, that we cannot hope to capture all important truths and values. There will always be suppressed voices not fully taken into account, which will eventually insist on being heard. So, second, we should acknowledge that the project will need redoing again and again, even though we may still hold that it is valuable and necessary. Third, we will be led beyond purely intellectual understanding. For we do not fully know *why* a master-model seems to us attractive or threatening, and uncovering hidden reasons is a valuable part of the process. Finally, though conflicts in any case tend to eventual resolution, candid dialogue between opponents reasonably equal in conviction and ability gives the best chance of new insight. One repeated aspect of the process will be the offering by one side or the other of attempted syntheses. These may be inadequate even to solve the issue as it has been posed, quite apart from later reformulations of it. But they are an essential element in the dialogue, and may progressively point the way to better solutions. I shall now try to apply these principles to the approach developed in this book.

8. Final Suggestions

Just as my analysis of understanding in Part A was only a starting point for the implications in Part B, so the previous discussion is only a preliminary. For ultimately we would need, I believe, nothing less than a new master-model to provide a guiding, though not constricting, standpoint for our times. Such a model draws on deeper than conscious roots, and begins to manifest itself in apparently unrelated ways; nor can we see, except in retrospect, which formulation of it best goes to the heart of the matter. Today many people retain from the mechanistic worldview a sense that physics gives the final explanation, but also believe or hope that this reduction is inadequate, so our culture is alive with attempted new syntheses. But all too often academic disciplines will not take them seriously, while their expositions lack intellectual rigor. We need here an immensely difficult combination of an imagination that takes seriously what may at first seem absurd, and a rigor that refuses to abandon critical thought. Now, however, I can only draw together some threads in my own approach that might provide a starting point.

The first thread is the scientific significance of the problems of organized complexity. By moving from the mechanistic worldview to focus on situations where whole and part strongly interact, we deal with aspects of reality that reflect more closely the mutualistic nature of our own minds. If we take this as a guiding thread, we echo a notion which was already old in medieval times: that *a human being is a microcosm of the macrocosm*; that somehow —just how, was always a matter for debate—our own nature reflects the nature of reality as a whole. For four centuries, as science steadily expelled an anthropomorphic understanding of the world, this view seemed increasingly naive. Today I find its older forms as unacceptable as ever. For example, one classic expression of it was the astrological belief that patterns in the heavens influence our lives—"as above, so below"; but, whatever resurgent popularity this may enjoy, I can conceive no mechanism—in the broad sense of an interaction of parts—whereby it might operate. Yet the general notion recurs, in a way fully committed to the scientific method, in the study of organized complexity. A striking illustration is the scientific acceptance of the "Gaia hypothesis". This treats the whole biosphere (the band of air, land and water which supports life) as analogous to a vast organism.[20] Against the earlier orthodox view that life merely adapted to its physical environment, it claims that living and non-living things interact with all the complexity of an organism, to produce self-regulating mechanisms that keep our planet within the narrow parameters needed for life.

To study aspects of nature where the organized complexity reflects the mutualism of our own minds, links with my plea to avoid reductionism. For it does not deny the significance of different levels of explanation. It encourages us to see ourselves as physico-chemical entities, as the biological result of an evolutionary process, as economic units, as the manifestation of often hidden social forces, and as much else besides. To all these it says "yes-but", and then aims to integrate them by examining their mutualistic interaction. Its basic significance-judgment is that we should reject both a reductionism that easily distorts the phenomena, and the criticalist claim that all overviews must inevitably do so. It aims rather at the ideal of an overview without distortion.

One focus of the debate would be that every worldview must offer some ultimate explanation of how and why things are—in the sense in which even "Things are due to sheer chance" is an ultimate explanation. Here, as we saw, so long as the mechanistic worldview could not explain the origin of life in its own terms, it accepted a Divine Watchmaker. But since Darwin, the concept of evolution has provided a reductionist framework for seeing ourselves as nothing but the outcome of a purposeless biological selection. So evolution has seemed to many to squeeze out all religious standpoints which conceived of ultimate reality as in any way akin to human consciousness. Yet for a yes-but approach, an evolutionary and a religious approach would be, not necessary antagonists, but only two more important aspects of our thought to fit together. Certainly, the possibility always remains that we might eventually reject a whole discourse; in this case, that scientific beliefs might eliminate all rational justification for religious ones. But our answer would depend on how these two discourses best cohered both with each other and with innumerable other considerations. Among those others, one would be that if, as I have suggested, we are ultimately but not wholly mysterious to ourselves, we could hardly expect the macrocosm to be otherwise; our understanding of nature, as of ourselves, would be something we can endlessly illuminate, but never exhaust. This undermines a tendency of the mechanistic worldview to see nature as a resource to be plundered, and encourages its replacement by a more environmentally sensitive ethic.   Further, if fuller understanding of ourselves requires deeper involvement, we may ask how that might also apply to our understanding of the world outside us. As Ch. VI suggests, many forms of involvement pass beyond intellectual understanding, and we might rethink, say, the claims of art to penetrate to a deeper level of reality.   There are also explorations of a rapprochement between the basic science of the mechanistic worldview, namely physics, and the extreme form of passing beyond intellectual understanding through the stilling of the mind.[21]   But now I can only relate these points to analytic materialism, where the conflict emerges most starkly. For this materialism, as a supreme attempt to fit the concept of a person into the mechanistic worldview, is at the opposite extreme from an anti-reductionism that treats us as the microcosm that is the model for understanding the macrocosm.

Here the central issue is, I believe, how analytic materialism could come to terms with the aspectual view of reality which I have offered. In my view, mind and body are two large-scale aspects of a person, which each collect many sub-aspects; "mind" covers our experiencing, thinking, etc., while "body" refers to an interconnecting set of physical, chemical, biological and functional levels of explanation.[22]   So the question posed by analytic materialism—namely, whether a person is two entities, a mind and a body, or only one, namely a body—is replaced by such issues as whether these two aspects are exhaustive, in the sense of covering all we can know about a human being, and how they might best fit into a wider worldview. As always in philosophy, this approach leads to its own problems. But its transcendence of how the whole debate has been posed, leading to further exploration of how we might be a microcosm of the macrocosm, is, I believe, a good starting point for coming to terms with the greatest issues that face us today.

ENDNOTES

1 "Worldview" has many senses. If we extend it to cover the orientation of our whole belief system, including unconscious elements, we all have at least an implicit one. Even if we restrict it to conscious beliefs, a denial of any overall point to life is often called a worldview. But I now apply it only to more constructive attitudes.
2 For a discussion emphasizing different points, and written in a different philosophical climate, cf. my *Freeewill and Determinism*, pp. 285-297.
3 The criteria can conflict, as when the protocols of experiments that deal with paranormal phenomena are scrutinized more stringently because results conflict with the core.
4 As two examples of a vast literature, an important earlier book is D. M. Armstrong *A Materialist Theory of the Mind* (1968), while a brief and vigorous later defence is Paul M. Churchland *Matter and Consciousness* (1984).
5 There are complex debates about whether materialism requires *abstract* entities, such as sets, which may be necessary for mathematics and so for science. But all agree it excludes immaterial entities, such as minds.
6 A common initial reaction is that this leaves out the indescribable "raw feel" of actual

experience, such as being thirsty. But that debate gets extremely technical.

7 Complexities avoided in this brief sketch include the subtly nuanced position of Davidson. While he espouses in many ways a science-based view, he also argues that our present beliefs, which for him seem to include much of our commonsense, could not be radically wrong.

8 We could draw comparisons and contrasts here with the authority of Marxism in Communist countries. Such features as its vision of the state's withering away reflect Enlightenment optimism. But its cruder forms, in treating the texts of Marx, Engels and Lenin as authoritative, virtually harked back to the medieval tradition. Yet while I can see a case for treating Bible or Church as a superhuman source of wisdom, I can see none for according such status to these modern intellectuals, however shrewd their insights may sometimes have been.

9 Even if, by some currently unimaginable extension of present methods, we could develop a calculus of probabilities to apply here, we would still have to decide to *trust* the calculus when it took us beyond our intuitions (Ch. V.3). If we tried to formalize that decision, we would have to trust *that* formalization, and so on. For though we may often rationally trust a calculus beyond our intuitions, we cannot avoid our responsibility for placing trust in it, which ultimately requires an unformalizable judgment.

10 Technically, materialism can deal with putative immaterial predicates by (1) reducing them to others compatible with material ones, as in the earlier thirst example; (2) eliminating them as having no real application to the world, as it would do with the notion of demon possession; or (3) relaxing what counts as a reduction of one property to another (see later), in ways that still preserve the mechanistic worldview. (1) and (2) have relatively clear criteria for success or failure. (3) is a matter of degree; here materialism may run the risk of death by a thousand qualifications as it attenuates its position in reply to criticisms of specific reductions. The notion of significance is relevant in all these contexts, but particularly in (3).

11 In terms of the later notion of a reduction, I claim that, though there will be natural-scientific *descriptions* of the relevant states of affairs, no reduction to those concepts can capture their significance.

12 Since commonsense is permeable by science, aspects of the scientific description may always become relevant. E.g., if the science proved to be totally deterministic (which on present theories seems unlikely), it would have implications for commonsense views about human freedom. But the limiting factor is that science can become commonsense only insofar as it enters into our dealing directly with the world.

13 The causal approach in Ch. XI.5 would say that such matters can be dealt with scientifically, through sociological study. But that path must bring "science" closer to the German "Wissenschaft", which can apply both to the sciences and to the humanities. So analytic materialism appeals rather to the repeated expansion of the scientific method into new aspects of the structure of matter (Sec. 3). One day, it insists, rigorous mathematico-experimental methods will in principle chart the complexities of the brain which represent our thinking. I too hope so, but my concern is with the *significance* of such an achievement for our worldview.

14 It has rarely discussed these issues. But its only approach, I think, could be in terms of possibility (3) in fn. 10.

15 Warren Weaver "Science and Complexity" (1948) pp. 536-544.

16 The mechanistic ideal requires a hierarchical structure of molecule-atom-particle relationships, where each can be reduced to just one micro-level pattern. But this fails even in biochemistry, where, say, DNA molecules have such vast diversity of structure that they can represent the genes of unique individuals. Hence DNA is not a purely chemical concept, but a functional-chemical hybrid that is partly picked out by its role in guiding heredity. However here the explanatory power still normally flows upwards from a micro- to a macro-level.

17 The part-whole relation in statistical explanation needs more discussion than I can give it here.

18 It also has another root in an admiration of formal structures. With formalization, it is usually an unqualified gain to dispense with a putative entity. But how far this applies to

non-formal contexts is a further vast, and vastly underexamined, question. Cf. also next fn.
[19] Though Ockham's Razor is an undoubted maxim of good reasoning, it cannot itself establish the conclusion. For, first, refusing to multiply entities "beyond necessity" cannot itself indicate what the criteria are for necessity. Second, it does not directly bear on an aspectual approach, since aspects are not entities (see fn. 22). Finally, the maxim must be balanced against others, such as that mentioned in Sec. 8.

[20] J. E. Lovelock *Gaia: A new look at life on Earth* (1979).

[21] The growing list of books that approach this issue from various directions include those of such eminent physicists as D. Bohm *Wholeness and the Implicate Order* (1983), B.McCusker *The Quest for Quarks* (1983), and P. Davies *The Mind of God* (1992). McCusker (pp. 150-151) notes how many of the founding fathers of quantum mechanics were interested in the question. From the other direction, many books, and such groups as the Transcendental Meditation Movement, approach the argument from the stilling of the mind. In general, among these discussions perhaps the most influential is still F. Capra *The Tao of Physics* (1976). For some of my own views, see my "New Horizons: Reflections on the Future of Religion and Science" (1986).

[22] If, like analytic materialism, we approach the matter ontologically, aspects are not entities, but sets of predicates or statements. However many of them are expressed in intensional, and often vague and indeterminate, terms, so they do not fit neatly into formal analyses.

WORKS CITED

Achinstein, P. *Law and Explanation.* Clarendon, 1971.

Alston, W. P. *Philosophy of Language.* Prentice-Hall, 1964 .

Armstrong, D. M. *A Materialist Theory of the Mind.* Routledge, 1968

——. *Belief, Truth and Knowledge.* Cambridge Uni. Pr., 1973.

Aune, B. *Reason and Action.* Dordrecht, 1977.

Austin, J. L. "Other Minds". *Philosophical Papers.* Oxford Uni. Pr., 1st edn., 1961.

Ayer, A. J. *Language, Truth and Logic.* Gollancz, 2nd edn., 1946.

Baker, G. P. and Hacker, P. M. S. *Wittgenstein: Understanding and Meaning.* Blackwell, 1980.

Barnes, B. *Interests and the Growth of Knowledge.* Routledge, 1977.

——. *T. S. Kuhn and Social Science.* Macmillan, 1982.

Berger, P. and Luckman, T. *The Social Construction of Reality.* Doubleday, 1946.

Bernstein, R. J. *Beyond Objectivism and Relativism.* Blackwell, 1983.

Blackburn, S. *Spreading the Word.* Clarendon, 1984.

Bloor, D. *Knowledge and Social Imagery.* Routledge, 1976.

Bohm, D. *Wholeness and the Implicate Order.* Ark, 1983.

Bradley, F. H. *Appearance and Reality.* Clarendon, 1897, 10th imprn. 1946.

Brzezinski, J., Di Nuovo, S., Marek T., and Maruszewski, T. (eds.). *Creativity and Consciousness: Philosophical and Psychological Dimensions.* Rodopi, Amsterdam, 1993.

Buber, M. *I and Thou.* Trans. R. G. Smith. T. & T. Clark, Edinburgh 1937.

Campbell, Joseph. *Hero with a Thousand Faces.* Meridian, World Publ. Co., 1956.

Campbell, Richard. *From Belief to Understanding.* Aust. National. Uni. Pr., 1976.

Capra, F. *The Tao of Physics.* Fontana, 1976.

Casey, E. *Imagining: a Phenomenological Study.* Indiana Uni. Pr., 1976.

Chalmers, A. F. *What is This Thing Called Science?* Queensland Uni. Pr., 1982.

Churchland, Paul M. *Matter and Consciousness.* M.I.T. Pr., 1984.

Collin, F. *Theory and Understanding.* Blackwell, 1985.

Collingwood, R. G. *The Idea of History.* Clarendon, 1946.

Cousins, M. and Hussain, A. *Michel Foucault.* Macmillan, 1984.

Dallmayer, F. R. and McCarthy, T. A. (eds.). *Understanding and Social Theory.* Notre Dame Uni. Pr., 1977.

Davidson, D. *Inquiries into Truth and Interpretation.* Clarendon, 1984.

Davies, P. *The Mind of God.* Simon and Schuster, 1992.

Derrida, J. *Positions.* Trans. A. Bass. Chicago Uni. Pr., 1981.

Descartes, R. *Descartes: Philosophical Writings.* Ed. G. E. M. Anscombe and P. T. Geach. Nelson, 1966.

Deutscher, M. *Subjecting and Objecting: An Essay in Objectivity.* Queensland Uni. Pr., 1983.

Emmet, D. M. *The Nature of Metaphysical Thinking.* MacMillan, 1945.

Evans, G. and McDowell, J. (eds.). *Truth and Meaning.* Clarendon, 1975.

Evans-Pritchard, E. E. *Witchcraft Oracles and Magic among the Azande.* Clarendon, 1937.

Feyerabend, P. K. *Against Method: Outline of an Anarchistic Theory of Knowledge.* New Left Books, 1975.

Flax, Jane. *Thinking Fragments.* California Uni. Pr., 1990.

Flew, A. G. N. (ed.). *Logic and Language.* Blackwell, Series I, 1951; Series II, 1953.

Forman, R. K. C. (ed.). *The Problem of Pure Consciousness*. Oxford Uni. Pr., 1990.

Franklin .R. L. "A New Science of Consciousness?". *Religious Studies,* 1983.

——. "Creativity and Depth in Understanding". J. Brzezinski, S. Di Nuovo, T. Marek and T. Maruszewski (eds.). *Creativity and Consciousness: Philosophical and Psychological Dimensions.* Rodopi, Amsterdam, 1993.

——. "Experience and Interpretation in Mysticism". R. K. C. Forman (ed.). *The Problem of Pure Consciousness.* Oxford Uni. Pr. 1990.

——. *Freewill and Determinism.* Routledge/Humanities Pr., 1968.

——. "Knowledge, Belief and Understanding". *Phil. Quart.,* 1981.

——. "New Horizons: Reflections on the Future of Religion and Science". Uni. Tasmania Occasional Paper 43, 1986.

——. "Recent Work in Ethical Naturalism". *Amer. Phil. Quart.* Monograph No. 7, 1973.

——. "The Concept of Reality". *Aust. Jnl. Philos.,* 1986.

——. "Would Freewill Make Social Science Impossible?". *Diogenes,* 1983.

Furlong, E. J. *Imagination.* Allen and Unwin, 1961.

Gadamer, H-G. *Philosophical Hermeneutics.* California Uni. Pr., 1977.

Gadamer, H-G. *Truth and Method.* Sheed and Ward, 2nd edn., 1979.

Gettier, E. "Is Justified True Belief Knowledge?". *Analysis,* 1963.

Gordon, R. M. *The Structure of Emotions.* Cambridge Uni. Pr., 1987.

Groenendijk, J. and Stokhof, M. "Semantic Analysis of wh-complements". *Ling. and Philos.,* 1982.

Hacking, I. *Why Does Language Matter to Philosophy?* Cambridge Uni. Pr., 1975.

Hamlyn, D. W. *Experience and the Growth of Understanding.* Routledge, 1978.

Hannay, A. *Mental Images: a Defence.* Allen and Unwin, 1971.

Harman, G. "Positive versus Negative Undermining in Belief Revision". *Nous,* 1984.

Harman, G. *Thought.* Princeton Uni. Pr., 1973.

Hormann, H. *To Mean—To Understand.* Springer Verlag, 1981.

Hume, D. *Treatise of Human Nature.* Selby-Bigge edn. (1960 repr.).

James, William. *The Varieties of Religious Experience.* Fontana, 1960.

Joachim, H. H. *Logical Studies.* Clarendon, 1948.

Jung, C. G. and others. *Man and His Symbols.* Pan Books, 1978.

Kant, I. *Critique of Pure Reason.* Trans. N. Kemp Smith. Macmillan, 1953 repr.

Katz, S. (ed.). *Mysticism and Philosophical Analysis.* Sheldon Pr., 1978.

——. *Mysticism and Religious Traditions.* Oxford Uni. Pr., 1983.

Kneale, W. and M. *The Development of Logic.* Clarendon, 1962.

Kuhn, T. S. *The Essential Tension.* Chicago Uni. Pr., 1977.

——. *The Structure of Scientific Revolutions.* Chicago Uni. Pr., 2nd edn., 1970.

Lakatos, I. and Musgrave, A. (eds.). *Criticism and the Growth of Knowledge.* Cambridge Uni. Pr., 1970.

Lakatos, I. *Proofs and Refutations.* Ed. J. Worrall and E. Zahar. Cambridge Uni. Pr., 1976.

Lloyd, G. *The Man of Reason.* Methuen, 1984.

Lonergan, Bernard J. F. *Insight.* Darton, Longman and Todd, 1958.

Lovelock, J. E. *Gaia: A new look at life on Earth.* Oxford Uni. Pr., 1979.

Lyons, W. *Emotion.* Cambridge Uni. Pr., 1980.

Manninen, J. and Tuomela, R. (eds.). *Essays on Explanation and Understanding.* Reidel, 1976.

McCusker, B. *The Quest for Quarks.* Cambridge Uni. Pr., 1983.

McIntyre, J. *Faith Theology and Imagination.* Handsel Pr., 1987.

Melchert, N. "Mystical Experience and Ontological Claims". *Philos. and Phenom. Res.*, 1977.

Mill, J. S. *A System of Logic.* Longmans, 8th edn, 1947.

——. *Utilitarianism.* Many edns., incl. Everyman 1948.

Miller, D. W. and Starr, M. K. *The Structure of Human Decisions.* Prentice Hall, 1967.

Moore, G. E. *Principia Ethica.* Cambridge Uni. Pr., 1903.

Norris, C. *Derrida.* Fontana, 1987.

Norris, C. *The Deconstructive Turn.* Methuen, 1983.

Orme-Johnson, D. W. and Farrow, J. T. *Scientific Research on the Transcendental Meditation Program.* Vol. I, M.E.R.U. Pr, 1976.

Palmer, R. E. *Hermeneutics.* Northwestern Uni Pr., 1969.

Parrett, H. and Bourveresse, J. *Meaning and Understanding.* W. de Gruyter, 1981.

Phillips, D. Z. (ed.). *Religion and Understanding.* Blackwell, 1967.

Plato. *Republic.* Many edns., incl. Everyman, 1935.

Pollock, J. L. *Contemporary Theories of Knowledge.* Rowman and Littlefield, 1986.

Polyani, M. *The Tacit Dimension.* Doubleday Anchor, 1967.

Popkin, R. H. *The History of Scepticism from Erasmus to Descartes.* Harper and Row, 1964.

Popper, K. R. *Objective Knowledge.* Clarendon, 1972.

——. *The Logic of Scientific Discovery.* Hutchinson, 1959.

Pritchard, H. A. *Moral Obligation...Essays and Lectures.* Oxford Uni. Pr. repr. 1968.

Putnam, H. *Meaning and the Moral Sciences.* Routledge, 1978.

Quine, W. V. O. *Word and Object.* M. I. T. Pr., 1964.

Rescher, N. *Cognitive Systematization.* Blackwell, 1979.

Rorty, A. O. *Explaining Emotions.* California Uni. Pr., 1980.

Rorty, R. *Philosophy and The Mirror of Nature.* Blackwell, 1980.

Rose, M.A. *The Post-Modern and the Post-Industrial.* Cambridge Uni. Pr., 1991.

Ross, W. D. *The Right and the Good.* Clarendon, 1930.

Russell, B. *Logic and Knowledge.* Ed. R. C. Marsh. Allen and Unwin, 1956.

Ryle, G. *The Concept of Mind.* Hutchinson, 1949.

Sayre, K. *Cybernetics and the Philosophy of Mind.* Routledge, 1976.

——. *Recognition: A Study in the Philosophy of Artificial Intelligence.* Notre Dame Uni. Pr., 1965.

Shope, R. K. *The Analysis of Knowing.* Princeton Uni .Pr., 1983.

Skinner, Q. *The Return of Grand Theory in the Social Sciences.* Cambridge Uni. Pr., 1985.

Sloman, A. *The Computer Revolution in Philosophy.* Harvester, 1978.

Sober, E. *Simplicity.* Clarendon, 1975.

Strawson, P. F. *Individuals.* Methuen, 1959.

Stroud, B. *The Significance of Philosophical Scepticism.* Clarendon, 1984.

Tarski, A. "The Semantic Conception of Truth". *Philos. and Phenom. Res.* 1944. Repr. H. Feigl and W. Sellars (eds.). *Readings in Philosophical Analysis.* Appleton-Century-Crofts, 1949.

Thomas, L. *The Lives of a Cell.* Futura Pubns Ltd., 1976.

Toulmin, S. E. *Human Understanding.* Vol. I, Clarendon, 1972.

Unger, P. *Ignorance.* Clarendon, 1975.

Urban, W. M. *Beyond Realism and Idealism.* Allen and Unwin, 1949.

Urmson, J. O. *Philosophical Analysis.* Clarendon, 1956.

Vendler, Z. *Res Cogitans.* Cornell Uni. Pr., 1972.

Waismann, F. "Verifiability". A. G. N. Flew (ed.). *Logic and Language*. Blackwell, Series I 1951.

——. "Language Strata". A. G. N. Flew (ed.). *Logic and Language*. Blackwell, Series II, 1953.

Warnock, M. *Imagination*. Oxford Uni. Pr., 1976.

Watkins, J. *Science and Scepticism*. Hutchinson, 1984 .

Weaver, Warren. "Science and Complexity". *Amer. Scientist*, vol 36, 1948.

Weinsheimer, J. C. *Gadamer's Hermeneutics*. Yale Uni. Pr., 1985.

Whitehead, A. N. *Modes of Thought*. Cambridge Uni. Pr., 1st edn., 1938.

Wilber, K. *The Atman Project*. Theosophical Publ. House, 1980.

Wittgenstein, L. *Philosophical Investigations*. Blackwell, 1953.

Wright, G. H. von. *Explanation and Understanding*. Routledge, 1971.

Ziff, Paul. *Understanding Understanding*. Cornell Uni. Pr., 1972.

INDEX

Absolute Idealism 60, 77–79, 88, 151, 181, 193.
Achinstein, P. 7, 199.
agreement, as basis for reasoning 113–118, 126, 130, 135, 165, 170, 174.
Alston, W. P. 97, 199.
analysis. *See* philosophy, analytic.
analytic materialism *See* materialism.
Aristotle 52, 53, 60, 76.
Armstrong, D. M. 38, 112, 196, 199.
articulation 12–13, 16, 27, 29, 36, 43, 45, 56, 78, 96, 106, 116, 150, 155, 164, 166, 168, 169, 171, 189, 192.
aspect 19, 21, 23, 33, 58, 106, 157–159, 164, 187, 192, 195, 196, 198.
assertability conditions *See* truth conditions.
astrology 156, 194–195. *See* witchcraft.
Austin, J. L. 112, 199.
belief 14, 23, 25, 28, 37, 38, 43, 44, 58, 59, 66, 89, 92–94, 96, 97, 99, 103–106, 108–110, 117, 121, 122, 126, 130, 136, 137, 151, 155, 166–168. — *See* belief system; justification; truth.
belief system 14, 18, 19, 21–23, 27, 45, 56, 58–59, 106, 111, 117, 130–131, 135, 136, 149, 158, 159, 171, 179, 183, 196.
— and sub-systems 19, 21, 22, 45, 48, 56, 58–59, 66–67, 100–101, 120, 130, 142, 157, 158, 183, 187.
Bernstein R. J. 88, 127, 145, 199.
binary oppositions *See* postmodernism.
Blackburn, S. 160, 179, 199.
Bradley, F. H. 88, 199.
candor, rule of 102, 103, 105, 107.
causal and justificatory modes 136–139, 165, 173, 174, 175, 178, 181, 188.
cause, causation 13, 44, 76, 80, 110, 136–139, 150, 185.
Charity, Principle of 101, 111, 130, 146.
circles, vicious and beneficent 117, 122, 123, 125, 130, 133–134, 139, 152, 154, 158, 165, 166, 172, 188.
coherence 27–28, 34, 36–38, 44, 55–57, 69, 71, 91, 96, 101–102, 104, 114, 136–137, 150–151, 158, 166, 184, 195. *See* truth.

concepts 20–21, 44, 70–71, 111, 114, 116, 144, 154, 156, 159, 188.
conscious and unconscious 21–22, 64–65, 66–67, 123, 135, 157, 164, 170, 194, 196.
constructivism and criticalism 34–35, 78, 79, 84–86, 136, 141–145, 154, 156, 170, 181, 185, 193, 195.
Copernicus, Copernicans 121, 123, 182.
creativity 35–37, 48, 55, 66, 70, 145, 166, 178.
D'Agostino, F. vii, 60.
Davidson, D. 88, 129–131, 145, 146, 197, 199.
decision procedures *See* rational assessment.
deconstruction *See* postmodernism.
defeasible justification, defeaters 104, 108–112, 118, 133.
delimitation 16–17, 21, 34, 118, 153, 192. *See* transcendence.
depth *See* understanding—depth of.
depth psychology 21–22, 24, 64–69, 72, 120, 148, 179, 189.
— and symbols 66–69.
Derrida, J. 140, 143–145, 147, 199.
Descartes, R. 52, 59, 146, 179, 185, 199.
detached intellect 63–64, 67, 147.
dialogue 119, 122–127, 145, 170, 172, 178, 194.
Dixson, M. vii, 72.
Einstein, A. 31.
elegance 30, 31, 108, 116, 184, 185, 192.
Ellis, B. 50.
Emmet, D. M. 50, 199.
empiricism and rationalism 76–78, 80–81, 86, 113–114, 118, 141, 182, 185.
Enlightenment, the 38, 67, 77, 81–82, 86, 122, 125, 129, 135, 141–143, 163, 164, 175–178, 183.
epistemology *See* theory of knowledge.
error, possibility of radical 126, 129–131, 134, 158.
essences *See* postmodernism.
esthetics, esthetic appreciation 32, 33, 65, 69, 78, 184.
Euclid, Euclidean 53, 59, 60, 77, 80.
evaluation *See* fact; statement.

Revisioning Philosophy

The series seeks innovative and explorative thought in the foundation, aim, and objectives of philosophy. Preference will be given to approaches to world philosophy and to the repositioning of traditional viewpoints. New understandings of knowledge and being in the history of philosophy will be considered. Works may take the form of monographs, collected essays, and translations which demonstrate the imaginative flair of examining foundational questions.

The series editor is:

David Appelbaum
Department of Philosophy
The College at New Paltz
New Paltz, NY 12561